Redneck Mothers, Good Ol' Girls and Other Southern Belles

A Celebration of the Women of Dixie

By Sharon McKern

The Viking Press
New York

303.7

Copyright © Sharon S. McKern, 1979
All rights reserved
First published in 1979 by The Viking Press
625 Madison Avenue, New York, N.Y. 10022
Published simultaneously in Canada by
Penguin Books Canada Limited

LIBRARY OF CONGRESS CATALOGING IN PUBLICATION DATA
McKern, Sharon S
Redneck mothers, good ol' girls, and other Southern
belles.
1. Women—Southern States—Social conditions.
2. Women—Southern States—Biography. 3. Self-percep-
tion. I. Title.
HQ1438.S65M3   301.41′2′0975   78–13329
ISBN 0–670–59249–8

Printed in the United States of America
Set in Videocomp Compano

In memory of
THOMAS W. MCKERN
1920–1974
still my bridge
over troubled waters

Contents

Prologue

> *. . . all theory, dear friend, is gray,*
> *and green, alone, life's golden tree.*
> —GOETHE

I t is a special vanity of Southern women to believe that they are different from other American women, perhaps in the way that a wide Technicolor screen differs from a narrow black-and-white one. For those whose roots are buried outside the boundaries of the old Confederacy, such analogies (rightfully) rankle; still, the myth and mystique have been perpetuated in so many novels, screenplays, and songs that most Americans believe that Southern women *are* special. They may not want to emulate us or copy our honeydew drawls, but they know (and always have) when we're around.

There was a time, to be sure, when whistling "Dixie" was considered bad form: the only people who puckered up and did it were the ones who ran around at night dressed in sheets.

But the South is on the rise again, partly because of women like the ones who people the pages of this book. In what was for so long the nation's poorest, most backward-looking region, prosperity is on the rise. Seventy percent of U.S. population growth today is in the South. Such explosive growth has left us as urban as Americans who make their homes in New Jersey, and many of us live now in suburbs superficially indistinguishable from those that ring Chicago. There's nothing innately evil about the "Americanization" of Dixie, of course, and a good deal of it can be viewed as welcome evidence of progress. But a native daughter has no desire to lose her Southernness in the process, and she fears homogenization more than snakebite. She views air conditioning as a mixed blessing, arguing winningly that if refrigerated air has helped to trigger this unprecedented influx of Yankees, then the right-smart thing to do is get rid of the air conditioners, and *fast*. She sees the K-Marts and McDonaldses and Holiday Inns littering a landscape once draped in honeysuckle and figures that from now on, it's all downhill with the brakes off; there may be no way to avoid the minor collisions and resulting contusions, but she can hope at least that nobody gets permanently maimed in the crash. Whatever you choose to do with your heritage, she's going to hang on to hers.

She'd rather eat a bug than lose *that*.

A Southern belle of any variety is born, not made (some of us can be made, too, but that's grist for another mill), and the place she is born is in her special history. From our earliest years, we are taught two separate histories. I learned one in school, in the company of other children and out of books. The other I learned after supper, in the company of fireflies and chiggers, on the veranda at the back of my parents' house. The twilight version wasn't an organized history, but one relayed in fragments—in no particular order—through stories about great-great-grandparents and uncles and aunts and others who had set the traditions I would live by. It was a long time before I realized that these men and women had done nothing more remarkable, really, than survive in a world that made survival a tricky bit of business, especially for women.

This may explain the fact that most family tales centered

about strong *female* forebears. There were anecdotes, too, about my male ancestors; I heard about my grandfather, who started out in business with Howard Hughes but dissolved the partnership when he decided Hughes never would amount to anything, and about my great-grandfather, who till the age of ninety-six hiked to town and back daily (a distance of eleven miles) with a broom slung over his shoulder, for no reason other than that it seemed to him a good thing to do.

But most of the stories I heard after supper had to do with Southern women who dared to be different—so different, in fact, that I remember wondering as a child what point there was in conforming in this land of pork, pone, and pragmatic dementia. Some of the old anecdotes my parents had learned from their parents and grandparents; others were told first-hand. Always, the stories conveyed a tradition of women who combined strength with femininity, courage with eccentricity. Nobody ever said that these were traits I should emulate, but it was clear from the relish with which the anecdotes were told and re-told that these were the very traits that elevated the women in my family from the ordinary to the heroic. In addition to such specific admonitions as "nice girls don't," "it never hurts to marry a doctor," and "remember who you are," I learned then at my daddy's knee that there are in the Southern tradition certain feminine qualities likely to get me through life with amazing grace and a minimum of hassle. And, since nothing happened to disabuse me of this notion, I found it easy enough to carry through childhood and adolescence into adulthood the unshakable conviction that Southern women *are* unique: they have it aced.

But exile is supposed to give one perspective, and mine has. Living outside the South (and in two other countries as well) taught me something about the awesome commonality of women everywhere. Circling home after nearly a decade away taught me something about the phenomenal tenacity of regional stereotypes. Time and television, the two great cultural Cuisinarts, had done little in my absence to erode the myth of Southern difference, which for Northerners and Southerners alike always has exceeded even the *facts* of difference.

Then came the research for this book, which taught me not to chunk rocks at facts, either.

One is that Southern women loom larger than ever now as national folk heroines, and in bold new guises so outrageously audacious that they threaten to eclipse the popularity of the old-style Southern belle. Americans who once insisted on viewing all of Dixie's darling daughters as silken-lashed imitations of the petulant and capricious Scarlett O'Hara now regard them as breezily impudent backwoods babes fabled for their raw wit, cracker-barrel candor, and constant readiness for good-natured rebellion.

This is news to elicit a rebel yell or two for those of us who preferred all along to spend our spare time rigging trotlines over leading reels. Besides that, it was as good an excuse as any (and better than most) to re-explore the South I remembered. If there were still real women behind the rowdy country-cousinism of the faddish new plastic-fantastic Redneck Mothers, Good Ol' Girls, and other new-style Southern Belles, I'd have to track them down before I wrote about them. More play, I thought, than work. I began with two battered tape recorders, a map, a list of friends scattered through the eleven states of the original Confederacy, and a handful of letters of introduction to Southerners I hadn't met. But the South has a way of closing down over its own like the jars in which we once captured fireflies out on the veranda, and Southern women have a way of splicing others into their lives. Why not stay an extra week or two or three in Birmingham to stay up late, trading memories and sipping bourbon with Cherie Colston? Or linger one more night in

Belzoni to sink into the feather bed in the front bedroom at Ethel Mohamed's great old Victorian house? Or return to Nashville for the third time to sit in on Stella Parton's new recording session and give us a few more days to swap our tales of work and love? After the first seven thousand miles of backroads driving, I knew I'd be exploring the South on its own terms, in its own time. It would take longer this way, involve many more thousands of miles. But distance is part of the heritage, and there's a lot to be learned sitting with a new friend on a sunny front porch, talking while our hands did the work of shelling black-eyed peas. What began as a simple survey became a long-term involvement. A few weeks on the road stretched into a full year. Simple questions and easy answers turned into shared documentaries revolving around the Southern experience.

So I drove, and talked, and lingered longest where the talk was best, questioning women who boasted no special expertise other than their own experience and expectations, talking with sociologists and psychologists and other academicians accustomed to sorting out the complexities of social geography, with women who have never traveled far enough from home to cross a county line, and with celebrities whose very provincialism rocketed them into the limelight and made the world their Technicolor stage. There *are* redneck mothers and good ol' girls, rebel queens and rhinestone cowgirls, honky-tonk heroines and belles of every age. All real. All proud. All worthy of celebration. They're passionate and compassionate, unbelievably candid, fully aware in their own fashion of what it means to be female and Southern in the seventies. They know their rights. They know how to get what's coming to them. But they're not afraid to step back once in a while and have a good laugh at themselves, either.

Just as long as you understand they're having the last laugh.

Women like these wrote the book on originality and individualism. In the truest sense, they wrote this one as well. I told them the title, and they took over from there. From the day I started driving through their cities and towns, they offered themselves as willing hostesses, informants, chauffeurs, confidantes, teachers, historians, interpreters, sources, guides, research assistants, go-fers, publicists, and enthusiastic participants in this work. Not all are Southern women, for more than a few good ol' boys offered their assistance too (though some volunteered help of a different sort than I had in mind), and a couple of dozen Yankees lent aid as well. It is appropriate but regrettably impossible to thank each of them in these few pages, but they know who they are and they know how they add to the reservoir of Southern comfort that I hold, always, in the back of my mind.

I'd go to the well with them any time.

Some must be singled out for special mention, because their contributions are so central. In Birmingham, Alabama, Cherie Colston aided and abetted me in this re-exploration from the beginning, and suffered through the hard times at the end, when my need to get it all in (and inability to do so within the limits of a single volume) made my teeth ache and my head throb. In Vicksburg, Mississippi, Gordon Cotton steered me to women without whom this book would be incomplete. In Decatur, Georgia, Pauline Rose Clance gave me time she could not spare, and insights only she was qualified to provide. In Montgomery, Alabama, Louise Mohr gutted herself to talk with total candor of the darkest (and brightest) moments of her life, came to my rescue when the little Mercedes turned on me at last, and (perhaps unknowingly, though I doubt it) gifted me with a link, longlost, that lets me visit at will my dearest friend and nearest spiritual twin. In Atlanta, Faith Brunson pointed me in directions I needed to go and gave me her friendship: she defines the word, I think, as cautiously as I do, and she may deduce from this a measure of my joy in knowing her. In Lovejoy, Georgia, Betty Talmadge opened her home and her heart, with warmth and hospitality uniquely hers, at a critical juncture, and this was a precious gift too. In a dirt-floor shack in an Appalachian settlement so tiny it lacks a name, Gretta Townsend cleaned my wounds and iced down my sprained ankle when I tried, despite my better judgment, to walk a stone path and chew gum at the same time; her sister Berry taught me to make hog-maw salad and gave me a charm for warding off the evil eye. In Nashville, Stella Parton let me impose far too often on our friendship, trusted me with special secrets, asked little, gave much, and let me tag along with her, coast-to-coast, to meet some of my favorite sequined superstars. Stella and Dolly, I owe you both.

Bob Hall, editor of *Southern Exposure,* put me in touch with Southerners who are about as easy to reach by phone as the President of the United States. In Plains, Georgia, Mrs. Allie Smith, who tired long ago of the celebrity that comes with being a presidential mother-in-law, and who shudders still at the thought of another interview, took me in and submitted to my questions. Kitty Wells, equally unenthusiastic on the subject, was a gracious hostess and shared some private thoughts on what it is to be the queen of country music.

Woodville, Mississippi's favorite transplanted Yankee, Ernesto Caldeira, put me in touch with Mary Stuart, America's best-known soap-opera superstar, and guided me to Mary McGehee, one of the most direct and likeable Southern women I know. Greenville, Mississippi's Sylvia Jackson gave me more than she knows. In Birmingham, Alabama, Marie Jemison proved patient and cooperative beyond reason. Tandy Rice, Nashville's ablest, most power-charged talent representative, put at my disposal his vast and valuable resources. Sue Hensley walked a precarious path between discretion and candor in nearby Madison, Tennessee, giving me a glimpse into the life of the Carter Family,

Johnny Cash, and June Carter. In Belzoni, Mississippi, Ethel Mohamed gave me a day-and-a-half of down-home hospitality, good company, and warm nostalgia, and pampered me so extravagantly that I'm still tempted to run away from home to go live with her. Vicksburg's Blanche Terry, and her daughter Ginnie Raymond in Tuscaloosa, Alabama, dovetailed their interviews so that I might compare at my convenience the lives of mother and daughter. In Memphis, Tennessee, Dianne Vaughn earned my loyalty for as long as she wants it.

A few Southern women gave me spectacular insights by virtue of their expertise in their respective fields and more time than I could reasonably ask of them. Among them: Heidi Betterton in Hammond, Louisiana, Brenda Bell in Maryville, Tennessee, Sandra Bell in Natchez, Mississippi, Harriett Prevatte in New Orleans, Louisiana, Joan Perry in Birmingham, Marie Woodard in McComb, Mississippi, Mrs. Dizzy Dean in Wiggins, Mississippi, Gusta Street in Collinsville, Alabama.

I owe special thanks to Austin, Texas's Pepper Huddleston, Birmingham's Peggy Presley, and (as always) Jeanette McPhail Smith. I'm particularly grateful, too, to David Kent, Frank Page, Micki Fuhrman, and Bill Keeling at the Louisiana Hayride in Shreveport.

All these women and men shared with me the exhilaration of finding answers to hard questions. There are four others who shared the pain that comes with a labor of love. Rebecca Singleton, my editor and Southern soul-sister, offered suggestions so spectacularly ingenious and helpful that I was embarrassed at failing to come up with them first; she gave me help of a different kind (and continues to do so) on a scale uniquely Southern, and I am incapable of the sort of mathematics necessary to tally my total debt to her.

I owe even more to my new family.

My husband, Jack Whitaker, endured the neglect, preoccupation, erratic absences, and frenzied mood changes that I bestowed so freely upon him during this year of research and writing. He rubbed my neck, fed me vitamins, guarded my privacy, gave me love and reassurance and occasional lost weekends when I deserved none of these, and did not file for divorce. He *did* come dangerously near complaining on one or two occasions that this might not be the most enjoyable year of his life, but I am able in my gratitude to him to overlook this verbal mishap. Brenda Whitaker proved to be patient, compassionate, and mature beyond her fourteen years, and gave so freely of herself to help me that I am obliged to conclude she is the most desirable step-daughter in all of Dixie (or anywhere else). Jeffrey Whitaker, who is not exceedingly fond of doing laundry, running household errands, cooking his own dinner, and keeping his stereo at low volume, did all these things and more so that I could work; it may just be that he's a special good ol' boy.

And, finally, some very personal appreciation to a few of those who helped in major ways to get this book written: Vera Ard, Robert C. Armstrong, George Bacon, Cheryl Blackerby, Lindy Boggs, Donna Breeden, Lawrence Brandenburg, Isabelle Cannon, Mrs. Henry Cannon (a.k.a. Minnie Pearl), Mary Cain, Toni Carpenter, Barbara Carroll, June Carter, Edna Cash, Johnny Cash, Beth Childress, Charles Clem, George Clinton, Linda Colgate, Ken Colston, Helen Cornelius, J. Felton Covington, Jr., Elisabeth K. Dart.

Joy Davenport made this book possible.

There are more: Yana Davis, Marjorie Dennis, David Dews, Buford Dowell, Shelia Dunnivant, Sue English, and "Sally Ann Ferguson," who spoke with such candor in her loyalty to me that I was obliged to substitute a pseudonym for her real name.

And more still: Joe Gaines, Verda Gibbs, Annette Gnospelius, Olivene Godfrey, Sally Ann Gresham, Barbara Griffin, Vernell Hackett, Sheldon Hackney, Winnie Harper,

Arleen Harden, Mr. and Mrs. S. T. Hawkins, Mrs. H. Hayden, Mary Hayes, Inez Henry, Lady Bird Johnson, Mary Helen Johnston, Mark Kilborn, Gurubachen Khalsa, James W. Lambert, Betty Lee, Rosemary Lucas, Barbara Mandrell, Mary Maples, Beatrice Martin, David Mathews, Katherine Grafton Miller, J. Balfour Miller, Donna Milligan, Eula Morrow, Edna McCain, and Edna McKay.

Olivia Newton-John was an unexpected informant, and she deserves special thanks. So do Eta Nichols, Nancie Parker, Dolly Parton, Webb Pierce, Francis Pitts, Charles A. Pomerantz, Penny Reeves Pryor, Jacque Pulley, Joel Rachelson, Jim Raymond, Ruth Reed, Maxine Reese, Jean Robitscher, Mary Sawyer, and Dinah Shore.

I'm not quite through. How can I omit Vi and Hugh Smith, who rescued me from a winding road somewhere in Appalachia, where I'd gotten lost, and escorted me out and on my way to Granny Nichols? Or Kathy Speakman or Hattie Stacy or Norton and Barbara Styne or Joe Taylor?

Thanks too to Teresa Taylor, Rose Thadford, Gail Thomas, Susan Todd, Jerry Jeff Walker (whether or not dressed in his big-yellow-bird suit), Perry Wayne, Bob Weeks, Ann Whitaker, Brother Harlo White, Jan Wiley, J. R. Williams, and Ann Williamson.

And six more who showed their grit: John and Maureen Jenkins, John Giles, Bryan Spires, Jr., Lee Rohn, and Billy Don Rieves.

Not to mention the Ephalunt.

True Grits & Cracker Power:
New Strains of Scarlett Fever

Southern women are Mack trucks
disguised as powder puffs.
—REYNOLDS PRICE

There is, and always has been, something unique and special about the women of Dixie.

Now this is a notion that enrages some who know the South and many more who do not. Americans tend to tolerate almost any form of ethnicity except that of prideful separatism. And I have heard it suggested (though this may surprise you) that Southerners are, oh, 'bout semi-prideful.

For all their flag decals and patriotic bumperstickers, Southerners are no more and no less "American" than people who live elsewhere in the nation. But they are products of their own distinct historical experience, and they feel this most keenly. In this complex and contradictory land, the past isn't dead: Faulkner was speaking for Dixie when he noted that it isn't even *past*. The men and women of Dixie see the boundaries of the South as more than mere administrative lines etched across the face of a map. In the Southern psyche, such borders encircle a collective state of mind (one not entirely rational) and of heart. It is this persistent sense of separate nationhood that permits Southern men and women to retain their essential provincialism even as they move further into the mainstream of the larger society. It is this sense of shared losses and shared gains that helps to perpetuate the larger-than-life Southern stereotypes that alternately delight and repel other Americans. One of these is the Good Ol' Boy, another the Redneck. Both now are celebrated in song and in story.

But it is the Southern *woman* who truly grips the nation's imagination.

It is she who best typifies the vigor and progressiveness of today's South without surrendering the sense of family and reverence for tradition that Southerners hold dear. She may plunge lustily into the future, but not without keeping track of where her forebears are buried. She may focus now on substance, but not without retaining her right to insist on form. The Southern woman is resilient, courageous, emotional, charismatic, adaptable, energetic, given to wild flashes of insight and to mercurial moods as well as bold histrionic flourishes. She values *place* over *time.* She prizes sentiment, nostalgia, rhetoric, imagery, and hyperbole (though not necessarily in that order). She is amazingly tough and stable beneath her façade of practiced eccentricity.

And she's got a remarkable line of bullshit.

It is true that there's a dark side to her nature. She can be selfish, proud, vengeful, mean, manipulative, and (by all means) racist, whether she is white or black. At times she seems to regard intellect as a dubious virtue; often her world view extends no further than the end of her nose. There are those who say she has more sides than the Pentagon and is three times as dangerous. She mixes grace with hatred, polished manners with naked violence turned against the handiest random target. But this is her darker nature, and one not specifically the province of women who inhabit the lower-right-hand corner of the United States. Paul Hemphill once noted that there is a theory, at least partly valid, that one reason racism in other parts of America was late in receiving notice was that Southern racists were so much more colorful.

The Southern woman has been analyzed, idolized, criticized, and misunderstood. She has almost never been ignored. She is fully aware that her special quirks and eccentricities provide the rest of the nation with some of its most notable myths and anomalies.

The essence of her fabled "mystique" eludes those who would define it in concrete terms; an awesome amount of printer's ink has been spilled in settling instead for descriptions of her silken strategies and serpentine evasions, her audacious manipulations and elaborate charades, her unparalleled sense of timing and finesse. Traditionally, the Southern woman is depicted as a master magician, a Jezebel illusionist so skilled in her craft that she refers to neither plan nor premeditation when casting her spells.

Never mind that this magic consists of little more than a series of evolved techniques, most so finely honed by heritage and habit as to be largely unconscious: her power remains electrifying even when the illusions are stripped away. She may resort at times to kittenish tricks or sly manipulations, but she's never yet found herself wholly dependent on them. Her greatest charm comes from her idiosyncratically wayward ways—her freewheeling independence, her irreverent candor, her *yahoo* readiness to thumb her nose at convention—and her unparalleled penchant for survival.

> *But for all the modesty of*
> *her spreading skirts, the demureness of hair netted*
> *smoothly into a chignon and the quietness of small*
> *white hands . . . her true self was poorly concealed. The*
> *green eyes in the carefully sweet face*
> *were turbulent, willful, lusty with life,*
> *distinctly at variance with her decorous demeanor.*
> —MARGARET MITCHELL

It wasn't modesty and decorum, you recall, that drew us to Mitchell's Scarlett; we were captivated by her audacity, awed by her strength and will—and won over at last by her determination to *survive.*

Like Mitchell's Scarlett, the Southern woman is beyond all else a skilled survivor. There is in her an element of steel and stamina, and an uncanny knack for remaining essentially untouched even by catastrophic change. Throughout the decades—through slavery and secession, invasion and defeat, postbellum poverty, emancipation, reconstruction and integration—Southern women have shown their true-grits ability to outlast (and therefore outwit) adversity. Today's tough-minded, hard-driving, bad-ass Redneck Mother is descended from the same tradition that spawned the old-style Southern Belle, so revered for her sweetness and her centuries-old code of genteel femininity. The two are in fact soul sisters, spiritual twins shaped by the same rural environment and derived from the same cultural context. They differ far more in style than in substance, suggesting alternatives rather than contradiction: Redneck Mother and traditional Belle are but variations on a Southern theme. Many themes permeate Dixie's history, and the Southern woman, shaped by her past, is a product of them all.

The most central theme is survival.

Both Redneck Mother and old-style Southern Belle derive from a tradition that pays eloquent lip service to the desirability of social conformity while putting its hard money on individualism, for perfectly valid reasons, most rooted in the Southern past. The women of Dixie have been shaped far more by historical influences than have their masculine counterparts. Typically they married young, worked hard, and stayed put (usually for generations) in the towns and hills, farms and plantations where they settled. The men were mobile: they traveled forth, politicked, evangelized, marched off to war, or simply moved on in the wake of an ever-expanding Southern frontier. Their women remained imbedded in the local soil, soaking up the flavor of a changing world through roots that seldom branched into the next county. To settle in the early South and survive its swamps and pests and awesome isolation is to have emerged, if at all, a hardy, hell-bent-for-leather, high-styled individualist.

There are those who argue that there is no room for provincial individualism in what is called the "New South." And it's true that Dixie lies vulnerable to creeping homogenization in the face of urban and industrial encroachment. Taller buildings, wider freeways, standardized Holiday Inns, and fast-food franchises combine to make the South appear almost identical to the rest of the nation. Industry—lured by dazzling tax breaks, relatively cheap labor, newly enacted right-to-work laws, moderate climate, and plentiful power resources—has responded by littering the soft-edged Southern landscape with factories and office buildings. The classic Southern provincials seldom appear in their most colorful past guises. No more rebel governors to rant against fluoridation as a Communist plot to poison our water, or exhort us to place our faith solely in the "three friends we have in this world: God, Sears & Roebuck, and Eugene Talmadge" (in West Virginia, of course, one substitutes Senator Robert C. Byrd for Talmadge and adds Monkey-Ward and Carter's Little Liver Pills for a total of five steadfast *amigos*). Not too many barrel-bellied cracker sheriffs lurking behind the billboards out on the old Interstate to beat up on bearded college kids and fleece the Yankee tourists. Not many billboards, in fact. And hardly any delicate half-clad ladies to rock and hum and stare vacantly into space while remaining, as Dixification has it, dependent on the kindness of strangers.

Why, you could shake every kudzu vine 'tween Tulsa and Tallahassee and never find no glow-in-the-dark plastic Jesuses for sale.

Today's Southerners have acquired a veneer of sophistication. They're embarrassed by such relics of the past, dismissing them as, well, *tacky.* These people now watch network television even after football season's over. Some read big-city newspapers. Most have traveled out of state, or vacationed abroad, or attended some Eastern college, or worked in a distant Northern city. When they return to the rural South they bring with them an updated, *Americanized* frame of reference. Many talk and dress, walk and court, and behave in general not so differently from *regular* people—say maybe folks who got their raisin' in Seattle. Or Buffalo.

Change? Mercy sakes. *Lawdy Mamma!*

But the South has changed before and remained unchanged. Many of the old attitudes and convictions persist. The South, however transformed, remains paradoxically the same.

And so do its women.

Dixie's daughters share a rich and eventful history, and they have grown skilled in the ways of survival. They have mastered the difficult art of graceful accommodation. They have learned to adapt and adjust to the demands of an ever-shifting set of social circumstances. Yet always, stubbornly, they have remained unchanged.

No other women know so well the dynamics of their own social order, nor boast such a keen understanding of the finer points of power. Southern women have learned, slowly but very well, to take advantage of subtle loopholes in the social fabric and use these to expand their spheres of personal freedom. This is no small feat in a world committed, however futilely, to maintaining the status quo. The Southern woman is a product of a provincial, male-dominated tradition shaped by the rural past even in the reality of an urban present. But she is a product, too, of the South's peculiar heritage of individual courage, semi-organized rebellion, and velvet-hammer militancy. The same Southern tradition that places such a premium on social conformity prizes individualism even more, and all but guarantees eccentricity as a feminine prerogative. Given society's tacit approval to vent one's most cherished peculiarities, Southern women respond much as other Americans might: they take it not only as their right but their obligation as well to live up to their billing.

Now we are practiced poseurs, each of us; life in any human society is an endless acting-out of roles, assumed and assigned. But in the South, where the bizarre is ordinary and the ordinary spectacular, role-playing assumes dramatic new dimensions. Whatever role they choose—rhinestone cowgirl or backroads rebel, up-country aristocrat or Appalachian redneck—Southern women play with style and total commitment, for they understand better than most that roles played well carry them nearer their personal goals. What emerges is a whole new folk tradition, with a whole new cast of superstar eccentrics indigenous to the Southern soil: Redneck Mothers whose audacious words and ways give belligerent voice to attitudes and biases the rest of us hide behind code words. Good Ol' Girls who follow the yeasty, gallivanting tradition of freewheeling forebears. Cosmic Cowgirls in their sleek pre-faded jeans and high-chromed pickups. Rebel Queens in all their dowager-glory, who shed aristocratic preoccupations and seek new causes. The women of the South have risen again to serve as contemporary folk heroines.

And not a second too soon, either.

The old clichés don't wash with the realities of contemporary life. Even the traditional Southern Belle, so long the favored fantasy outside the South, seems now a romantic pretension. And in a sense she is, though she continues to serve Southern society in valid if invisible ways. Dixie's prideful daughters long have chafed at the notion that they were perceived outside the South as so many high-bosomed, firm-bottomed semi-Scarletts, turned out like doughnuts from a pastry machine to bat their silken lashes, stamp their tiny feet, and pout prettily in the manner immortalized by Vivien Leigh. This is the most time-worn and unimaginative of all regional stereotypes: it was perpetuated largely by the same people who persist in regarding Dixie as one great magnolia grove densely dotted with revival tents, baton-twirling academies and throngs of happy pickaninnies. Not a bad place for the menfolk to gather to burn an occasional cross when the huntin's bad an' the fish ain't bitin', but an illusion nonetheless—and one the South can do without.

The problem is that the Belle was drawn more from fiction than reality. In earlier years, nearly all the classic Southerners were: Margaret Mitchell's belles and gentlemen soldiers; William Faulkner's half-wits and nymphomaniacs; Erskine Caldwell's low-rent po' white trash; Richard Wright's maimed blacks. Toss in one faithful mammy, a rawboned moonshiner or two, a stoic black cook gifted with rare-but-simple human wisdom, and you've got it: the celebrated Old South was one long Tobacco Road save for the carefree aristocrats gamboling on Tara's lush lawns. "Po' white trash," "hillbillies," and "crackers" make good reading, but it is only by the loosest interpretation of the census figures that as much as 10 percent of the antebellum white population can be classed as poor whites. There weren't many aristocrats, either: a mere 10 percent can be placed with Scarlett's Irish daddy in the plantation-owner class, and only 5 percent boasted twenty or more slaves. The vast majority of antebellum whites were middle-class yeoman-farmers and their families, who usually raised only a single money crop and sustained themselves with the harsh realities of subsistence farming. What little there was of the mythical Plantation South lasted a mere seventy years in most parts of the South. The landed gentry and their mag-nolia-and-iron ladies made the quantum leap from poverty to decadence within the span of a single generation and in a far shorter time moved on into postbellum decay, leaving later generations to hanker after an idyllic Golden Age that never was.

Americans who learned 90 percent of what they know of the South from the Selznick film (and the other 10 percent in the Atlanta airport awaiting their flight connection to Mexico City) have never quite snapped to the fact that the fabled Southern Belle was for the most part a colossal provincial put-on. When Southern women camp it up, flirting and simpering and shrieking at the sight of mice, what they're doing is taking a few satirical swipes at the whole institution of Southern femininity and indulging, for amusement's sake, in a bit of playful self-parody. The truth is that the old-fashioned Southern Belle, helpless and vain, could not be taken seriously by women long accustomed to getting their hands dirty when the ox is in the ditch. Southern women as a whole are steeped in the values of the Puritan work ethic, and they reserve some harsh judgments for women who aspire to no more in life than maintaining a seventeen-inch waist and serving as an ornament on the arm of some good ol' boy like Billy Clyde Puckett. This is not to suggest that the old-style Belle is obsolete, for she serves now as in the past a valid purpose in role politics. But for the most part the authentic curl-tossing, foot-stamping, reel-leading, nostrils-flaring Belle has cashed in her chips. Would-be belles who pant hungrily after the chance to play Homecoming Queen in the parade's lead convertible or trot after a rhinestone-studded Miss America crown are cheap imitations that reduce the legendary Belle to a tinny tinkle nearly so faint as to warrant exclusion from the folk tradition.

But those Yankees, don't-you-know, they're 'bout semi-romantic and right-smart naïve, and they're still operating under the delusion that every sloe-eyed coed in Dixie is a

Southern Belle unless she's got a mouth on her big enough for eating peas out of a jug. Coeds are too young, too inexperienced, and too undercapitalized to carry off a proper Bellehood. Brides may be sufficiently high-strung to be passed off as thoroughbred semi-Belles, especially if Daddy has sprung for the ultimate full-scale Southern wedding with its twenty-four paired attendants, multiple matrons of honor, twin ring-bearers, quintuplet flower girls, and a reception to follow for 750 of the bride's closest friends.

Among the Southern debutantes, only a remarkable few make superstar semi-Belles. The ultimate presentation is that of Charleston's blueblooded St. Cecilia Society, founded in 1762 and so properly elitist that it bans all press mention of its activities, membership, roster of current and upcoming debs, and the annual ball itself. Several years back, one St. Cecilia debutante saw her name linked with the Society in the Atlanta press, provoking a panic-stricken contemplation of her fate: should she simply withdraw in shame or await the demand of her withdrawal? Would the Society and its followers ostracize the young woman's family or offer its collective condolences?

In Savannah, most but not all the very best young women come out at the Cotillion Club's Christmas Ball. Here publicity is permitted, even encouraged, a fact that has the self-conscious cream of Savannah aristocracy squirming in doubt: might the debut be seen as *advertising?* Wise parents evade the issue by shipping their debut-age daughters off to Europe for the holidays. Elsewhere in the South, however, the debut continues to thrive as the final tribal ritual of a nice, upper-class Southern white girl, and debutantes still enjoy the special perks that come with the honor of being chosen a year-long semi-Belle. It isn't that the perks aren't deserved: each debutante has survived, since kindergarten days, the relentless scrutiny of blue-haired aristocrats who constitute selection and sponsoring committees.

In some Southern cities, attempts are made to link the coming-out balls with some *au courant* cause like conservation, or community service, or architectural preservation; the hope is that presentation might then be seen as less frivolous in an age where the debutante system seems a bit creaky. In Columbus, Georgia, the annual Heritage Ball entails the presentation of each deb in a different restored townhouse or mansion. Ostensibly, such settings reflect the time-honored tradition of Southern hospitality and graciousness. Actually, the Ball was conceived in 1968 to benefit the Historic Columbus Association. Contrary to rumors floated by rival cities, Columbus debs do not wear 'round their waists ribbons advertising the Association's annual membership drive.

Short-term semi-Belles do not evoke memories of the legendary Scarlett: their glory days are too brief, the challenge forbidding. True bellehood, after all, is a state of mind: to translate that state into living legend takes considerable commitment, some native cunning, a certain practiced panache, and more than a measure of mellowed maturity. The New Belle is a bit older, then, than the average coed; she's been around the track a time or two (though the mileage doesn't show). There are two things (my mother said) only time can bring: wisdom and experience in dealing with the mysterious male ego, and expertise in playing a heroic role with true Southern-fried charisma.

My mother does not read Germaine Greer.

New Belles are dazzlingly feminine. No faded jeans for them, no Redneck Power T-shirts, no chunky heels or crazed thrift-shop chic; instead, simple fluid jersey or billowy chiffon, high-heeled strappy sandals and mist-sheer stockings (yes, Virginia, even in summer, 'less you want to go 'round like po' white trash). The New Belle may snort cocaine through a solid-gold straw, may indeed hump her way alphabetically each month through the white pages of the telephone directory. But she knows not to smoke on the street. She may be unable to articulate her code of conduct, but she has a fine sense of fitness, a sure and certain feel for what is Proper and what is Trashy and what is bad form besides.

The New Belle is aware of the feminist movement, shares its most basic tenets if none of its tactics, and knows her own human worth. Usually, she's well informed or well educated or both. She does not have a job; she survives not on Daddy's money but through occasional windfalls and brief flurries of free-lance work in journalism or local television. She sees no harm in accepting expense money from men, but only from those she'd have slept with anyway (turning tricks is Trashy). She'll bleed as willingly as anyone for equal pay and day-care centers, but in her *own* time and in her *own* way (read: when no men are watching). She sees no reason to trade the exhilarating headiness of style for the realities of substance when she might have both. Nor does she see as mutually exclusive the complex sexual power plays she so relishes and the feminist battles she (quietly) supports. Why not, she thinks, have it *all?* Usually, she does. Meanwhile, she makes use of all the traditional feminine wiles, often gaining a reputation as a Feminist Sellout and True Bitch (because she ends up, invariably, with all the better men). Given the choice of playing Scarlett or Melanie, she'll opt for bitchy over mealy-mouthed any day.

There aren't many New Belles around: the role exacts an awesome toll in time, money, and energy. Still, it's a challenge nearly irresistible to Southern women primed in the tradition of high-risk gambling, and a few spectacular big-league Belles remain at large to captivate the general populace. My friend Pepper Huddleston is one despite limited funds. I can't tell you how she does it, and she's not talking; I suspect she manages by sheer wit and will and some very fancy footwork. Pepper takes an occasional temporary job (though not in summer, for this would cost her her tan); otherwise, she offsets her lack of capital with high-power energy and high-voltage charm. Perhaps it is because she moves so fast (normally, we glimpse only her blurred outline) that no one notices the deficiency.

Barbara Howar is another. She once scaled the pinnacle of social success in Washington, from which power base she made the cover of *Saturday Evening Post,* was photographed dancing with then-President Lyndon Johnson for *Time,* and made *Newsweek* as well. This outspoken former debutante from Raleigh, North Carolina, served as arbiter of taste in clothing to the Johnson daughters, mixed as a favored insider at Kennedy parties, helped redesign Lynda Bird for her interlude with actor George Hamilton, and entertained the press by feeding them gossipy quips cheekily directed at high government officials. She got away with it all: the nation's capital was ready, it seemed, for a beautiful and irreverent woman endowed with a soupçon of down-home flair. Disaster struck when she exceeded the implicit boundaries of Southern eccentricity; her fall from grace came on the basis of just two indiscretions (one, unfortunately, with a presidential aide). Doors slammed shut all over D.C., and the audacious insider was *out* in the length of time it takes a rumor to cross town in the capital city of gossip.

But what Washington hadn't bargained for was Howar's uniquely Southern ability to outlast adversity. In the way that Southern women have, she bounced back with a frank autobiographical account of her rise and fall. Her book, irreverent but absolutely candid, brought her rising like a backroads phoenix from the social ashes. She's more interesting now, bloodied but unbowed, than ever before. For all her charm and beauty in those early pinnacle years, she commands far more respect for having shown her ability to capitalize on disaster: once again, a Southern woman turning crisis into personal advantage.

True grits.

But Huddleston and Howar are exceptions. For the most part, even the most spectacular of the New Belles have been eclipsed by earthier Southern provincials. In a mass impulse that has taken on faddish overtones, Dixie's down-home daughters have been wildly romanticized in recent years.

Cracker power.

The new provincials are heroines with a honky-tonk twist, reflecting an entire nation's fascination with things country. Everyone's automotive aspiration now is a battered pickup truck; fashionable attire has come to consist of faded jeans and rattlesnake belt. In a region infamous for its book bannings, monkey trials, and crusades of the Anita Bryant genre, it's chic to be Redneck. Suddenly Southerners are finding themselves credited with unique native cunning, backroads wisdom, and cracker-barrel wit; such assumed qualities add to a mystique built on the unfounded but oddly pervasive premise that to *be country* is to be honest and straightforward, trustworthy and strong, and finely attuned to the rhythms and cycles of one's home region. Hence the evolution of the Counterfeit Redneck Mother, an entity certain to baffle the authentic number who must deal with the fact that she no longer has the woods to herself. The hills fairly teem with weekend cowgirls dressed in Big Mac overalls, who commit grammatical homicide with every drawl or twang, and roll their own Bull-of-the-Woods cigarettes (or, in the case of the Hippie-Counterfeit, their own dope). Such fake provincials as this serve only to show how far the Redneck craze has come. True redneckism cannot be shucked on Sunday night: an authentic Redneck Mother *is* one for life. Now you can get yourself some fine, handsome Redneck Mother and scrub her up good and give her a sleek veneer of civilization. She's not stupid (for she knows enough to act dumber than she is when she knows something and smarter than she is when she doesn't). You can buy her some decent clothes and nag her into wearing stockings. You can teach her not to say "hot damn!" and "nigger" in public, and you can trade her chipped jelly glasses for a set of good water goblets. Do all this and more, and she'll still be redneck in all her most basic attitudes and values. Worry all you wish about the "Americanization" of Dixie: the redneck core is impervious to change or dilution.

That's part of the provincial appeal. The new Southern stereotypes—the Redneck Mothers and Good Ol' Girls and other Southern Belles—are regional variations, updated for the seventies, of the same reliable heroines we honored in earlier years.

There is a kernel of truth in each of these stereotypes. It can't be otherwise, for all stereotypes are grounded in reality, and all serve real and valid (if hidden) purposes. But the larger-than-life central-casting figures plucked from Dixie to serve as contemporary pop-cult heroines have acquired considerable polish in translation. What they represent is the provincial South without its oft-criticized hard edges, reflecting today's emphasis on *country*, a return to older values. Without consciously turning to the South, people in other parts of the U.S. long for some of its values: family, home, community, roots. Yet the rebel's romantic appeal is valued still, especially if brushed with the common touch and leavened with a bit of irony. It is a time for down-home figures whose bluntspoken presence suggests a few rebel-hearted alternatives to the regimentation of daily living. Fantasies of the free life live on in the lyrics of country music and in the audacious mannerisms of outspoken Southerners. Rednecks. Good Ol' Girls. Rhinestone Cowgirls with unpredictable grammar and down-to-earth views. These are new-style heroines uniquely suited to the times.

Whatever polish they acquire in translation, the pop-cult caricatures are rooted firmly in the Southern soil. The women of Dixie *are* different from women elsewhere, just as we've all suspected for so long, and often they differ in substantial and measurable ways. As a group, they differ from non-Southern women in the nature of their family ties and in the frequency with which they remain lifelong natives in the states in which they are born. They have their own no-nonsense notions of community responsibility as well as their own ideas of how to care for their sick, aged, and poor. They react differently to the basic ideas of the feminist movement and to current feminist strategies. They're unusual for the ways in which they maintain their female friendships. They are unique among American women in their near-metaphysical attachment to the land itself. Usually, they express their ethical and religious commitments in ways that are uniquely Southern. More importantly, they *perceive* themselves to be different from women elsewhere. And on this basis, they recognize their kinship with one another. They share a provincial mindset which, drawing them together, sets them apart from women whose roots are to be found outside the borders of Dixie.

This does not mean that Southern women always think and act in tandem (though often they do). They've responded as *individuals* to the problem of getting on with life, just as they've responded as *individuals* to the shaping influences of Dixie's collective history. There is a remarkable homogeneity to the women of the South; they produce a blend, one that reflects the common needs, values, and aspirations of a unique breed of American woman. Even so, their individual lives and lifestyles are diverse.

Southern women are uniquely equipped to juggle apparent opposites. They accept up front (and always have) that life itself is an endless paradox. They are molded in a tradition that routinely pairs civility and violence, conformity and individualism, style and substance: it is unlikely that they see contradiction in the Southern ideal that demands of its women both strength and traditional femininity. The tradition of combining these traits gives Southern women a decided edge over their contemporaries outside the South: it is *learned* rather than inherited behavior that has worked a circumspect feminine revolution in Dixie. In the decade from 1960 to 1970, the number of women in the South's civilian labor force rose by more than 40 percent, much of the growth in technical and professional fields. Yet few Southern women are willing to lobby publicly for feminist causes, and almost all reject out of hand militant strategies designed to achieve parity with men. The velvet hammer approach *works,* and this is why it is employed in nearly every aspect of life by Dixie's daughters.

It serves the purposes certainly of the Good Ol' Girl, whose current popularity eclipses even that of her masculine counterpart from whom she derives her label. She's earthy and sensible and breezily unpretentious, as much a product as the Good Ol' Boy of their common heritage, or more. She's quick to lend a hand to friends and neighbors, all of whom proclaim her the "salt of the earth." She votes if she remembers to, and returns her library books on time. She is blessed with unfettered cheer (one reason she's so likeable) and stores of energy so boundless as to border on the obscene (the Good Ol' Girl cooks, sews, cleans, knits, skis, rides, scouts, refinishes furniture, raises bromeliads and African violets, takes night courses in Self-Improvement, does a bit of crochet and crewel embroidery, writes occasional poetry of the type that rhymes, and maintains voluminous diaries and scrapbooks). She may or may not have a college degree, but she almost always has A Job; if so, she is earnest and capable, serious and reliable at work. She is a climber, an achiever, a woman determined to *get ahead;* if necessary, she will jog uphill all her life in order to do so. Nobody ever told her that hard work doesn't lead inevitably to victory, and so she's more likely than not to succeed.

Even so, she is powerfully male-oriented. However she lusts for her own power and money and status, she's convinced that these traditional male indices of success won't in themselves keep her warm at night, so she sees to it that the largest chop on the plate goes to the male to whom she looks for support, whatever her own occupation or earning capacity. She has learned to measure her own worth; but she won't accept her own rating until *he* looks at it and judges it valid. She masks her own ambitions behind a façade that is traditionally feminine. She is first and foremost, she says (and quite often, too), her husband's helpmeet. She will devote all her public charm and energy to advancing his career, whether he likes it or not. Meanwhile (for she didn't fall off the back of the turnip truck yesterday), she makes damned sure there's plenty of time and energy left over for her personal pursuits. Somehow, there always is. Society awards the Good Ol' Girl full credit for wifely loyalty, and gives her a staggering number of extra points for spunk and sheer mindnumbing stamina.

Being a Good Ol' Girl has nothing to do with birth or breeding; it cuts across all social and economic and (in recent years) even racial lines. It is, more than anything else, a mindset based on the assumption that honest effort and unflagging determination bring inevitable rewards. Convictions like these, deep-held despite constant evidence to the contrary, make the Good Ol' Girl positively bulletproof: nothing can penetrate her unsinkable good humor, and nothing can keep her from her appointed rounds.

No woman fits the regional stereotype exactly. But in all her most basic values and attitudes, Lady Bird Johnson is the quintessential Good Ol' Girl. During her husband's life, she followed unswervingly in his peripatetic path. The bulk of her small family inheritance and her first familial loan financed his initial political campaigns. The bulk of her energies later was devoted to activities that would support and enhance his political image. So deeply involved was she in his life and work that she often used the royal "we" when referring to her husband ("We are beginning to really explain to the world about Vietnam"). Lady Bird cheerfully hosted thousands of impromptu gatherings, welcoming political throngs Johnson invited home on impulse and without notice. She took it upon herself to mediate Johnson's quarrels; often, she followed behind her husband, softening with gentle words the pain inflicted by Johnson on friends and staff members.

Throughout her marriage, Lady Bird Johnson served as her husband's valet and personal manager. She laid out his clothes each morning, paid his bills, filled his lighters and his pens, placed his pocket items within his easy reach. Because he disliked low shoes and full skirts, she wore neither. She worried endlessly and publicly how she might please him; once, when he disliked a gift she'd selected for him, she turned in anguish to her journal: "I am chagrined with myself. There must be something I can give him that would surprise, excite, elate him. The only thing I can think of is to learn how to do my hair, keep my lipstick perfect, and be devoid of problems." She is a remarkably democratic woman, largely free of pretensions, but she can rattle off genealogies as capably as any blue-haired Southern aristocrat, keeping track of names and relationships that span four generations ("Actually, one of Lyndon's ancestors was one of the three joint founders of the D.A.R. She was Mary Desha, a granddaughter of Joseph Desha, brother of Lyndon's great-great-grandmother, Phoebe Ann Desha Bunton."). All along, she managed to channel portions of her resources—her time and money and energy—into quiet investments of her own. By the time Lyndon Johnson attained the presidency, Lady Bird had built a multimillion-dollar business empire in her own name (without once missing, I'd bet, an appointment with her hairdresser).

Far more evocative of the provincial world of feed stores and paper fans is the fabled Redneck Mother. The original model worked as a gum-smacking waitress in a roadside diner or as a night-shift assembly worker, or peddled plastic Jesuses from orange-crate stands beside the highway. She was perennially pregnant, and was never seen in public without a crown of pink plastic curlers (it may be that she was readying herself for a grand event we know nothing about). She spent most of her spare time hauling about wet screaming children and mangy dogs in a battered pickup plastered with bumperstickers that read KEEP YOUR HEART IN THE USA OR GET YOUR BUTT OUT; usually, there was a Winchester racked in the rear window and a fifth of Jack Daniels beneath the seat. What the Redneck Mother held sacred was Mom, the flag, police, armadillos, turnip-green pie, and 'taters. What she hated most was hippies, pot, draft-dodgers, limousine liberals, and people who admitted to taking welfare. What she feared most were change, God, and federal confiscation of her firearms (in just about that order). She was celebrated first in song by Ray Wylie Hubbard, who lambasted her for her provincial Momism, a habit that committed her to passing on to her sons all the prejudices and social limitations she'd inherited in her lifetime.

In the stereotype promulgated by those who have taken this Southerner to heart, the Redneck Mother has been cleaned up a bit, emerging as a likeable, oft-emulated Southern eccentric with a charm and cachet all her own. Her freewheeling style, her irreverent candor, and her freedom from sex-role agonies win her a good deal of notice from both sexes. No awards for good taste, you understand: just a good deal of notice. Her taste in art runs typically to acrylic crucifixions and garish bullfight scenes painted on black velvet canvases. She has a bad habit of whitewashing old tires, half-burying them in her front yard, and planting them with spindly marigolds. Her bedroom is strewn with pillows stitched in satin thread to read "SWEETHEART."

The Redneck Mother may or may not have offspring: the label has far less to do with motherhood than with a certain diehard spirit of unbridled independence and lack of regard for convention that is uniquely redneck. This is a woman who thrives on unorthodox behavior and takes her greatest joy in pursuing unconventional goals. She is well accustomed to killing her own snakes. She bills herself as the freest and most rebellious of all Southern women; she does in fact boast the freest vocabulary. The Redneck Mother makes a point of striding ostentatiously where other women fear to tread, not in the name of women's rights (she couldn't care less and, besides, she believes we each make our own) but in order to suit her own whims and comforts and to indulge her penchant for shocking the sensitivities of more conventional souls. She's delighted then to while away a rainy afternoon in a kicker tavern, drinking beer and hustling pool with the Good Ol' Boys; they admire her for her gall, for her ribald humor, for her lack of feminine game playing, and for the fact that she's not averse to getting laid. Unlike other Southern women, she doesn't mind getting herself talked about: her only fear is that she *won't*.

She has been known to cart around more biases and prejudices than you can fit comfortably into a Chevy quarter-ton. If she has overcome her natural propensity for racism, then she articulates racial bias anyway from a deep-seated need to induce shock and outrage. Her rebellion and her autonomy are foils designed, consciously or not, to mask her reluctance to compete in the popularity stakes and ritualized mating games many Southerners play full tilt. She may thumb her nose at convention, but she does so from the safety of her informally sanctioned redneck role, and she takes care to keep within the bounds of provincial eccentricity.

Barely.

Janis Joplin was a rip-roaring, hard-driving, wild-ass Redneck Mother who challenged the outer limits of the role. She cursed like a sailor, disdained bras before nipples came into vogue, wore her hair wet and wild, drank almost anything she could get her hands on, and snorted the rest. It's a good guess the bulk of her rebellion stemmed from her inability to play the Belle or perfect the Good Ol' Girl role. She was forced to go it alone without the protection and reassurance of the acceptable labels—a pioneer.

That's true grits, too.

The Cosmic Cowgirl is a blatant Southern fraud fascinating for her mixed social aspirations. Typically, she's a Sophie Newcomb graduate who carries her own ivory-inlaid pool cue and frays the hems of pre-faded jeans acquired at exorbitant cost from the second-floor boutique at Neiman's. She is captivated by the new respectability of the Redneck Mother, and envious of the redneck's unbridled independence. But, conformist at heart, the Cosmic Cowgirl can't quite make the leap. Instead, she plays part-time redneck. She assumes the exaggerated redneck drawl, toys with redneck expletives and experiments with redneck biases. She is, of course, a country-music junkie, a high-style groupie who spends her vacations traveling to Nashville or Memphis or Austin to dig the Cosmic Cowboy scene, to follow the wild and woolly after-hours perambulations of Willie and Waylon and even good ol' Jerry Jeff. She once made it with Willie's third back-up guitar player; she will tell you in lurid detail (and with considerable pride) the subsequent uses to which she put Kwell shampoo. You may as well listen, because you're not going to hear the lyrics anyway: the Cosmic Cowgirl keeps up a nonstop commentary so that you can fully appreciate what's going on down there onstage: now-listen-right-here-Jody's-gonna-harmonize-see-then-Willie'll-come-in-alone. Tucked in her sequined jeans is a hip toke of mellow grass, in her denim halter a tiny vial of energizing cocaine. Meanwhile, it should not escape your notice that the Cosmic Cowgirl's mother was one of the Birmingham Montgomerys (see-how- *bad*-I -am-but-just- remember - I've-got-*breeding*). She can't quite hack the redneck disregard for the traditional measures of Southern status.

No grits: just cracker chic.

There are other Southern stereotypes, rebels all, to be encountered later on, and real-life women as well. Whatever roles they play, all are linked by a common problem: that of being a woman *now,* of defining and achieving status of one sort or another, of striving in different ways to reap a measure of success and satisfaction in a system where most values and standards have been set by males. The women who people the pages of this book, for the most part, have seized imaginatively on the idiosyncrasies of the Southern tradition in tackling that overriding problem. They act in the context of their culture and history, and they are best viewed within that context: working and playing, venting their rage, living with family and friends, avenging their wrongs, plying kittenish tricks or simply cultivating their flowers and vegetables in the midst of explosive change.

Changing with the times, yet remaining the same, as Southern women always have.

They are Dixie's *real* women—dynamic, resourceful, and free, with a sense of Southern-fried charisma that rivals Scarlett at her best. There may be lessons to be learned from their dealings. Provincialism is not a way of life reserved specifically for women who inhabit Southern climes, nor are such inventive approaches to life as theirs. But backwoods Southern provincialism offers some creative social loopholes that can be used to expand spheres of personal freedom and enrich the quality of everyday life; a traditional fondness for these informal loopholes has created a corps of uniquely Southern experts who are heroic in their perpetuation of individualism and irreverence, eccentricity and femininity, faith and hope and charity.

But perhaps the greatest of these is Faith . . .

To a Manner Born:
Growing Up Eccentric

I was an oddity and I realized
that, and it was a big help to me.
—BETTY TALMADGE

Faith Brunson, that is, renowned in Atlanta for her habit of driving to work in pouring rain in an open convertible, a shower cap on her head.

Now this might be the first thing Atlantans will tell you about her, and it passes more often than not as a high-spirited example of the sort of down-home eccentricity in which Southerners take such pride. Brunson is one of those incomparable native daughters who manage the tricky feat of playing out a larger-than-life regional role while evoking all the *real* attitudes and values that transform the feminine caricature into a folk heroine. She plays life largely for the quality to be wrested from it, and it pleasures her some to feel wind and rain in her face. This is an attitude grounded in the tradition of old-fashioned American innocence, and Southern only in that it persists most obviously today in a region where men and women alike still take time to find, in the texture of everyday life, unself-conscious enjoyment. Brunson's rainy-day jaunts speak far more eloquently of a regionally shaped individualism than of the celebrated Southern penchant for eccentricity, though by reason of heritage and upbringing she lays legitimate claim to the latter.

Brunson can also claim extraordinary professional success. She's senior buyer for the book department at Rich's department store, an Atlanta institution only slightly less venerable than Coca-Cola and one that annually turns more merchandise than any other single retail outlet south of metropolitan New York. She's legendary in the highly specialized book trade for her homegrown elegance and for her on-target instincts about where the winds of popular taste will drift next. So impressive is her professional track record, in fact, that major publishers pay heed when Faith Brunson predicts the success of a new release or faults a cover illustration; trade gossip has it that more than a few make it a point to check with her before deciding how many copies of a book will be produced in its first printing. A friend says she is "sheer energy—unquenchable, unstoppable, irrepressible." A colleague describes her as headstrong, capricious, witty, and wise and, should that sound too much like a Hallmark greeting, rushes to add that dealing with Faith when she's riled is something like trying to crawl feet-first through a wind tunnel. She can be cyclonically outspoken, and often is. But like most Southern women, Brunson pays considerable attention to small courtesies, even in times of open conflict or heated dispute. She may use extraordinary tact and patience when dealing with others, but the softness of that Southern style can be deceptive.

In other words, *watch out.* Faith Brunson suffers gladly neither fools nor second-raters. Nor was she trained to.

All the creativity, autonomy, and level-eyed pride she brings to her work are mirrored in her private life, and stem from her Emersonian regard for individualism; like most of her Southern sisters, Brunson believes in the individual and in what the individual can accomplish. It's a conviction instilled in her by what she calls a "very typical upbringing" in a "very typical little town nobody ever heard of" in southern Mississippi. From the beginning, Brunson inhabited a nonconformist world punctuated by that brand of eccentricity so intriguing to those who live outside the borders of Dixie. It was only as an adult that she was able to pinpoint those eccentricities. As a child, she saw nothing odd or unusual in the fact that she had an aunt who spent a good deal of time rocking peaceably in a closet, and a father who habitually mowed the lawn in a linen suit, long-sleeved white shirt, necktie, and vest.

Doesn't everybody?

Her mother—part silken-lashed belle, part fiery activist—was a maverick schoolmarm in a series of backroads schools where she taught all twelve grades and took room and board with local families as part of her salary. Miss Molly was a familiar figure throughout southern Mississippi, largely because she found it necessary to change jobs every year or so. Her gypsylike existence and erratic employment record were logical by-products of her crusader's zeal: she was determined to teach hygiene to rural children whose hair she so often found teeming with lice. Among the Brunson family treasures are her early diaries and a yellowing clutch of letters from irate school superintendents bent on having Miss Molly's job if she didn't straighten up and stick to what was in the books. A rebel at heart, Miss Molly continued to scrub heads and change jobs for fifteen years before marrying at last at age thirty-two. She'd broken some seven engagements and a considerable number of hearts before she met Faith's father in a tiny town called Foxworth, Mississippi. The meeting was a romantic encounter—the stuff of which movies once were made—handed down and recounted with hilarity years later by Brunson and her sister, Gretta.

Foxworth (population 200) consisted of little more than a one-room schoolhouse, train station, post office, and a small general store that functioned, as such small-town establishments generally do, as the town's informal social club. It was where the locals gathered on weekday afternoons to buy chocolate drinks and mingle.

"My father happened to stop in there, just off the train, to get a drink. And he saw my mother, and he asked somebody standing there who she was. And they said, 'That's Miss Molly Ellen, she's the schoolteacher.' And my father just walked up to her and said, 'I'm I. J. Brunson, and I'm going to marry you.' Well, my mother was *furious*. They hadn't even been introduced! And she said to herself, *'this old fool.'* But she married him two years later, after a crazy kind of courtship."

Mr. Brunson was obliged to do the bulk of his courting from New Orleans, where he owned an insurance agency and tended a few stock investments, and the free-spirited Miss Molly led him a merry chase.

"Once he was coming through Foxworth on the train— the train didn't stop unless someone was getting off—but he'd written my mother to come to the station and wave at him. She was at the station, all right, but she was standing there surrounded by four men, laughing and talking. He raised the window and waved his white handkerchief, and she never even saw him while the train went through. We have the letter he wrote afterward. You can still squeeze tears out of it."

Eventually the activist-belle succumbed to Mr. Brunson's charms, formal as they were ("he always dressed in linen suits in summer, with pistol legs, and always with a vest; he never owned a sportshirt and I never saw him without a tie"). They settled in Columbia, Mississippi, and were married quite happily for a quarter of a century before his death.

I. J. Brunson wanted three daughters from this marriage, and he got two of them.

"He wanted to name them Faith, Hope, and Charity. Can you believe this? I got Faith because I was the first. When my sister came along, he wanted to name her Dorothy Hope. But my mother said, 'No, you named the first one and I'm naming this one, and it ain't gonna be Dorothy Hope.' And she named her Daisy Marguerite, Daisy after a favorite niece and God knows where she got the Marguerite."

Faith and her mother called the new baby Gretta. Mr. Brunson, beleaguered but unbowed, either called her Margaret, which was not her name at all, or Baby, except in moods of spirited self-assertion, when he called her Dorothy Hope, which startled the child into submission. Years later, Gretta's firstborn would be christened Catherine Hope. This child isn't called Hope, either. But no matter: the name is a loving link between generations that could not meet—and quiet tribute, tendered with misty-eyed humor by two sisters, to the bond they share.

Such small tributes as this, shorthand reminders of times and occasions gone by, are common in the South. Here *place,* roots and tradition, heavily reinforces identity, whatever individual avenues are explored later on. Greater even than place is a strongly developed sense of family. The South is powerfully appealing to its own, and part of that appeal, far more than moonlight and magnolias and a freewheeling brand of down-home madness, is an American alternative built largely on the warmth and security of its commitment to family and kin. So valued is that commitment that it is reaffirmed on a near-daily basis in the form of private jokes, code words, anecdotes, christenings, and gestures of symbolic nature. All these and more are tributes to an endearing sense of personal and regional history no other American shares. If life in the South seems to move more slowly than it does elsewhere, it may be because Southern women have the good sense to live in two tenses. Whatever the distance between them, however complex their individual schedules, Dixie's native daughters manage to come together often to compare notes, to reminisce, to trade old memories of valiant times and vanished troubles and to share new perspectives on a common past and so develop even closer ties. There is reinforced identity in this ritual too, and more than a few mental jolts: every Southerner has reeled with the occasional realization that much of the process of growing up Southern was, well, a bit more *eccentric* than it seemed at the time.

Faith Brunson has had a few more jolts than most. For one thing, her father was never called by his first name. His friends knew him as Mr. Brunson or as The Senator, a nickname bestowed in pleasured acknowledgment of the fact that he *looked* as if he should be a senator, though he never stood for public office. The family, too, called him Mr. Brunson. Though his name was Ira Joshua, no one ever called him Josh, or I. J., though initials often serve as names in the provincial South.

"My mother called him Mister Brunson, always, and he always called her Miss Molly, and we never thought anything strange about that until we grew up, and then we thought it was terribly, terribly funny."

Mr. Brunson slept with a wool scarf about his neck and his socks on, and covers piled six times as high as those on Miss Molly's side of their standard double bed. He was quite cold-natured, and he habitually shivered with cold even under such wrappings as these.

"After I was grown, I'd say to my mother, I'd say, 'How in the world did you crawl into bed with all those covers and have sexual intercourse with somebody you're calling Mister Brunson?' And she'd blush and say, 'I don't want to talk to you about it.' "

In the small-town South, religion is so much a part of everyday life that its basic tenets are seldom questioned. Brunson didn't question them in childhood. What puzzled her was the necessity of attending church so *often*.

"My mother was on a first-name basis with God and Jesus and all the angels. So we went to church every Sunday and every other time it looked as if they might crack the door to let us in. From the time I was little-bitty until the time I got out of high school. And that was one of the reasons I wanted to graduate from high school—so I could get out and go to Ole Miss and not ever have to go to church!"

Even Aunt Babe (truly Brunson's aunt, a fact worth noting as, according to Southern fashion, most any woman over the age of forty is called Aunt by somebody) seemed perfectly normal to Faith, at least during childhood.

"Aunt Babe didn't get married until she was fifty. She didn't want any children and she didn't take any chances. She wanted to get through menopause first. That's *true.* She couldn't stand children, she couldn't stand drinking, she couldn't stand *anything.* And she was very cold-natured besides.

"Anyway, she finally got married, and she lived with her husband for nine years. Then one day—she was fifty-nine at the time—she decided she'd had enough of *that.* So she called my mother and asked her to have my father pick her up that afternoon. Well, of course she despised my father— he'd been divorced and in the South back then you simply *did not* marry a divorced man—so she absolutely *despised* him. But he went and picked her up that day, and from that point on until she died at eighty-four, she visited around."

Visiting Around is a time-honored Southern tradition which serves multiple purposes. First, it frees maiden aunts and others of the bother and expense of maintaining their own homes; they simply rotate among their kin, visiting one after the other, at intervals ranging from six weeks to six months or longer. Second, Visiting Around provides each child with close-range exposure to her extended family; aunts, cousins, grandparents, and other relatives are an amorphous, loving, bickering mass that parades singly or in pairs through the household to offer diversion, oral history, and free baby-sitting services. Everyone benefits.

When Aunt Babe Visited Around at the Brunsons', she staked her claim to the guest room with the walk-in closet. As she was very cold-natured, she wore the Sunday edition of the *Times Daily Tribune* between her dress and her petticoat: it cut out the draft. The walk-in closet served the same purpose.

"We'd walk into her room and the closet door would be cracked, and she'd be sitting there reading her Bible in an armless rocker with her galoshes on, and a shawl, and the *Tribune* in her dress. We'd say, 'Oh, Aunt Babe's in the closet.' "

> *. . . we always took care of our eccentrics.*
> *There was one fellow who used to run up and down*
> *the street, thinking he was a streetcar,*
> *and nobody bothered him.*
> —EUDORA WELTY

As a child, Brunson saw nothing odd in Aunt Babe's behavior. During her teenaged years, though, she thought Babe a bit *peculiar,* and was agonizingly embarrassed.

"She'd walk through, and we'd hear this *crinkle,* and our friends would say, 'What's that noise?' Well, I'd have died before I'd have said, 'Oh, Aunt Babe wears the *Tribune* between her dress and her petticoat.' "

Now if you've never had an Aunt Babe of your own, you won't be able to imagine just how difficult it is to keep one under wraps. The word gets out. And so it should, for gradually in the South we learn to take paricular pride in such family crazies. They suit the Southrn sense of fancy. They set us apart and make us speal. Our friends are livid with envy. By the time Faith ached college age, she'd performed the mental quickp that transformed Aunt Babe from adolescent embarsment to treasured pet eccentric. The real shame in the

South, you see, comes with having no family crazies at all.

So appealing is the "Southern madness" to those who live within the borders of Dixie and those who live without that it has been suggested that in the South eccentricity is a tribal aberration expected of all. The truth of it is that more than a few cherished eccentrics—like Brunson's Aunt Babe and my own Aunt Bonnie Lela Crump—serve real and valid purposes far exceeding their entertainment value. By personifying the strong individualism prized among Southerners they perpetuate that standard. They lend credence to the underlying liberality of the provincial world. They broaden the very definition of normalcy and so widen all life's options. And they provide compelling alternative role models for the young, suggesting by their very presence that there are a good many different ways to get through life and not all of them have to do with conforming, even to the most highly touted cultural ideals.

Brunson remembers no pressure to conform.

"When I was growing up in the South, girls were challenged to be *different*, to be better than anybody else, just as the boys were."

Miss Molly saw the handwriting on the wall early in the game and knew that Faith would be forever a nonconformist. A rebel herself, she made but one, futile, gesture to stem the tide.

"I came home from school one day and Brother Cane was in the living room. In those days we called the minister of the church *Brother*. And he knelt down and said a prayer and told me he wanted me to become a missionary in China. Well, I translated that out: my mother had called him up and said something like, 'Will you please come over here because I-can-see-it-all-now, she's going to end up one of the most-wanted women on the FBI list unless I can get her into China as a missionary.' Of course *that* went down the stairs and out-of-doors. And I said, 'Brother Cane, you are very dear and sweet, but I don't want to be a missionary in China, or even Japan.'"

> *There was always that feeling, and I think*
> *there is even now, an inner*
> *thing that just says, "I've got to be better,*
> *I've got to be different."*
>
> —FAITH BRUNSON

"So I had a wonderful childhood, and I went off to college for four years, and my only sister finished a year behind me. I majored in business administration. It was the easiest course, and, my God, this was nineteen forty-one. No female from a little town like that ever thought about a career. Back in those days girls who weren't married by the time they finished college worked in the bank or did nothing. I never even thought about what I was going to do, never thought about a career, and I had a *great* time."

She had no premonition that this tuition-backed reprieve from maturity would expire a year after graduation. But even in the soft-edged South, you can't eat magnolias. Mr. Brunson, then seventy-five years old, was well aware of that. When Brunson finished college she stayed at home a year, a fairly common ritual among young Southern women. Gretta graduated a year later. Then Mr. Brunson had some startling plans for the two of them.

"He called us in and told us we'd lived in a small town all our lives, and he wanted us to go to a city and stay two years. *We could not come home for six months!* And then we were to decide whether we wanted to live in a city or a small town. He said we weren't equipped at that point to make a decision. He told us we could pick any city in the U.S., just as long as it was too far away to come home on weekends, because that would defeat the purpose of going. We thought he was *insane!"*

Mr. Brunson gave Faith and Gretta $300 apiece and telephoned a nephew in Atlanta ("who he had not seen or heard from in thirty-one years!") that his daughters were coming there and would contact him if they got into any trouble.

"Then he put us on the train. No advice. He said he wasn't giving us any advice because we both had college educations and, besides, he'd already told us everything we needed to know. I was *furious!* I was just furious over this whole thing, because I'd known everyone in that little town, and at the university as well, and here I was, a stranger in Atlanta, *miserable.* I was going home every day. I packed every night."

She and Gretta picked up a newspaper and started culling through the classified ads.

"I applied for a million jobs—this was nineteen forty-five, right after the war—and if you could sign your name and distinguish a typewriter from a refrigerator, you could get a job. There were more jobs than people. So every time I applied for a job, I was offered one. And several paid more than a hundred and forty-five dollars a month. But for some reason I took the job at Rich's. They didn't tell me I was going to have to work half a day on Saturday. I said, 'Well, I'm not going to work on Saturday for *anybody.'* I came from a small town, and that was the day you had off. And I haven't had a Saturday off since, and that's been nearly thirty-two years."

Gretta went to work at Rich's, too ("somehow, she managed to live on that hundred and forty-five dollars a month; *I* never did"), and both chose to settle permanently in Atlanta.

"But I have a tremendously warm feeling about the little town I grew up in. I was having lunch recently with a friend of mine from Atlanta and an author from another city, and the author asked where I was from. I said, 'I'm from Columbia, Mississippi.' And my friend said, 'Faith, *really,* after all these years you can say you're from Atlanta.' And I said, 'No, I can't; I'm from Columbia, Mississippi. I live in Atlanta and I love it, but I'm not *from* Atlanta.' "

> *I would not live one inch above the Mason-Dixon line. I would shrivel and die, I would be perfectly miserable.*
> —FAITH BRUNSON

Neither of Brunson's parents ever urged her to find a husband; their concern wasn't that she marry, but that she know what she was doing if she did. There've been a few serious involvements and one formal engagement, which Brunson canceled; she was candid enough, some twenty years before it was fashionable to admit it, that she had no interest whatsoever in traditional domesticity.

"What really tipped it was that I was having absolute *nightmares* about fixing his breakfast and washing his socks. I mean, that's what really did me in. It's that stupid. But I never felt insufficient being single."

Few unmarried women Faith's age, especially among those who grew to majority outside the South, are so serene and self-possessed on the subject of marriage and motherhood. Faith can afford to be: she has had the options, has still, and, besides, the South has never attached any great stigma to spinsterhood. What is stressed here is *clan,* and Southern clans abound with unmarried aunts. The entire region is made up, for the most part, of *natives.* Mississippi, Brunson's home state, leads the nation in its proportion of residents born in the state (nearly 90 percent, compared with the 44 percent typical for the Western states). Many Southern families have lived in the same general territory for generations; extended family ties preclude isolation and loneliness, one reason Aunt Babe could bide her time, waiting to marry till she was past her childbearing years. Miss

Molly wasn't in any hurry, either, to tie a knot that would last a lifetime. And Brunson, reared in a family fiercely devoted to the notion of rugged individualism, never felt the obligation to prove anything to anyone except herself.

"By the time you're forty, you know who you are, and all of a sudden you're *free,* you can enjoy it all. You know what you want to do, and you really don't give a damn as long as you maintain your own standards."

There was the matter, for example, of her church letter.

"In my church the membership is called a 'letter.' Now you think of a physical letter, a certificate or something that says Faith Brunson is a member of this church. Well, I belonged to a church here in Atlanta and I got so turned off that I decided to stop going."

She called the church and asked for her letter.

"They said, 'Now don't be ridiculous.' And I said, 'Well, I've decided that I'm not going to belong to the church for a while, so I want my letter.' And they said, 'But everyone's letter has to be *somewhere.*' I said, 'Do you mean I can't get my letter? Do you mean that there is really no such thing, that it's a *myth?*' And they said that unless I intended to resign from the church and declare myself an atheist, my letter had to be in *some* church. So I told them, 'Okay, just leave it there and mark it inactive, because I do not want to look as if I'm participating when I'm not.' But let me tell you: *there's no such thing as a letter!* You'll scare them to death if you call up and ask for it."

Like many other Southerners, Brunson distrusts computerization. She calls it "living by the numbers." She carries on a nonstop personal crusade to prevent the invasion of her privacy by computers.

"If I hadn't already established some credit in my earlier days, before I got on this thing about the numbers, I wouldn't have a charge account anywhere. United Airlines sent me an application unsolicited, and on there it said that

I've had an established credit rating for thirty years. But they had to have my social security number and my income. So on all those things, I wrote 'none of your business.' And I got a form letter back saying I'm not suitable for credit. But nothing bores me quite like conformity."

Faith Brunson clearly is not destined to be bored. Since 1945, starting as a secretary in Rich's public relations department, she's found an excitement in her work that defies description. Even so, speaking in crescendos, she tries to describe it.

"I love the sound of a department store. I've spent my whole life here, and I can't work anywhere else. I'd rather hear the click of a register and the hum of conversation on the selling floor and the banging of a truck bringing in merchandise than listen to the finest symphony in the world. Those sounds are my own personal symphony, and I love it."

From the public relations department, Brunson moved reluctantly ("I couldn't add, I couldn't even write a sales ticket") into a short-lived merchandising job in women's sportswear, where she credits "a fantastic lady named Catherine Rice" with giving her the crash course she needed later to survive and thrive in the book trade.

"She's now eighty-four years old, worked in the store for fifty years and is now retired. She started working here as a wrapper, but eventually she became one of the outstanding merchants in the country. She was a member of the Board of Directors before it was fashionable to have women on the Board. I trained under her and stayed there eighteen months. Then one day they called me in and said they wanted me to be the book buyer. And I said, 'You've really flipped your wigs this time.' So they put me in the book department. I had no training at all."

Two weeks after she moved into Rich's book department Faith attended her first American Booksellers Association convention, where she was ignored by male book buyers who had no notion that the wit and wisdom under Brunson's Buster Brown haircut equaled that of anyone in the trade.

"I went to a meeting and they talked in codes like R-S-V-B. I found out later that meant revised standard version of the Bible. And I said to myself, 'I'm getting out of here, they're talking in codes and I'll never learn this business.' Well, I came home and I was *so mad* I didn't take a day off in two years. I worked myself to death and learned the business, making all these rash statements and taking all these wild chances, and by luck they turned out to be right. Some thought I was a genius, but it was plain unadulterated luck."

Perhaps. But she spotted the potential of Macmillan's *Oh, Ye Jigs and Juleps* before the publisher did. Same with *Doctor Zhivago* and Pat Boone's *Twixt 12 and 20.* A few years back, she plucked from the stacks of books she keeps beside her bed a new book by an unknown British writer ("on a kooky subject—about rabbits"), read till dawn, then called the publisher to increase Rich's order and announce emphatically that the book would top the best-seller lists in the coming season. *Watership Down* proved an historic seller; Rich's was one of the few stores in the country that boasted ample stocks when the book peaked in sales.

In nearly twenty years of matching book orders to customer demands, she's had plenty of trials and amazingly few errors. And if she has a way of making the tough play look easy, it's because she is so totally involved with her work. No detail is too small to command her attention. Once, when the Rich's book department sold prints and other artwork as well as books, a customer was distressed by a print reproduction of Sallman's *Head of Christ.* She'd always thought, she told Brunson unhappily, that Christ had *blue* eyes. Faith asked the lady to wait, rushed the print over to the art department, and returned with a print with blue eyes daubed in. On another occasion, a woman approached her on the floor and demanded "a Bible with Jesus talking to himself in red." Brunson, a product of the Bible Belt herself, knew exactly what the lady wanted. She pulled out the red-letter version of the King James Bible and offered it to the customer for examination. The woman opened it at random to the Old Testament section and complained, deeply aggrieved, "He ain't talking to himself in red in this one." So Brunson opened the Bible to the New Testament section, and there were just three words in red on the double page. Her customer looked and snorted her disapproval: "Well, He ain't saying much."

But she bought the thirty-dollar edition.

Such close attention to details results in the sort of customer satisfaction that is so much a part of Rich's national reputation, for which Faith feels a personal if old-fashioned responsibility. As far as further advancement within the store, however, she's not ambitious, partly because she sees no sense in wasting a perfectly good present by worrying about the future, partly because she's totally satisfied with her life as it is now.

"I only want to be Rich's book buyer. I'd *like* to be the best book buyer in the U.S. But I'm not interested in being an officer or a division head in the store. This is a typical female attitude, you know, toward work. Females will make specialists of themselves, gain a real reputation within a particular field, and then refuse advancement because they're much more interested in being a specialist in that one field. That's what appeals to me. I'd rather be a big fish in a little pond."

She hasn't taken a vacation—even a day off—in two years.

"My days off are when I go out of town on business. I'm an egomaniac because if I cannot be Number One, then I'm not interested in being Number Two. And being Number One means that I've got to put a lot of other things second to this job. I'm careful about only one thing, and that's my relationship with my sister and her family. She's my only sister. She weighs a hundred and sixteen pounds, and she's the only perfect person I know."

At fifty-three, Faith Brunson is a powerfully attractive woman, partly because she's so oblivious to her charm.

"I always wanted to look like a Southern belle, five-foot-two, eyes of blue. But no matter what I did, I ended up looking like a girl scout, you know, this haircut, which was styled in a Mississippi barber shop when I was four years old. It was called Buster Brown then, and I've always worn it. Again, not conforming, because for so many years this style was simply not 'in.' Then fashion caught up with me, and I was just *furious.* Because all of a sudden, everybody had my haircut, including Julie Andrews. And people would say, 'Oh, you have Julie Andrews's haircut.' And I would say, 'The hell I have, she's got *mine!'* "

Whatever her words, it's unlikely Faith Brunson ever regretted her failure to play the role of Southern belle: she finds obvious enjoyment in nonconformity and derives considerable pleasure in the brand of individualism emphasized by her regional history and by her own family. Both are enormously freeing traits: detached from notions of what one *should* be, she's always had the freedom to be what she *is.* From Miss Molly and Aunt Babe, she learned that there are a good many different ways to be both human and female. She knew thirty years ago what the feminist movement is just now getting around to saying: that in order to survive as an individual, it is necessary for a woman to be a coherent statement in herself. Brunson is just that: her pride and professionalism, her individualism and occasional eccentricity, her personal integrity and credibility, and her candor and quick humor reflect deep-held values that are

distinctively Southern. She has been able to reject the traditional domestic role because her history, both personal and
regional, has taught her the difference between being alone
and being lonely.

There are very few women in the South who do not know
the feeling of being alone. For the old Southern code defines
women by their connectiveness to life: by their forebears, by
their husbands, and by their children. These are legitimate,
valued connections. But Southern women straddle two
realities simultaneously. The traditional code may define
them by traditional connections, but the code of individualism, also Southern, permits them to define themselves.

And that code, lifted to the level of elective eccentricity,
serves as an informal social loophole through which Southern women can escape the confines of a third definition,
which is grounded not in reality, but in literary romanticism.
The literary tradition of the antebellum South was neither
great nor abundant. The overwhelmingly rural, pioneer nature of the region precluded a large reading public. Illiteracy
was the rule rather than the exception among colonial
Southerners, and this hardly made for a highly discriminat-
ing reading public. But what literature emerged from the
antebellum South reflected the conditions and values of
early Southern society, including the common misconcep-
tions of the time.

Many Southerners mistakenly believed that they were
descended from noble Cavaliers, and a few actually viewed
the South as a romantic medieval world miraculously transplanted to nineteenth-century America. Early Southern
writers skipped over the reality that many Southerners were
descendants of the criminals, drunks, and paupers who
bought passage to America by voluntarily binding themselves to colonial landholders as indentured servants and,
when their terms of forced service ended, acquired land for
themselves. Instead, they wrote of a Southern aristocracy

renowned for its rich hospitality, pampered women, devotion to family, and code of honor. In a region captivated by romanticism, honor becomes critically important. If a Southern male was insulted or slandered, honor demanded that he challenge his adversary to a duel. Closely connected to the concept of manly honor was the cult of Southern womanhood. Southern males who felt it mandatory to protect their own honor were obliged by extension to defend the honor of their women. The romantic ideal portrayed Southern women as chaste, morally pure, unfailingly Christian—sheltered belles with soft skin, sensitive souls, and plenty of leisure time in which to plan for their next ball.

The truth of it was that most women in the antebellum South worked harder than field hands. They married early and spent long hours cooking, cleaning, washing, sewing, making soap, bearing children and raising them. Not even wealth lifted the domestic burden, for the wives of the few rich plantation owners acquired even greater responsibilities with the addition of slaves to their households. They supervised slave labor, including that of the sickroom, kitchen, laundry, planting, and harvesting. Yet the reality did nothing to expel the romantic ideal; it was simply incorporated into the legend: Southern woman was exceedingly strong beneath her decorous demeanor and feminine façade.

The war itself enhanced that legend. The Civil War is known as a "woman's war," for it was Southern women who were among the most ardent advocates of secession, and Southern women who made the greatest sacrifices for the South's lost cause. When hostilities erupted in the spring of 1861, women urged their husbands, sons, and lovers to enlist. Throughout the South they showed their disapproval of males who did not volunteer for military service. In Selma, Alabama, women carried out a prolonged "pout and sulk" campaign to promote enlistment. Many broke their engagements to men who were slow to enlist. More than a few sent their beaus skirts and petticoats with instructions to "wear these or volunteer."

As the war progressed, the women lost much of their ardor for battle, as did their men. But they remained firm in their support of the Southern cause. And even after defeat, many continued to urge unrelenting resistance to the hated foes of the North. After the fall of Vicksburg, occupation forces installed a Yankee minister at the Christ Episcopal Church and included in the service a prayer for the President of the United States. As Gordon Cotton, director of Vicksburg's Old Courthouse Museum, tells it, "There was a huff and a rustle of skirts, and the women stalked out in protest. The local commander issued a stern ultimatum, but the women refused to return. There would be no prayer for Abraham Lincoln in *their* church. The men didn't have the nerve to do that. But the women did."

Some years after the end of the war, Cotton continues, a certain Senator Williams from Yazoo County was talking with a Northern friend in the U.S. Senate.

"The friend asked why the rebel army had continued to fight when they knew the defeat was certain. Senator Williams said the Confederate soldiers were simply afraid to quit and go home because of the women."

The Southern male, whose dominance both sexes accepted in antebellum times, could not logically regard as inferior the woman who had successfully managed farm or plantation during his absence. And so the Civil War provided a springboard of sorts for women, from which they leaped beyond old circumscribed female spheres into many earlier reserved for men. Southern males might have been slow to recognize women's changing status; certainly they made no haste in granting them suffrage or admitting them to the medical and legal professions. But women enjoyed far more freedom—and far more responsibility—than before. The logical next step was for husband and wife to pool their energies in an effort to cope with the enormous problems of the postwar years. And this is what most actually did. Especially since the war, women of the South have contributed their energy and judgment to family enterprises—farms, plantations, and stores—and assumed wider control of these. They retained, usually, the control of the household.

The tradition of strength combines with the value historically assigned to individualism to grant Southern women a remarkable measure of personal freedom. And the time-honored Southern escalation of individualism into eccentricity encourages women to find niches of their own.

And Brunson's Aunt Babe? Well, she kept in touch, as maiden aunts do, until the very end. She may in fact have set some sort of a record for last-minute communication. She was, you recall, a prodigious reader of the Bible. She carried it into the closet with her. She discussed it with anyone who'd listen. She made it a point to read it a bit each day. Brunson, on the other hand, had gotten out of the habit.

"I don't read the Bible anymore. Hadn't read it for years. But one morning I woke up at one A.M. Wide awake. I had this *compulsion* to read the Bible. So I got up and scrounged around for it, and I went in and read Matthew, Mark, Luke, and John. Straight through. And then I went back to bed and slept till seven. And then my cousin called from southern Mississippi and said Aunt Babe had died that morning. And I said, 'Well, she got a look at me on the way through.' "

Keeping in touch is part of the heritage.

Country Sweet:
            Thoreau-backs & Trailblazers

It's hard to have deep roots
under concrete.
—DOLLY PARTON

Just as there's more to the South than moonlight and magnolias, there's more to Southern woman than romanticism and down-home madness.

Below each dainty, well-turned ankle there's a heel solidly planted in backroads dirt.

Southern woman is committed to preserving what is valid from her past. And that past is firmly rooted in the old rural values: in the provincial love of place, the sense of family, the emphasis on clan virtues, the everyday courtesies, the near-tactile empathy with the land itself. Never mind that most of us now are urban creatures: Southern women are rural in mind and in spirit, and most of their reactions spring from attitudes held over from earlier times. They're bound, physically and psychically, to the Southern soil—and to the notion that to cling to it is to survive and flourish even in the face of explosive change. City-bred Southerners talk of a vague but persistent longing to return to the land. City-dwelling Thoreau-backs restlessly retrace their roots on weekends and holidays. Those who have remained in the smaller towns and on the farms would have to be pried like abalone from rock from their country-sweet acreage along the South's muddy backroads.

The provincial South persists most vividly in its smaller towns and villages, and on the farms where it is still possible to know first-hand the special assets of the Southern soil. But those who fall heir to these know that country can be bitter as well as sweet. Census figures—those that show rural population growth surging ahead of urban growth—paint a false picture of backroads prosperity. Since 1970, non-metropolitan areas have grown in population twice as fast as the urban centers. Yet they harbor more than a third of the region's elderly, and nearly half those living below the nation's official poverty line. Smaller towns know urban distress as intimately as any metropolis; but often they are arbitrarily excluded from federal grant programs and forced to tote the load of costly improvements that play hell with the budgets of aged and needy residents. As for farming, that's usually a matter now of selling pigs to buy feed. Tapeworm and pellagra went out with Dixie's one-crop economy, but today even the best-informed farmers live in a near-chronic state of economic strain, and most others are marginal.

The rural South has never been a land of ease or material comfort, except briefly and for a very few. Even so, it is the rural South far more than the urban one that sustains Southern women and keeps them distinct. It is here that the old traditional values find their greatest expression, here that family and place supply the essence of identity.

Little else is needed.

"Not much profit in farming now. Just pleasure, and trying to make ends meet."

Mrs. S. T. Hawkins is sixty-nine years old. She's lived her entire life in Calhoun County, most of it on the 210-acre farm near Bruce, Mississippi, that she's worked with her husband since marriage. She's a handsome, down-to-earth country woman without frills or refinements, a relaxed and energetic lady with a level-eyed view of life and a soul-sustaining pride in the knowledge that she and her family hold title to the land that surrounds her.

> *If a person has a piece of land,*
> *they __have__ something.*
> *Land is special in the South.*
> —MRS. S. T. HAWKINS

One suspects, listening, that this is a woman who is grateful for the good times, unruffled by the bad. Through all her words runs the unmistakable chord of Southern satisfaction that is so often born of a strong sense of identity and contentment.

"It's a hard life, farming. But it's a free one. You're your own boss. The main thing is what you enjoy. If you enjoy farming, that's the thing for you to do. You do the best you can with what you've got."

The South, she says, is special: she would live nowhere else.

"I think it's the people. You can start down this road right here, and you won't walk far because somebody will stop and pick you up."

Her husband, S. T., agrees.

"We've still got good neighbors," he says. "My grandson built his house right out yonder by the lake, sometime last spring. He hired a man that knew how to read a blueprint and everything. And the time come to wire it. And one of the neighbors come over and wired it. The carpenter said something about that. He just couldn't understand why that boy'd come wire that whole house and not charge a red cent for it. Well, the way it is here, someone's always helping. Someone's always doing something for somebody else. For nothing. But it's money you're saving."

S. T. worries that the South is changing: the old values

seem to be gone with the wind, and the new, commercial ones are crass and suspect. Mrs. Hawkins is more optimistic. But in provincial female fashion, she sits back while her husband holds forth, nodding her agreement and approval when she can.

"One thing that's hurt," says S. T., "is too many people trying to make money instead of trying to raise a family. We've got kids around here eighteen and twenty and twenty-one years old that don't even know what a day's work is. I don't care how much education you've got. If you haven't got the experience to go with it, what do you know? Down South, you've got that experience that the South had. Well, you can read books. And you can tell just what the book said. So what?"

It's too much, at last, for Mrs. Hawkins.

"I *like* to read," she protests.

But S. T. holds the floor, and he's pessimistic:

"There was a Baptist preacher here awhile back, and he says times was going to get better. But according to the Bible, they won't. It done pulled over. I think we done seen its best days."

Mrs. Hawkins objects. *These,* she says, are the good old days:

"We've lived through the First World War, the Second World War, the Korean War. We've gone from the ox-wagon to the tractor to the car. I remember when I saw the first car. The first Ford, and the first tractor in Calhoun County. I was amazed! But we didn't have lights. We didn't have water. We didn't have the conveniences in the home that we have now. It costs more to live, but you get more for your money than you did back then. I wouldn't have it back the way it was. Not for a minute."

This is a woman who lives in the present, with few complaints and no regrets for the years she has spent on these two hundred acres. The provincial world is a small one, but all she ever needed or wanted, she says, she found here: land, family, church.

The Hawkinses are Primitive Baptists. Somebody once asked S. T. Hawkins what he'd be if he weren't a Primitive Baptist.

"I'd be ashamed!" he snapped, like a Mississippi turtle in churning water.

For Mrs. Hawkins the church is an integral part of life, as much secular as sacred. It's more than a spiritual mainstay: for most of her years the church has served as the center of her social life. Her commitment is absolute, but not unduly solemn.

"Sometimes we'd get somebody to give us a party at night. We'd play games like four-in-the-middle and Charlie. We'd just have a good old whoop-up time. I tell you what, it's just about the same as square-dancing. But you couldn't dance in church, so you just changed the name! With Charlie, you line up on each side and you go get your partner, you know, and you sing a song. It was okay with the church if you called it a game instead of a dance."

But her great dedication is to the tradition of Sacred Harp singing. One of the South's most remarkable traditions, the Sacred Harp began in the 1840s as a nondenominational form of sacred music, and survives today, closely aligned with the Primitive Baptist Church, as vigorous community singing. Itinerant singing masters of colonial times taught young men and women part-singing with a musical scale represented by the sequence of syllables then popular in England *(fa so la—fa so la—mi—fa);* later, each syllable was assigned a distinct shape as an aid to sight-singing. Before singing the text to each song, "fasola folk" vocalized the syllables representing the notes, each according to shape; in time, the singing of the notes—to "put the tune in mind"— became a ritualized part of the service.

Shaped-note singing survives today virtually intact,

partly because of the singing schools and partly because the tradition is so firmly rooted in a rural lifestyle that has remained essentially unchanged for generations. Sacred Harpers travel considerable distances for weekend song-fests that re-create rituals far older than any participant. The typical meeting place is a small country church, often situated in a grove of trees near the graveyard; the locale is significant, for shaped-note singers seldom stray from the context of continuity. Inside, the church is usually bare of decoration. Singers arrange themselves on rows of wooden benches formed in a square, a side for each harmonic part, with an open space within for the leader. Benches for listeners line the aisles facing the singers. The strength of this tradition is equaled by the stamina of its adherents: shaped-note singers meet for all-day sessions, singing from nine in the morning till late afternoon with five-minute recesses on the hour and a single break for dinner. Before they finish, they may have run through as many as a hundred eighteenth- and nineteenth-century melodies from the old Sacred Harp book. They don't quit and go home till their vocal cords give out.

"It's been going on in this part of the country, well, back in eighteen-hundred-and-something my granddaddy Hawkins had one with three thousand people there. That's where we held it last Sunday, the same place. Guess it's been going on for over a hundred years. Nobody knows how long for sure."

Mrs. Hawkins nods her husband on.

"We've traveled around some. We've been in Alabama and Florida. We went down on the coast one time *just* to sing! For a big club outfit, you know? They paid all our expenses down there and back. Part of the people were from New York City, and they had never heard it in their life. And they wanted us to fly down there, but there were already four or five carloads of us."

"We don't have a group," says Mrs. Hawkins. "Anybody that wants to sing. We sing the notes first. The top line is treble, the next alto, the third line is the soprano, and the bottom line is bass. Each one sings their part. Everyone stays on the same time, and when the alto leads out the leading part hushes and you go right on. And when you get to a certain beat, that's when the other part comes in."

Traditionally, the Sacred Harp is a democratic institution, open to all who wish to sing. In practice, few are equal to the complexity of technique and procedure or to the dedication demanded by the art. Perhaps no more than a few thousand practitioners persist. Among them, the Hawkinses are famed for their knowledge of the old songs and for their skill in singing them.

Sacred Harp survives as a regional subculture, drawing on the strength of family ties and bonds with community churches. The music is entrenched in the rural pattern and passed on by those who remain committed to the local soil. While the church never adopted officially the songs of the Sacred Harp, singers believe strongly in the moral power of their singing. Every session is opened and closed with prayer; shaped-note singing is offered as religious tribute. Beyond its natural alliance with the Primitive Baptist Church, however, the Sacred Harp offers its remnant bands of followers a real sense of rural fellowship and a tradition of pleasure for its own sake. This isn't *performance* music, but group-singing. Foot-tapping music. Singers grin and nudge one another throughout the sessions, chatter excitedly between songs about the skill of this group, the progress of another since last meeting. Good-natured banter prevails at recess. Dinner-on-the-grounds ("that's what you want to get in on!") is a communal feast carted in boxes by singers accustomed to reaping their own harvests; it's a high-spirited social hour when they relax, heap their plates high, and mingle with the crowd, talking, teasing, trading mock insults, renewing old bonds and forging new ones. Everyone is known here, and the sense of identity is significant. Beyond its moral focus, the Sacred Harp is a means of bridging the distance that is so much a part of the regional heritage. In the isolation of the rural South, shared purpose and clear identity close a circle against the outside world. If that circle is broken at the end of the day, Sacred Harpers know at least that it will be formed anew with the coming weekend.

If you drop more than you can pick up,
somebody'll be there to help you.
—S. T. HAWKINS

"*These* are the good old days," Mrs. Hawkins repeats, patting the stout oblong book that contains all the old songs of the Sacred Harp.

The land means no less to Southerners untutored in the intricacies of shaped notes and harmonic parts. Nor, for many, is it necessary to commit the soil to production. To live near the land, to enjoy it, to keep it in the family, are enough. At fifty-nine, Mary McGehee has struggled for more than thirty-five years to retain her great-great-grandfather's plantation acreage near Woodville, Mississippi.

Bowling Green was no ordinary plantation, Judge Edward McGehee no ordinary planter. He settled in Wilkinson County in 1829 with his third wife, Mary Burress, and eight of the nineteen children he would eventually father. Originally, there were 1600 acres planted in cotton and corn. The grounds were littered with frame structures relevant to the work of the estate: a gin house, meathouse, cookhouse, carriage house, slave dwellings. The main house, an elegant columned structure built with imported brick, was completed in 1831, and served as a focus of Delta hospitality in antebellum times. On the first floor were spacious parlors designed for entertaining; in the library were books and portraits of honored family friends, Daniel Webster and Henry Clay among them.

It was from this luxurious headquarters that McGehee directed his varied interests; these were considerable. He owned other lucrative farms and plantations in Mississippi and Louisiana. He owned and operated the fifth railroad to be built in the United States; his was the first American line to use the standard gauge, the first to issue and print freight tariff, the first to adopt cattle pits. He build the first textile mill to be erected in the South. He owned the first cotton factory in Mississippi. He established the first bank in the region. As an early associate of Samuel Morse, he constructed the first telegraph line in Mississippi. He built the first Methodist Church in New Orleans. He founded the Bethel Methodist Church at Whitestown as well, providing slave labor for its construction and hiring a preacher at his own expense. He established the Woodville Female Academy. He was co-founder of Centenary College in Shreveport and helped to fund a number of other colleges in the area. He declined an offer from President Zachary Taylor to serve as Secretary of the Treasury. Judge McGehee looms as the single most prominent planter-philanthropist of the antebellum Delta; Bowling Green was a rich and aristocratic home and a legendary social center.

But during the Civil War, the Judge served breakfast to Confederate soldiers quartered nearby, and Union troops took exception. The McGehee family was given twenty minutes to retrieve from the main house any prized personal possessions, then forced to watch as Union soldiers set fire to the mansion; gin house and fields were torched as well. After the war, the Judge built near the ruins a large frame house that served the needs of generations of McGehees until it, too, was destroyed by fire in 1941. Mary McGehee was born in that two-story wooden structure, and she has managed by sheer grit and a full-time job in town to hang on to 675 acres of the original acreage.

"You have to work to make enough to farm, and you have to farm to make enough to work at any job in town."

I had expected her emphasis to be on the past. But she too is rooted firmly in the present. Her ties, most essentially, are to the land itself.

"I enjoy stories of the past. I really do. But I live today. I was born here, been living here, raising cows, loving it ever since."

She never made a conscious decision to serve as caretaker to her fifth-generation Bowling Green heritage.

"I came home from college in nineteen forty. Had two offers to teach school. One, that was up in northern Mississippi, was for sixty-five dollars a month, the other over here in east Mississippi for seventy dollars, and I had to take my own bed. I didn't want to teach school anyway. I didn't know what I wanted to do. So I came home. The house burned in forty-one, and my father was sick at the time. We had eight or ten families living on the place, just raising cotton and corn like they'd been doing forever. So when my father died in forty-three I said, 'Mama, I'll do it if I don't get any static from anybody.' Well, bless her heart, she didn't give me any."

She got off to a disastrous start.

"I bought a bull. First bull I ever bought. From a neighbor over here, Mr. Key. And I put that bull on the place. He stayed off by himself, not mixing with the herd. So I went home very upset, this being my first big investment, and I said, 'Mama, I don't know what to say to Mr. Key.' And she said *she'd* do it. She never was at a loss for words. But this time she really hesitated. Mr. Key kept saying, 'Well, Miss Mac, what seems to be wrong with the bull?' 'Course, he knew as well as anybody else. And finally Mama said, 'Well, he's just not *effective.*' It took me about three years to live that down.

"But I guess I grew up with my mother's philosophy. Live today. One day at a time. That's all you've got. Why worry about something you can't do anything about? I got *that* from my mother. She was a Virginian, and you couldn't talk to her three minutes that she didn't let you know it. Now she was a strong character: you should have known *her.*"

Mary McGehee has always had a freewheeling sense of independence of her own. She tried to enlist in the WACS in 1942. Because of a calcium deposit on one lung, she failed the physical.

"I could have gotten in later, but I didn't want to after that. Came back and started working, here and in town."

She worked for two years for the county agent, for fifteen as a linotype operator for Woodville's newspaper, the oldest paper in the state. In 1960, she went to work in the bookkeeping department of the Commercial Bank. Later, she worked as teller, then assistant cashier. Always, she worked full-time in town; always, she supervised the work at Bowling Green as well.

"It was just a regular plantation. Cotton and corn at first. But then the boll weevil arrived, and I finally gave up and went to the cows."

She still has her job at the bank.

"Trying to figure out how to retire. I'm fifty-nine. Fifty-nine-and-a-half, 'cause I'm counting the halves now. If I can figure any way to retire before sixty-two, I'm going to. Ever hear the expression 'sitting loose'? I'd like to build a log house out on this place with a front porch facing south, overlooking the pond, and sit there with my feet propped up all day long. They'll pass by and say, 'Poor old thing, there she sits.' "

But it's respectable, of course, to be a bit eccentric in the South:

"What's the point of getting old here unless you are?"

Even so, Mary's guardianship of the old plantation should

keep her occupied. At the insistence of friends, she permits, during Woodville's annual mid-March Pilgrimage Week, a stereophonic re-enactment of the burning of Bowling Green. Taken from an original account written by Mary Burress McGehee, it's an ambitious, high-quality production. The drama is produced by Ernesto Caldiera, a former producer for CBS television who was lured to Woodville by the chance to restore nearby Rosemont, the boyhood home of Jefferson Davis. Mary Stuart, star of television's long-running "Search for Tomorrow" and highly regarded "queen of the soaps," contributes the narration without fee. She's Southern by birth, too, and mindful of the heritage she shares with Mary McGehee. Mary is grateful to Caldiera and Stuart, but decidedly practical. If the production helps to cover taxes and maintenance expense on Bowling Green, fine; if not, she'll manage somehow, as she has in the past.

Mary's life seems to support studies at Harvard University which pinpoint Woodville as the Southern town most consistently typifying the traditions, customs, and culture of the antebellum South.

"It's just like any small town in the South. Maybe more so. It hasn't changed in thirty-five years, or forty, however many you count. When you get in trouble, there's not one soul who doesn't come. When the frame house burned, we had no water, but everyone from town was here, going in and carrying things out. We saved everything on the first floor, all the fixtures from two bathrooms, the mantelpiece —three of those, I think—the window casings and window panes. People couldn't do enough to help."

A free spirit who disdains fancy dresses and makes no secret of her fondness for good bourbon, Mary McGehee tends to be billed by townspeople as an early "libber." She's not: she's simply a down-home original who knows how to kill her own snakes and wastes little time worrying about the superficialities of appearance.

"When I started using this thing, this cigarette holder, Ernesto said I looked like the town character. I could care less. I'm not going to quit smoking, either. It doesn't bother me at all."

Such minor rebellions are low-key, relaxed, and good-natured; she has seldom been challenged for the right to do as she pleases, and doesn't expect to be chastised now. She has never felt any strong social pressure to marry, and she hasn't ("through the grace of God and the stupidity of man"). She has no regrets whatsoever. She's buoyant, serene, and content, thoroughly at peace not only with the present but with her personal past as well. She has nieces and nephews who will inherit what's left of Bowling Green together with any improvements she makes ("they love this place as much as I do"). She would live, voluntarily, nowhere else.

"You have an identity here you don't have outside."

Meanwhile, she continues to take pleasure in walking the land that belonged first to her great-great-grandfather, and in the knowledge that she has been able to keep Bowling Green safely in trust for the remnants of her family. She goes where she wishes, at her own ambling pace, does as she wants, and enjoys the company of a varied circle of friends who share her interests and her values.

"It's terrible being so happy with your life, isn't it? But I am."

In the South, place and family are the essence of identity, and they perpetuate the old, provincial values. Family here, of course, means *clan,* that huge and assorted horde of kin who cluster 'round to lend color, support, and diversity. They have a good deal to do with the development of the strength and high-styled individualism that distinguishes Dixie's native daughters. It takes no more than a dash of down-to-red-clay common sense to see why.

In the eyes of more rootless, mobile Americans, the

South's close-knit familial bonds seem rare and exotic.

The average American family relocates every six years, outdistancing the bonds of an extended family whose members, however meddlesome, might otherwise rally 'round to share in domestic responsibilities. It's a loss that has impact on the institution of marriage only slightly less profound than that of the boll weevil on Mary McGehee's first cotton crops. At best, it serves to isolate husbands and wives in lonely pairs: it is their lot to fill unaided all the gaps created by a new and insatiable American mobility.

Not so in the past—or, today, in the provincial South, where family ties rival the rampant kudzu for entanglement and tenacity. Whether they live in cities or on farms, newly married Southern couples even today typically take their place within an extended family, within a familiar social and economic community, within a shared context of regional history, and (usually) within a religious tradition. Institutions like these do far more than offer support in times of crisis; they provide the new union with a sense of direction. More often than not, marriage in the South is a means of transmitting old values, a way of assuring that the rhythms and cycles of life follow an orderly course through each succeeding generation. The nuclear family never had much currency here; in this crazy-quilt provincial world, grandparents, aunts, uncles, nieces, nephews, and cousins stream regularly through the household, and a raft of long-term neighbors crowd the porches.

This is yesterday's wisdom, alive and at work in Dixie today.

For those close family ties seem to nourish the flamboyant individualism so dear to the hearts of Southerners. Dr. Pauline Rose Clance, a conspicuously autonomous Southern academic who maintains a remarkable balance between femininity and personal freedom, knows why. A Southern woman herself and an experienced clinical psychologist, she views Dixie's daughters from two perspectives. And she's uniquely equipped to articulate the paradox of Southern womanhood.

"On the one hand, you have an emphasis on conformity and social adaptiveness. On the other, you have a heightened respect for individuality, for people who are eccentric or idiosyncratic in their behavior."

She traces the duality to the commonplace presence of extended family members.

Clance was born and reared in Baptist Valley, a small village in the hills of West Virginia. She took her doctorate at the University of Kentucky at Lexington, and makes her home now in Decatur, Georgia. But she has lived for long periods outside the borders of the South. She has had the chance to compare and contrast; she has the training necessary to define the ways in which Southern women differ from women elsewhere.

"What I saw when I lived in Cleveland and in various suburban areas outside the South was a social organization in which the extended family was the exception rather than the rule. A typical family consisted of a mother, a father, and their children; other family members lived miles distant. It struck me then: there were two adults trying alone to meet all the needs of their offspring. Only their biases, all the things they valued, were transmitted to the next generation.

"In the South, where people tend to live among their kin, there's a far richer diversity of values from which children may choose. My own father was a scholarly man, though he wasn't highly educated. He cared about books and reading. He valued intellectualism. And those are *good* qualities. But I had an uncle, too, and he was very different from my father. He loved hunting and fishing and having a good time. Knowing them both gave me options I wouldn't have had otherwise. I drew from both lifestyles, both sets of values."

Not a bad deal, this business of having on tap adults

removed from the primary responsibility for instilling values and administering discipline. More important, the extended family multiplies the number of behavioral models available to each child.

"I'd go spend a couple of weeks from time to time with my aunt. I'd go fishing or hunting on weekends with my uncle. I wasn't dependent on just two parents, just two models. I could see other adults and how they acted and what it got them in life."

A riotous mass of kin, loving or bickering, lends needed diversity, widens horizons. Southern children realize early on that life offers abundant alternatives. There are a good many ways to be human, to be Southern, to be male or female. The provincial child has exposure to numerous life-styles, and falls heir to the odd brand of tolerance that distinguishes those born and bred in Dixie.

> *Traditionally, the South has been quite tolerant.*
> *Localities tolerate the village atheist and the*
> *lonely radical. The family tolerates. The South,*
> *more than any other place, honors the strong*
> *individual stand, the person who says*
> *what he believes.*
> —SHELDON HACKNEY, PRESIDENT, TULANE UNIVERSITY

Clance believes too that the tradition of being simultaneously gentle and strong puts Southern women one up on their Northern sisters, who more commonly view these as conflicting qualities.

"I look at the messages people get about how to live their lives. I think the myth of the Southern belle was perpetuated as an ideal. Most women got the message: they realized early on they were expected to be gentle and feminine. At the same time, they knew that Southern women have always had great domestic and economic responsibility, and a good deal of power too. They're given permission for power and strength through an unspoken social trade, or bargain. So long as they are willing to pay homage to a male, they enjoy considerable behavioral freedom. I use the word *homage* deliberately. That's the trade. If a Southern woman is willing to give credit to a man, especially in a very public way, then society grants her the freedom to show her strength and influence without faulting her for lack of femininity."

Both Mary McGehee and Faith Brunson, who've built full and enjoyable lives without making trades in role politics, would argue the point. Yet it may be that they are two of the exceptions who serve to prove the rule. It's easier by far to play the traditional role, and the majority of women in the South exercise what freedom they have from within the context of traditional femininity.

Clance's father owned a successful lumber company. Her mother was a small farmer. There was no conflict between the two regarding status or power; Mrs. Rose deferred publicly to her husband and used her private power in ways that are deemed traditionally feminine in the South.

"When a doctor couldn't be found, my mother served as midwife for the women in our little valley. People saw her as a gentle, caring woman. They also felt she had a lot of strength. Yet it was my father who was placed on the pedestal. It was a small town, and people there knew who owned what. But if you asked, I think they'd say the farm belonged to my father, even though it was clear that my mother ran it, that she raised the cows and sold the cattle and brought in the crops."

By trading public for private power, Southern women gain behavioral freedom unsurpassed by women elsewhere. By cloaking that power in practiced femininity, they gain the right to rule the home roost; often they exercise considerable influence in the community. Both black and white Southerners live basically in a matriarchal society. Because of the lasting links here between church, family, and community, matriarchs (like Lillian Carter) enjoy awesome social power.

Even so, they defer publicly to their men.

"In front of company, in front of any outsider, even in front of the family, Southern women defer. They'll insist even to the kids that it's their daddy who's in charge, though all are aware that most major decisions are made by the mother."

Clance sees this arrangement as a highly creative way of working out the conflict of shared power.

"The Southern woman recognizes the reality of male power. She chooses to affirm male power rather than behave destructively toward it. In her affirmation she is able to affirm in much more indirect ways that she too has power —and considerable personal freedom."

Hard-core feminists foam at the mouth when confronted with this unspoken social pact between the Southern sexes, charging Dixie's darlings with self-demeaning sexual manipulation. Yet only a few Southern women find it repugnant to play the submissive public role in trade for expanded personal freedom. In any case, Pauline Clance thinks the need to bargain is temporary.

"There won't be as much need to do this in the future. But it *has* been a creative way of working things out in the past and present."

For those who choose to make the trade, the old Southern Belle role comes in handy; it provides a ready model for traditional femininity that is not always used in traditional ways.

The Southern belle: I have loved her as a friend, respected her as an adversary. A few women truly excell in the role; Sally Ann Ferguson* has raised it to the level of commercial

*Pseudonym, by request.

art. Ferguson is part of New Orleans' subterranean economy; her fortunes have varied with the times and with the expediencies of local politicians, but she's always managed to avoid those Southern *macho*-crazed whore bars where mean-eyed juiced-up honky-tonk cowboys assign themselves a nightly quota of asses to whip and show little regard for where the broken glass flies. She once ran a Mafia-backed whorehouse and stashed away some $100,000 a year. Those are untaxed dollars, don't-you-know, not bad pin-money for a little Shreveport girl who never made it to college. Call her a Midnight Cowgirl. Or a Hillbilly Hooker. In any case, she's a warm, candid, rebel-hearted and enormously likeable Southern woman who's made a profession of the traditional feminine role. In addition, she'd more than do to ride the river with. Now if you're some peckerhead Yankee who lacks the ear for such flowery provincial compliments, all I can say is that this is the highest praise one Southerner can bestow on another. What it means is that Sally Ann's a good ol' girl, and just about semi-delightful despite the hidden scars she bears from living life so long in the fast lane.

And if you're one of those militant anti-belle feminists, you're not gonna like what she has to say about you. No, ma'am. Not one bit.

"Well, I've lived all over the North, and I *know* Southern ladies are different. Northern women are very competitive with the men. They really don't know how to relax with a man. They're so competitive up there that when they get a man all they can do is worry him to death. They wheedle and whine and make demands. Whereas a Southern woman usually has a little life of her own on the side that she hopes her husband doesn't find out about, and she lets him alone. But she knows how to relax with him. No matter what kind of day she's had, she puts him first at night. She rubs his back and fetches him a drink and fixes him a mess of good old chicken-fried steak and lets him *enjoy* himself. Seems like Southern women are taught this, whereas Northern women are taught to compete. You know, to get a man, to get married at any cost. And that's the difference. They were taught to get a man, but we were taught *how.*"

In Dixie, women band together in groups from their earliest years to ponder the mysterious male ego and swap what Ferguson used to call "mantrap secrets." Some of these were technical tips passed down from her mother (brush front teeth with cold cream for an easy-gliding smile). Others, contributed by older, faster girls, dealt with the prevailing if often unfounded folklore of the day; many of these centered about the multiple uses of Coca-Cola (drop three aspirin into a Coke for a quick, cheap high; shake and fizz a bottle of Coke for an emergency douche). Most feminine secrets focused, however, on the sort of "ladylike" behavior designed to entice and tantalize males. A lady never interrupts when a man is talking. She never refers to past arguments (especially if she was reckless enough to win them) or asks prying questions. She never beats a man at chess or tennis. She laughs at all his jokes, even if she's heard them a hundred times before ("oh, Billy Clyde, you are just the *most fun!*"). She never talks too much about herself. Instead, she works hard at becoming a "good listener," especially on such subjects as football, baseball, and his latest 'coon hunt. She works even more diligently to perfect the role of the submissive female. She is nurse, nurturer, helpmeet, and she is destined to do a lot of fetching and carrying. Her primary purpose in life is to make herself desirable to the male.

Ferguson's mother was a woman who bartered public for private power. But, always, she was outwardly submissive to Sally Ann's dad.

"Dinner was on the table at a quarter of six because he got off work at five-thirty. And woe be to him if he stopped off for a couple of beers. But I remember that about an hour before my daddy came home, my mother would bathe and fix her hair and put on a nicer housedress."

Ferguson married at seventeen and followed the same super-feminine Southern pattern.

"I used to set the clock ahead an hour. My husband got up at seven, so I slipped out of bed at six. I'd make sure the house was absolutely clean. I'd bathe and put on my makeup and fix my hair. Then I'd creep on back into bed, so when he woke up and turned over to look at me, I was *perfect.*"

But she was young and high-spirited, and such single-minded dedication to the traditional role took its toll.

"It's always been hard for me to stay in a mold. As soon as I felt I was in a mold, I'd begin to get bored and then maybe I'd do something real freaky. I'd played the perfect little housewife for nearly two whole years. Then one day I went out to the base and I stole his car. I drove all the way to Clearwater, Florida. I picked up as many hot tomatoes as I could find hitchhiking on the road, and I stayed gone two days. He had the police looking for me because he thought I'd been kidnapped. And I never did do that again. I mean, I never stayed out for two whole days again. But I'd gotten crazy that first time, and I couldn't stop it. From time to time I'd get bored and I'd break loose and I'd go fuck off."

At home, however, she was ladylike and provincially deferential. And she kept her mouth shut. She had a year-old baby girl, was five months pregnant with her son, when her husband died in Korea.

"He didn't get killed in combat. He got killed in a jeep accident on base. He was drunk."

She says it non-judgmentally.

"I boogied on the insurance money. What do you do? You're nineteen years old, the government gives you ten thousand dollars, and you never saw so much money in your life. You buy yourself some new clothes and a car and you go through all the money. Fast."

When the money ran out, Sally Ann moved to New Orleans and started job-hunting. She wasn't trained to do anything but please men. Finally, she found work in a bar, where tips were proportionate to her well-honed ability to make a man feel relaxed and comfortable.

"Two months later, I found out I was working for the Mafia. I was thrilled, I was delighted. I thought, 'Okay, if I quit work, they'll *kill* me!' It intrigued me. I did pretty well there, so they let me start managing clubs for them. After a couple of years, I got tired of working. They pissed me off one night and I walked out. I'd met this madam in the bar a few months earlier and she'd said if I ever wanted to go to work I could call her. She explained *exactly* what she meant. So I called her. She invited me over, and a week later I had this great apartment and I had three phones and I was making about a thousand a week."

It wasn't a career she'd planned for.

"It was just until something else came along. Like everything else in my life. I never have felt like *anything* was my career. I think *career* is fantasy work. There aren't that many glamorous high-status high-pay jobs around, not for men and not for women."

That is a realism echoed over and over again by Dixie's daughters, and one of the common-sense reasons (though not the primary one) these women see so little point in feminist strategies designed to open "men's jobs" to women.

A second realism (one Ferguson braced hard for) never came to pass, at least not on the scale she anticipated. Until her first marriage, she'd been exceptionally chaste, guarding her reputation as she'd been taught was so crucial. Her initial marital transgressions were conducted with discretion, outside the city limits and so safely beyond the range of familiar eyes. When she stepped far more boldly off the given turf to enter the bar-prostitution circuit, she expected (one imagines) to be stoned to death in the streets. But she counted among her clients and acquaintances some of the city's most prominent males; often through these contacts she was welcomed at posh society parties where she was introduced (naturally) as a free-lance model. This sanitized version of her work fooled no one. But life in the South is so intimate, with passions so near the surface, that certain fictions are maintained as social restraints. Everyone knows the contradictions are there, but it's considered quite important (and good form, besides) to conceal them.

Sally Ann remains a prized party guest, ever in demand. Yet she has never had the feeling that the warm welcome habitually extended her derives solely from the novelty and naughtiness of the work that she does.

For one thing, her high status in the alternative culture gives her the romantic appeal of the superstar rebel. Ferguson is to street prostitution what Ferrari is to economy cars. Success may not be the perfect deodorant, but inside or outside the South it makes an intriguing perfume.

But far more important, she broke with convention in the honored Southern tradition of trading one larger-than-life role (that of the saucy-but-submissive homemaker) for another (that of the happy backroads hooker with a heart of gold). And she played the part so well that acquaintances were charmed rather than threatened by her wild-and-wicked trade. It's a demanding role but one that finds amazing acceptance in a Bible Belt region that takes such pride in the chastity of its women. One is obliged, like it or not, to pay homage to the inventive logic so inherent in the Southern mind.

Dixie never was the land of grand ladies, chaste and untouchably pure, that many Southerners would have it.

The South is enticingly, indisputably sensual, for all its traditional emphasis (much of it sincere) on Christian ideals, social conformity, and puritan virtues. It is sensual in its seasonal display of indigenous foods with exotic sweet flavors and mellow textures. It is sensual in its dank and humid climate, in its lush groves and densely wooded landscapes. It is sensual in its love for the soft liquid sounds and easy elisions of its honeyed speech. The South, indeed, is sensual in ways barely comprehensible to outsiders.

But where do you put the lust it inspires?

One can separate the "good women" from the "bad women," but then there arises the thorny problem of "debasing" oneself with the latter. In antebellum times, slavery provided a partial if undemocratic answer; in an ingenious feat of mental gymnastics, the Southern male reasoned that female slaves, being black and therefore "different," might be rawly passionate without being "bad." Hence the abundance of light-skinned slave children pattering about the old plantation.

Reality, however, intruded: the idyllic plantation days were numbered, and only a few white Southerners fit into the great-plantation class, anyway. The trick then was to manage—somehow—to transform "bad women" into good ones—not good enough to marry, necessarily, but good enough at least to mess around with. And so they embellished upon the socially redeeming stereotype of the country whore with a heart of gold. She is an inherently good woman, without a bad word for anybody, who was led astray by bad luck, circumstances, and the wickedness of the urban world; she retains, however, her provincial honesty and respect for family and concern for the masculine ego with all its urgent accompanying needs. Her spirit of camaraderie, her essential pride, her plain-spoken sense of humor and native (if salty) wit join with her legendary wildness in bed to make her a fit companion in the absence of one's wife.

Sally Ann Ferguson not only fits the popular stereotype, but lives up to it as well. When she defied the social norm, she did so within the context of high-color provincial idiosyncrasy. What she gained from her entry into the world of

store-bought love was a new and expanded personal freedom. She routinely crosses boundaries insurmountable for
other women, and she's never suffered from rigidly traditional sex-role standards.

"When I got married the first time, I found out that fuck-
ing was fun. It wasn't just a duty like I'd heard. So I tended
to be sort of promiscuous after that. People always told me
I had a very *masculine* attitude toward sex."

Outsiders are intrigued and captivated by her boldness.
Insiders are dazzled by her skill in portraying the traditional
feminine role. What dazzles me is the duality of her nature:

"Now I'm talking to you like this 'cause I know you. I
don't use this kind of language outside, you know. Put that
in your book too."

Amazing Grace (& Betty & Louise):
Evangelism in the Provincial South

I used to be an ungodly mess;
now I'm a godly mess.
—LOUISE MOHR

For all the growth and newborn sophistication of the Sunbelt cities, the South remains in large part a provincial domain where churches grow in wild profusion—and men and women alike are born again with amazing frequency.

The Bible Belt houses more than its proportionate share of smooth-talking hot-Gospelers who preach the sort of fire-and-brimstone fundamentalism that has always set records for bad taste and bad theology (or both). Hard-shell redneck evangelism is practiced more commonly now by sleek indoor charismatics and cosmeticized television preachers, but the canvas crusaders are commonplace still. Their exhortations ("But, *hallelujah,* there was one righteous man, *hallelujah,* Noah, *hallelujah . . .* ") play on apocalyptic fears and on the widespread conviction that the vengeful Old Testament God is determined even today to exact eyes for eyes and teeth for teeth—that we must each of us confess, repent, and appease, or else fry till well done. In its more orthodox institutional expressions, religion in Dixie has represented both the best of the Southern experience, teaching and acting from a position of social justice, and the worst, serving as a cultural bastion for those who fear change.

But, always, it has mattered profoundly.

At once varied and yet so similar, religion in Dixie is largely a Protestant affair. All faiths are represented, but evangelicalism predominates. It's a movement that cuts across denominational boundaries to include the Fundamentalists, who insist in all matters on a literal interpretation of the Bible, and the Pentecostalists, who practice such divine gifts as speaking in tongues and healing by prayer-power, and almost everyone else, from the Episcopalians to the Roman Catholics to the Jews to the off-beat healers and assorted tent revivalists.

Religion is an integral part of life in the lower-right-hand corner of the United States, as much a social institution as an instrument for winnowing the righteous from the spiritually doomed. The church calendar is awesomely crowded. Throughout the year there are revivals, when visiting preachers and their troops of traveling singers arrive to hold special services for a week or more, often two or three times daily. There are midweek prayer meetings, covered dinners, Vacation Bible Schools, prayer breakfasts and prayer brunches, revival luncheons, businessmen's prayer groups, church picnics, potluck suppers. There are teen groups, geriatrics groups, and groups for young Christian couples. There are religious retreats, church softball teams and bowling leagues, choirs, student preaching seminars, and recruitment programs ambitious enough to insure the salvation of every man, woman, and child in Dixie. If through some clergical oversight some weeknight goes unscheduled, it's always possible to drop 'round the parsonage to view aged Kodak slides from the preacher's last trip, subsidized by a faithful congregation, to the Holy Land.

Southern churches have been faulted more than once for galloping hypocrisy, and rightly so. While numerous black churches have served as important nurturing institutions for social change and civil-rights movements, white churches have served too often a constituency fiercely committed to the status quo. But for all their limitations, Southern churches offer both individuals and families a crucial life center. People there support one another in crisis and in celebration. They care for the sick, the needy, the aged, and the dying. They join in a tradition that gives continuity to life and validity to the old provincial attitudes. More than any other institution, the Southern church is rooted in the local soil and reflective of the local heritage. And it is relentlessly autonomous, a product of the provincial impulse to keep the church local, democratic, family-oriented, and community-centered. It is at the grass-roots level, in thousands of tiny community churches, that the faith thrives most vigorously. In this age of electronic evangelism, there are a few flashy urban Superchurches with plush wall-to-wall carpeting, rock-gospel bands, and pews to seat five thousand (or more) of the faithful. But the great majority of Southern church-goers still belong to isolated rural congregations of 200 or fewer.

Non-Southerners have tended to view these backwoods Christians with stereotypic eyes. Just let a few dozen gather any Sunday, and the outsiders freeze in horrified anticipation, braced for the time when the hillbillies start chunking snakes and speaking in tongues. But the patterns for such Southern exotica, for provincial emotionalism and fierce local autonomy, were set in colonial times. The Anglican Church easily established itself as the principal religious institution among the landed gentry—and blew it in the backwoods.

Well suited to the urban and village society typical of England at that time, the Anglican parish failed to meet the needs of colonial Americans. The Church of England, busy at home, seemed disinclined to adapt, creating a vacuum quickly filled by dissenting sects—Quakers, Lutherans, Baptists, Methodists, Presbyterians, and others—that arose and swept the back country of the South.

The newer churches, courting converts, made fewer liturgical demands on their members. Services were less formal and less rigidly structured. Most stressed emotionalism over education and faith over reason, common touches that appealed to the uneducated pioneers. Most were democratic, featuring the congregational form of church government over the highly structured traditional one, and inviting the active participation of lay readers. Many of the newer sects emphasized the necessity of religious conversion. The emotional release was great, the mass psychology of a revival service powerful. Revivals and camp meetings brought together large numbers of isolated rural people whose social contacts were otherwise limited.

It was with the camp meeting—an intense gathering of hundreds or thousands of people for days or weeks of continuous religious rites—that patterns were set for later provincials. Religious folk music had its origins here. So did the public confession of sin and the testimony of salvation. Preachers described heaven and hell in the most vivid terms, setting the style for highflown hellfire-and-damnation evangelistic oratory. Songs, prayers, and shouts from repentant sinners combined with the energy released by the crowding of so many people to create an atmosphere of electric intensity. So successful were these meetings that the revival was quickly institutionalized in most of the new faiths.

With urbanization came sophistication and refinement. City-dwelling Baptists and Methodists grew unsure about the religious excesses that prevailed at camp meetings. They formalized and refined their services, gradually eliminating what they came to view as the crudities of the past. In the rural South, however, churchgoers retained the old ways without interference from those who thought them unseemly. It is here that the faithful still find direction, dignity, and unself-conscious fulfillment in yesterday's rites and rituals. What evangelicals sometimes lack in sophistication or polish they make up for in feverish commitment. Even today there remain a remarkable number of sawdust-trail faith healers who peddle their canvas-covered version of the Christian gospel. In isolated churches members still deliver their own sermons, speak in tongues, and handle poisonous snakes in the routine worship of their God. The old fire-and-brimstone sermon is commonplace yet. So is baptism by total immersion, often in a mud-banked local river or lake so as to adhere more closely to tradition. The Southern dedication to Christianity is manifest even in the most secular reaches of society. Ads for hymn-singing events pepper the sports section of the Saturday paper. Signs along the South's backroads proclaim that JESUS SAVES, urge sinners to REPENT NOW, warn the faithful to PREPARE.

Always, there is spirited rivalry for lost and available souls. Nomadic faith healers post handbills that promise SIGHT TO THE BLIND, SPEECH TO THE MUTE, TUMORS NO MORE. Pentecostal fliers advertising HEALTH! SALVATION! MIRACLES! litter the parks in Atlanta. Over in Texas, Eldridge Cleaver pitches Jesus in a thirty-second TV spot sponsored by the Texas Baptist General Convention and directed by a Jewish-owned ad agency.

Grace always *has* been amazing.

Clearly the old-style religion, with its emphasis on the traditional values and its insistence on the born-again experience, fulfills a national need. Once patronized as redneck and tacky, the Evangelical movement indigenous to the South has burst the boundaries of the Bible Belt to win new converts at a clip unparalleled in American history.

There's a new look now, too, to the soldiers in God's evangelical army. It would seem that if the road to Hillbilly

Heaven has been recently resurfaced, it is Southern women who've provided the asphalt.

Southern women have been saddled with God's abundance of stereotyped ethical platitudes and, in many cases, rightly so: they've long served as models to clarify the values and ideals of Dixie. Most have found anchors in their local churches, where answers may be simple (*don't do it*), but at least are exceedingly clear. Certainly women have done most of the work of the church in the South, serving through such sexually segregated organizations as ladies' aid and missionary societies or simply rushing to the scene when any congregational need arose. In a region famed for its smooth-talking, Bible-thumping, soul-saving salesmen for Christ, however, the brightest superstars were male. Women hit the sawdust trail as tambourine ladies.

No more.

In the ongoing drama that is bedrock evangelicalism, Southern women have staged a quiet revolution in casting, and made off with the choicest leading roles. While church-women outside the borders of Dixie challenged the system head-on, clamoring for their rights as women, Dixie's revivalist daughters took a more cunning approach. They seized upon the highly personal charismatic focus of evangelistic leadership, ably blended down-home salvation with up-town show biz, and (in a masterful stroke of strategic genius) ignored entirely the issue of women's clerical rights.

If God calls, can man argue?

Ruth Carter Stapleton was called. So were Catherine Marshall and Virginia Lively. All play larger-than-life roles in the born-again South, but none is better suited to the part of lady evangelist than Louise Mohr. Captivatingly candid and, at sixty-eight, shockingly attractive, Mohr is generally conceded to be the region's most prominent female evangelist. Certainly she's qualified to speak out for Christ: her first encounter with Christ transformed her life.

"If you've been a broad-based heathen, honey, you're a broad-based Christian."

Listening to Mohr may be one of the world's most memorable experiences. One expects messianic fervor—and gets it, but has it served up in a mellow drawl, with elided *r*'s and altered vowels. The words pour out, smooth as homemade sorghum, soft as country rain, in a litany relentlessly articulate. But there's a salty wit, too, that tells of a close and affable relationship between Mohr and her maker. One senses that hers is a kind and loving God who nonetheless has posted a few rules, described appropriate penalties, and damned well means to keep His word. Even so, He's open to discussion and, occasionally, bargains ("you understand, Lord, that's forty-two days . . .").

Mohr's happy to talk, but she won't force an introduction.

"If you're clutchy or over-anxious, you'll destroy the very thing you're trying to get hold of. Just sit real loose. In His own time and in His own way, He'll see to it you come into a relationship with Him, and it'll be just the kind you need."

It took Mohr some forty-four years to meet the Prince of Peace, and though she is hard on herself for those early years before Christ, she wouldn't trade them.

"I *cannot tell* you how I feel for the people who've never sinned big. I *cannot tell* you what I think they've *missed!*"

Mohr was Southern-born, Southern-reared, and makes her home in Montgomery. License plates on cars here read "Heart of Dixie," and one takes the slogan literally. In this city, just one block apart, both the Civil War and the era of civil rights were launched. It was from here that the order went out to fire on Fort Sumter. It was here that Jefferson Davis took the oath of office as first president of the Confederacy. A block away, down Dexter Avenue, Martin Luther King, Jr., proclaimed the Montgomery bus boycott. Mohr is appropriately placed: she is a product of the South in a way and on a scale that few others match. But she chafes at the upper-class Southern upbringing that shaped her early years.

"I was my parents' only child, doted on and very sheltered, born a rebel and a nonconformist to a mother who had a royalty syndrome. So I was carefully reared a snob with an incredibly phony value system. I adored my father, who was head of my fan club; in his eyes I could do no wrong, so he left the dirty work up to Mother, which I know now was dirty pool.

"Anything I could get by with, I did. I always had power and I knew it, but I didn't know how to use it, or I used it for the wrong things. I discovered boys, and if it weren't for the ignorance and intense terror of the time, I'd have been the alley-cat of the century. When I was about fifteen, at this very fine private school—second oldest private school in the country, incidentally—the principal said to me, 'You know, Louise, you have enormous qualities of leadership and you refuse it.' And I said, 'You bet I do.'

"I have *never* wanted responsibility.

"I deliberately stayed a child because people don't expect responsible behavior from a child. And my husband, who I eloped with on the fifth day I ever saw him in my life, was a Jew. He was the only Jew I'd ever known. And my family disinherited me for six months because I'd done the absolutely unforgivable thing: I'd married a Jew.

"But I was looking for a leading man who could make me feel good for the rest of my life. So we got married.

"I wiped out his life savings in two weeks. I went to town and in three hours furnished our apartment without so much as a by-your-leave. I'd never asked anybody before. There'd always been money when I went off to school, and my father took care of me well. He went to the bank and deposited money in the checking account. I never paid a bill in my entire life till I was thirty-four years old. Never wrote a check. Six months after Sid and I married—the first time my father and my husband were together—my father said to my husband, 'Never before in their lives have Louise or her mother had to hassle with their money. I check their billfolds at night before I go to bed to see if they have money. I'll make sure she'll never have to ask you.' And, bless his heart, he did."

How lovely?

"Lovely! That's sick! *Sick!* It was absolutely outrageous indulgence. It relieved me of any responsibility of any kind. And I'd spent my entire life in somebody's lap or other, being totally taken care of. The eight-year-old emotional child in an adult body, and that's very *dangerous.*"

The Mohrs decided never to have a child, but after five years of marriage, they changed their minds.

"I ordered a boy. Literally *ordered* a boy. I said I wanted a son, and I got one."

Preparing for parenthood, they cast about for the appropriate social affiliations.

"If Montgomery had had a jet set, we'd have been right in the middle of it. We were into community up to our hairline. We were into *everything.*

"We joined the Episcopal Church very cold-bloodedly. It was a snob church, and we thought it'd be good for the baby if we belonged to a church. And the Church got exactly what it deserved. It demanded nothing of me, and it got nothing. We didn't even have confirmation classes. I think they thought if they put any strings on it, we wouldn't bite. And they were dying to get us, you know; I think they had dollar signs dancing in their eyes. So from the time I was twenty-six until I was forty-four, I was a card-carrying Episcopalian, and I didn't know the first thing about what it was all about.

"So my son grew up in a totally Godless household. He was never taught to say his prayers, he was never told a Bible story. He never saw a prayer book at home, he never heard grace in front of a meal. He never heard God or Jesus mentioned unless it was heard in our cursing.

"And I was no mother at all. I wanted this baby and he wasn't a month old, and I still had the trained nurse from the hospital. I'd found out I really didn't want to take care of a baby. He didn't sleep until ten in the morning. He was *messy*. So we hired a beautiful black woman who was a practical nurse and she was in our home day and night for the first five years of his life. He had me for a playmate. Sid would poke him in the stomach twice a day and say, 'Hi, fella.' But she was the only mother he had."

She's worked her way through the guilt.

"I finally reached the realization that I've nothing to beat myself about because I was only capable of the stage of spiritual evolution that I was at, which was practically point-zero. I was only capable of being what I was. There's no way that you can stand over a dandelion and make it turn into a camellia."

But that's a later realization. Before that were years Mohr found so pointless that she raced through them as though trying to beat life to the finish line.

"I became chairman of everything, president of everything, held every job you could hold, everything in the Junior League except president, which I never wanted because I didn't want the responsibility. And then they made me a regional director, and I had my second nervous breakdown to get out of *that*. I'd had my first nervous breakdown in forty-six. It's beautiful: nature takes over. And a nervous breakdown is one of the greatest face-saving devices there is. And then I became a borderline alcoholic. Broke all Ten Commandments. I've never murdered with a gun or a knife, but I've murdered with my tongue.

"I had no external problems at all, of course. I had a husband who loved me, parents that hadn't raised me too well but had never crossed me about anything. My husband never said no about anything, and it's remarkable that he didn't because if he had, I'd have walked away from him. Sid had exactly the gentle, permissive nature that he needed to absorb an infinite amount of hurt and hate and prejudice without hating me in return. He's a quite fantastic person. I owe him an enormous debt of gratitude.

"But I got more and more desperate from forty-six to fifty-four, eight years in which my doctor kept me propped up with all kinds of nerve pills. I never saw the first psychiatrist or psychologist. The Church was nowhere in the picture at all. I never saw anybody I considered a Christian that did anything different in their lives than I did. I didn't have anything for God or against him. He just didn't exist.

"I was forty-four years old. I had twenty or thirty years of life staring me in the face, and I thought, 'Well, what the hell am I doing to do with it?' I hated bridge. I was so bored I didn't know what to do."

She tried crawling out an eleventh-floor window at the Hotel Baltimore.

"I looked down into the street below to see where I was going to land, and I had to look past two legs that looked like they wore fur leggings. *Don't be ridiculous!* If you think I was going to be picked up in the street with hairy legs, you're *crazy*. So I got down out of the window to go shave my legs, and my husband came back to the hotel two hours before he could possibly have been expected. And that was why I didn't jump. But it was always my ace-in-the-hole through the years: I could always take my own life. I planned many, many lovely ways. I have one plan that's so surefire, so non-flop, that it's a *great pity* to have it wasted."

The months before her son left for college were particularly traumatic; for Mohr, it seemed "the end of the line," the start of her "unemployment."

"Things began to come into focus in the course of that summer. I wanted two things. The first was serenity. I had no idea what serenity *was*. I've been a violent person all my life. I overreact. I say 'good morning' as though I'm never going to say it again. I was a champion hater. I could hate somebody for the way they parted their hair. The other thing I wanted was service. Now *that* was ridiculous because I'd served every way you could serve. But this time I wanted something bigger than I was that I could lose myself in. But how could you lose a self that you've never found? I looked at my life and I saw nothing that really counted."

On September 16, the Mohrs were invited to a cocktail supper. It was the night of the day Peter left for Princeton for his freshman year.

"I accepted the invitation because I was sad, and what could you do with sadness but drown it? So I went to get drunk and I did, in front of a hundred and fifty people. The hostess bird-dogged me all evening, asking me rude and ugly questions, like was I interested in religion. Or would I go to the Methodist Church with her on Sunday morning to hear a Baptist talk.

"I've never been so insulted in my life!

"But I ended up going with her. I was hung over the next day, and it was the most ghastly thing I'd ever been to. It was the most God-awful display of emotionalism I'd ever seen. This horrible little man that looked like Chief Tail-twister at the Lions Club and all these teeth in his mouth. Talking about Jesus, and he loved Jesus. It was just like *fingernails on a blackboard.* I·sat there thinking, 'I'm going to be sick.' Until I decided he was crazy, and then I could be angry at his family for letting him make a public spectacle of himself. I felt sorry for him, because insane asylums were highly populated with people who thought they were God the Father or Mary the Virgin or God the Son. And I thought this was one they hadn't caught up with yet. So I left that awful place when that common little man got through."

When Mohr arrived home that day, she found leaning

against her front door a small inspirational book.

"I took that book upstairs and sat down on a chaise lounge and read it right straight through. Expecting nothing. I just had to read it. I don't know why. It just seemed like the thing to do, and I didn't have any battle royal about it whatsoever. When I finished reading it, I closed the cover on the back of the book and for me a door opened to a world I'd never known existed.

"I looked beyond that door and—I know how corny this sounds, I'm sorry, but that's the way it happened—I saw a perfectly beautiful scene with this absolutely unearthly breeze. And standing in the center of a road was God the Father. He looked just like the pictures I'd seen of God the Son, but it was God the Father. There was no mistake about that. He had His arms stretched out toward me and I looked into His face, I looked into His eyes, and for the first time I knew without knowing *how* I knew that I was totally loved exactly *how* I was and exactly *where* I was. That I could never ever be loved any more than I was loved at that instant. There was nothing I could ever do that could make that love any less, no matter how bad I was. And I knew somehow too that I'd never be the same.

"All I said was 'help.' It was the first prayer that I'd ever prayed. And all I can say is that all the forces of Heaven poured in to fill up the vacuum that was me. I wasn't looking for Him. I wasn't expecting Him. I didn't ask Him to come into my life. That means *nobody* is safe. When He is ready to move on you, sister, *He moves* and you *know* it! There wasn't any question in my mind that something very revolutionary had happened."

She thought for the first year that she was losing her mind: "I didn't mention what I'd seen to my husband for a year and a half, because I was afraid he'd have me committed. Upper class, darlin', don't get converted. For Heaven's sakes, that's for the middle class and the lower classes. I'd never known anybody in *my* walk of life that this had ever happened to. So, you know, I was forty-four, and I'd always heard that when women reach a certain age they're apt to go a little queer. And I thought, ah, yes, change-of-life, old girl, and it was. But it wasn't the kind I thought.

"Love. That's my thing. Other people superimpose other stuff on it and try to turn it into all kinds of other things, doctrines, dogmas. Love is all of this. It's kind of like love in Him becomes the center point in your life. Everything works out from that. I was a woman who didn't know how to be a mother to one little boy. Now I'm a damned spiritual *brood.* Everywhere I go, I litter."

Eventually Mohr's husband had to know.

"I'd hidden my books. I hadn't read the Bible in bed at night, which is the way women queer the whole business for men. When I talk, I say, 'For God's sake, read the Bible on the pot, read it *anywhere,* but your husband does not go to bed at night to watch you read the Bible! So don't do that!' But Sid came home from the office one night and we talked, and he looked at me very fixed and he said, 'I don't know what it is you're doing and I don't know what it is that you've got, but you're a different person than you used to be, and I'm at a happier place than I ever thought I could be.' And God unzipped my mouth about a millimeter, and I said, 'Well, you might say I've learned a little bit about how to live.' And he said, 'Do you have a book about it?'

"And I hit those stairs like a bat out of hell and all the way up I said, 'Oh, Lord, which book do You want him to have?' And I zeroed in on one and brought it down to Sid. I didn't peep to see where he was or if he'd turned down the corner of any pages. Ten days later he started the first businessmen's prayer-breakfast group that we can find anywhere in the Southeast. It was very simple for him, because, you see, here was a man who was born good and had spent his life living up to the Jewish ethic. But it's hard to beat being made new. I was handed a brand new life at the age of forty-four, a brand new world, brand new interests, even a brand new prayer language."

I speak in tongues.
I have for seventeen years;
it's old hat with me.
—LOUISE MOHR

Mohr converses with God like she talks with anyone else.

"I'd say, 'Hey, Lord, this is Louise, listen,' because I was afraid He'd forget from one time to another who I was. I'd gotten in so recently that I'd never had a formal arm's-length relationship with God. It's a very free-flowing conversation. It's a dialogue. He says, 'Hey, Louise, listen,' which is not in any sense irreverence. It's simply closeness. Children do not stand outside the door and say, 'O mighty and most merciful mother, may I enter into your divine and august presence.' They come barreling in and tell you what they want, and sometimes they even forget to say 'thank you.' "

Mohr chose to spread the Godly word, working through small groups.

"I do not walk under anybody's banner. My primary ministry now is with the Junior Leagues. I do Faith-at-Work conferences as a speaker, as a workshop leader. I charge no honorarium. It's enormously important that I give away what God has given me so freely. This also keeps me from being a professional Christian. I guard my amateur status *fiercely.*

"The beautiful part of it, darlin', is that God can take even vessels that abuse and misuse the wonderful gifts that He gives and still use them. I mean, if God waited for perfect people to use, there wouldn't be anybody used since Jesus went home. I mean, you know, He's the only one that had it made. There are as many ways to God as there are people.

Now *I* am a carriage-trade Christian."

Twenty-two years ago, God told Mohr she would one day tell her story to the Junior Leagues of America.

"I said out loud, 'Lord, that's the craziest thing You've said yet.' Well, He never said another word, and I just hung that on a hook in my mind. But nine years later I was standing up before the Omaha Junior League, followed by Atlanta and Lincoln, Nebraska, and there it went. What God said in 1957 was the truth. And He told me about six or seven years ago He'd have twenty Junior Leaguers who'd take over my ministry when it got so big I couldn't handle it anymore. They'll fan out and sing the song with the words that I use. If we can get all of this background, breeding, money, know-how, training, advantages, intelligence, education, and power—now this is your privileged five percent—if we can get this plugged into the power of God and put it to use for Him, God knows what can be done."

Mohr keeps a pace that would kill a women twenty years younger; she's on the road most of each month.

"It's a way of life, sweetie, and it's exhausting. I'm only really alive when I'm doing my thing, so alive that I forget I have a body. Now it's hard for me to get gussied up and ready to do it. It used to be exciting and fun; now it is really sacrificial. And I usually dread it before I get there. But once I'm there and start doing it, I'm so lifted out of myself with the excitement and joy of watching dead people come to life. Baby, that's *addictive.*"

But when Mohr comes in off the road, she's blissfully down-to-earth.

"I get in and I've had holiness up to *here.* And I fix myself the biggest drink you've ever seen and I sit down and say, 'Shit, shit!' and I drink my drink and I feel like a new person. It gets me back in balance. I *loathe* piety, it stinks. I cannot stand it."

Followers and advisors keep urging Mohr to write a book

telling of her born-again experience and her growing ministry.

"Well, a book is like a pregnancy. When you get pregnant you deliver in due course whether you want to or not, and in the fullness of time it all comes out. Well, God has not yet impregnated me with my book. I haven't had morning sickness or anything. He gave me a title four years ago, and it's absolutely *marvelous.* I can even see the title of the book and it is 'How Odd of God,' and then in smaller letters, 'To Choose a Mess Like Me.' Isn't that a marvelous title? But the contents are not there.

"Knowing God the way I know Him now, when the time comes He'll provide everything, right down the line. I won't have to do a thing except walk in the path He lays down. But I'm getting awfully tired of running into this all the time. At least three or four people in the grapefruit line, 'Oh, the lovely talk you made, what's the name of your book, haven't you written a book?' It's reached the point where I want to say, 'Oh, *crap* on you and your book!' "

This carriage-trade Christian doesn't think it peculiar that her ministry seems to be aimed at the upper-income levels of Southern society.

"I package Christianity so it's acceptable to them. There's nothing, really, that's more apt to separate you from God than being a fat-cat. That's one reason for the people with power and money to get desperate enough for this to happen. They have what I call the five perilous P's: pleasure, plenty, popularity, possessions, and power. The more money you have, the more blind alleys you have to chase up and down looking for the answer. The more power you have, the more ways there are in which to run."

She thinks Southerners are more accustomed to evangelical fervor than Americans who live elsewhere. It seems a logical place from which to direct her ministry.

"We are the Bible Belt. I think we're acknowledged by the

rest of the country as being more spiritually oriented. Certainly this is true as far as the Junior Leagues are concerned. It has to do with the South's agrarian economy plus the fact, I think, that people here have suffered intensely. You find a reliance on God here you don't see elsewhere. I don't doubt that the War Between the States contributed largely to the Southerner's reliance on God. I'm certain it's what has made the Negroes so God-oriented. Now we've finally had a president that came right out of the heart of the South, and it looks like God is kind of crazy about it Himself."

Mohr talks rather nonchalantly about the supernatural world.

"I don't see visions. I've never seen a guardian angel. But I know that I have two. Wouldn't you know it'd take a day-shift *and* a night-shift for me!

"I know that by the tiniest, tiniest margin, almost so tiny that it would be indefinable, I am more spirit than I am flesh now. It's been gradual. It's been a process of over twenty-four years. And I know that when I crossed that line and became by this tiny, tiny margin more of the spirit than of the flesh, I would literally not survive more than six months —physically—if I ever jumped ship."

Mohr sees the born-again experience as a process of "co-creating with God." And God makes the blueprint.

"Your part is to let Him. And I want to tell you, for a self-centered activist, it ain't no breeze to get up and let somebody else do it!"

But she clearly has no regret for the person she was B.C.

"I have accepted my humanity, fully and completely, because that's what God made me. He made me a human being. If He wanted me to be an angel, He'd have made me an angel. That's a different breed of cat. But He made me a human being. That was rough material. That was the clay He chose to model. So my humanity was my most valuable asset, because that's what keeps me and God collaborating together, creating of the mess I made of the person He created me to be. If I hadn't been the person I was then, there would be no way I could be the person I'm being for Him now. There's no way I could identify with the people that I identify with and that identify with me.

"Now I know that I spent forty-four years of my life looking for a man to master me.

"And God trained me for everything He's got me doing right now. I'm living a life of blissful irresponsibility. I'm God's business. Since I'm His responsibility, I don't have to worry. I am a container that contains Him. I have nothing to do with it. He does it all."

So drop-kick her, Jesus (gently), through the goal-posts of life.

Rhinestone Cowgirls:
  Bright Lights & Country Music

I like rhinestones.
They shine and make me happy.
—DOLLY PARTON

Even in the South, where weak-watted radio stations play Hank Williams every four minutes (and feature between songs electronic preachers who peddle baby chicks and autographed photos of Jesus Christ), country music was for a very long time a musical elbow in the eye of polite society. Even in the early sixties, country was considered the exclusive property of backwoods yokels who favored shitkicker boots, Moon Pies washed down with Arr-Cee Colas, and dim-lit bars with backed-up johns and coin-operated pool tables. Some spurned country music as redneck; before the rise of redneck power, *redneck* was a word that conjured up images of lynchings, Ku Kluxery, and hog-waller politics. Others pronounced the music *hillbilly,* which was even worse. The haystacks-and-hayseeds hillbilly stereotype, rooted in our own urban provincialism and ignorance, was perpetuated by the music itself. Lyrical themes were limited: the songs spoke either of a maudlin longing for home or of good love turned bad by cheating wives, wayward husbands, and the seedy lure of honky-tonk life.

We embraced Southern fiddle music, making it respectable by calling it folk, and debated the finer nuances of such tunes as "Bile Them Cabbages Down." We embraced the tricky rhythms and fierce gyrations of work-songs imported by slaves who set the music to work for them in the fields; the beat synchronized with the monotonous motions of corn-shucking, rice-fanning, cotton-picking. We embraced the blues, liking its flatted notes and undercurrents of philosophic resignation. We embraced jazz, calling it culture. We embraced gospel, both the sad old Negro spirituals and the exuberant black hymns of praise. With one exception, we took to heart all the varied rhythms indigenous to Dixie.

Country was another pair of socks altogether.

Country music was whoopin' and hollerin' and pourin' beer on your head come payday. Country was girl-type singers got up in fancy spangled britches, Maybelline make-up, and peroxided curls piled to the highlands. It was turning down the car radio when you stopped at a red light so nobody'd know you were listening to Bob Wills. Chances were, you weren't. As recently as 1960, only eighty radio stations in the United States carried country music on a full-time basis, and none of those knew just how much longer they'd be on the air: country music had been swamped by the pounding deluge that was rock'n'roll.

But like they say down in Macon, church ain't out till the fat lady sings.

All the time the sophisticates were howling and holding their sides at the nasal twangs and cornball lyrics that were their notion of hillbilly music, gut-bucket country was winning converts faster'n a stump-tailed cow moves in fly-time. The initial catalyst was World War II, which brought thousands of non-Southerners to boot camps and military bases in Dixie, and sent thousands of guitar-picking Southerners northward toward lucrative jobs in Yankee defense plants. When the dust of battle cleared, country music was no longer confined within the geographic borders of Dixie. Radio piped down-home sound to transplanted Southerners and to new aficionados across the nation. Recording companies found a growing market for country discs. Country artists began to travel outside the South, following new and displaced audiences. First-generation city-dwellers looked to country music for nostalgic evocations of the life they'd sacrificed for the apparent promise of the city. And urban-rooted Americans began to see in country lyrics the virtues of the simple rural life that would serve as an indictment of the evils of urban industrialism.

Country music has always mirrored the social and economic milieu in which it is rooted, and commercial country developed out of the folk culture of the rural South. The music has absorbed, over the years, influences from a multitude of non-white, non-country sources, but it is a form created and disseminated by rural, conservative, white, Protestant, Anglo-Celtic Southerners. Their down-home values prevail: country lyrics link together to form a musical morality firmly grounded in the provincial heritage. Melodies are secondary. Many, in fact, are unabashedly ripped off from earlier classics, with the most minor adjustments, if any. "It Wasn't God Who Made Honky-Tonk Angels," then, made free use of the hit it was intended to rebut, "The Wild Side of Life," which in turn lifted *its* melody from an early gospel song, "The Great Speckled Bird." Waste not, want not.

No matter: it's the Southern working-class lyrics that sell. There's not much advocacy in hard-core country, and precious few poetic flights of fancy. The music speaks plainly, without frills or ambiguous embellishments, to a harassed and embattled class of wage-earners and their wives, who read the hard-facts-of-life lyrics right into their own lives and feel considerable kinship with those who sing the words. Maybe you never had any sequins on your jeans, but if you're a Good Ol' Girl whose husband ever came home mean-drunk from the potato-chip factory, you're going to feel a surge of down-home sisterhood for Loretta Lynn when she warns her old man, "Don't Come Home A'Drinkin' (with Lovin' on Your Mind)."

Country is a grass-roots, foot-stompin', shit-kickin' music that deals in unvarnished reality rather than dewy-eyed romance. It's for grown-ups who've racked up some mileage. There's never anything ambiguous about the words, the tunes are simple enough to recall, and themes are universal if few in number. There's lovin', leavin' home, cheatin', drinkin', ramblin', and old-time religion. The sacred songs range from eighteenth-century gospel classics like "Amazing Grace," to forties-vintage born-again testimonials like "I Saw the Light," to gonzo-contemporary tributes like "High on Jesus," in which the singer scores for peace and prefers Christ to a nickel sack. The ramblin' songs, a response to rural restlessness, offer up free-wheeling fantasies of the open road for Americans who are (or feel) locked into a life of resignation. Drinkin' tunes, guilt-ridden or pleasure-bent, usually have to do with love turned bad. Generally, these are set in the honky-tonk, that seedy hillbilly haven where sin and corruption abound. Whether lured there by the bright lights and blaring music or drawn by a need to escape into boozy revelry, honky-tonk heroes invariably find they create more problems on the premises than they solve. A typical lyrical response is to try to shift the blame to someone else, and it's astonishing how often God catches it in the teeth.

Well, now, the honky-tonk, that there's *male* territory, don't-you-know. There might be some honky-tonk angels here, all right, and a few "wild wild women." But such females clearly are unsuitable for long-term lovin'. A man might fall in lust with them, but never in love. True love's reserved for women who don't hang out in beer joints—like the little woman, who's been left at home tendin' babies while everybody else goes out drinkin' and honky-tonkin'.

Somebody has to keep those home fires burning, and those who do keep an eye on those who choose to flee the nest. Leavin'-home songs have been updated a bit in recent years, but even now in country music home is as much *what* as *where* you come from. Earlier lyrics reflected considerable guilt and a good deal of you-oughta-take-a-rope-and-hang-me repentance for leaving in search of greener pastures. Odes to home and Mama were country staples (it's unnecessary to circle back home, as long as you write a song of anguished self-flagellation for staying away). In a more mobile era, leaving home inspires far less guilt. When a Rhinestone Cowgirl sings now of home, her mood's more likely to be one of nostalgia than repentance, and usually she's not too proud to admit she's more'n a mite relieved to find she *can't* go home again. It doesn't matter much whether Dolly Parton writes a romanticized account of country life, as in "Tennessee Mountain Home," where life is "as peaceful as a baby's sigh," or offers up more candid views of life "In the Good Old Days (When Times were Bad)" and "anything at all was more than we had." She *remembers,* all that's required to keep the homefolks happy as dead pigs in sunshine. The real shame comes in forgetting. A Rhinestone Cowgirl knows better than to go back on her raisin'.

Or, as they might put it down 'round Waycross, ain't never been no whistlin' woman nor crowin' hen that ever come to any good end.

The course of true love never ran too smoothly in country music, and cheatin's been the inevitable result. Of course, we didn't hear much about cheatin' in the early years of commercial country. It might be a fact of married life more often than not, but one didn't go around talking (or singing) about it. Divorce was almost never mentioned: country people don't believe in serial monogamy, and Southerners have a penchant for lost causes, anyway. When love turns sour, they tend to stay put and make the best of it. Meanwhile, the odds are good that one of the partners (traditionally, the husband) is going to start looking elsewhere for solace, and you can bet your great speckled bird he's going to pay for it. Country lyrics may let him sample the wild side of life, but he'd do well to remember that in the end his cheatin' heart's gonna tell on him.

Southern sin does not go long unpunished.

There's no economic parity when it comes to the wages of sin in country music. Here, as in the tradition that spawned the genre, people are presented in traditional male-female roles (*read:* double standard).

In hard-core country even now, lyrics usually present the male viewpoint, especially when there's some extra-curricular grabbin'-and-gropin' goin' on; more often than not, the cheater has an excuse. Marty Robbins takes the devil-made-me-do-it tack: he *wants* to go home to poor ol' Mary, who's waiting and weeping, but what can he do? The Devil Woman's got a-holdt of him and won't let go. And if you can't hang it on Satan, you can always blame the wife. Maybe she cheated first (always the very best rationale for gropin') or maybe it's just that the fire's gone out at home. Again, only hillbilly poet Billy Joe Shaver reckons frankly that if the Devil made him do it the first time, the second time he did it on his own. But good ol' Billy Joe's a rare bird: few others 'fess right up like that.

Retaliation is rare even today. The little woman, betrayed by her ramblin' man, stays chastely at home singing mournfully about men who turn out to be poor marital risks. In country music, slippin' around is not usually a feminine option. The woman is left stoking the home fires and consoling herself with complaint and accusation.

And though there has to be another woman somewhere with her own story to tell, we don't get her side of it very often either. Wicked wretch that she is, messin' with somebody else's man, who'd listen?

Women always got shorted in country lyrics, and they didn't fare any better as performers. It wasn't until the early fifties that they emerged as country stars; till then they played supporting roles as accompanying singers, members of male-dominated groups, or comediennes of the backwoods-rustic variety. Because women in country music tend to be as conservative as the tradition from which they spring, there was little rebellion in the ranks. Women might be fleeing the farms to find work in the city and competing more openly as well as more successfully with men, but that cut little ice in Nashville, where female attitudes failed to keep pace with their changing economic status. There was no hint through the mid-sixties that country songwriters were going to break down and grant women sexual parity with men, either. Social change, rampant even in conservative rural life, had little impact on country music. Women were locked into narrow stereotyped molds.

"Back then," says Lydia Anderson, "there were just two kinds of women: good and bad."

Anderson, a high-spirited late-night deejay at KVET in Austin, Texas, cut her teeth on kicker music. At thirty, she was the first woman in the region to anchor an all-night radio program. And if the city of Austin can be said to have a mascot, it's Lydia. Her life is a blur of discs, fans, phone calls, and backstage passes. She's on a first-name basis with every student, musician, night-shift worker, and club-owner in town, and with most of the name performers who pass through. She breakfasts with Willie Nelson, lunches with Tammy Wynette, gossips long-distance with Larry Gatlin. Local newspaper editorials sing Anderson's praises; fans dispatch to the station a steady stream of tributes: candy, notes, long-neck beers. Anderson maintains a vast network of contacts with country's reigning superstars, who remember her birthday and invite her backstage while bigger names cool their Tony Lamas out front. Nobody knows more about what's going on in country music than Lydia Anderson.

"Until very recently," she says, "country lyrics maintained the old double standard. You were either the good wife, sitting at home, or you were the bad 'other woman.' When a man ran around on his wife, it was human weakness; when she ran around on him, she was a tramp. We never heard the woman's side, at least not until nineteen fifty-two."

That was the year Kitty Wells recorded "It Wasn't God Who Made Honky-Tonk Angels," opening the floodgates not only for aspiring Rhinestone Cowgirls but also for the sort of woman-to-woman message music relatively common in country today.

" 'Honky-Tonk Angels' was written in answer to Hank Thompson's 'Wild Side of Life.' The lyrics to his song implied he'd been taken in by a honky-tonk angel who pretended to be something she wasn't; the lyrics to hers said, 'Okay, turkey, listen here, you got in trouble all by yourself.' It was the first time a woman told her side of the story, and it made Kitty Wells the queen of country music. It really turned things around. Now we hear female entertainers sing that 'it's the right time of night for makin' love' and 'love is where you find it when you find no love at home.' But the music has broadened its appeal, too. Why would a song about a man cheating on his wife interest a fourteen-year-old? Young people couldn't relate to the old lyrics. But everybody can relate to the new songs."

For all its liberalized lyrics and broadened appeal, country music still reinforces the old traditional values.

"That's why people like it: it gives you the old guidelines. People have to have *some* rules. Traditional country music makes the rules clear.

"What do you think of when you think of the South? You think of home, family, church. And that's what country music's all about. The old values. The entertainers believe in them, too. When Tammy Wynette was here, we talked about three hours, and most of the time what we were talking about was faith, about the fact that we have Jesus to lean on. Connie Smith's very religious. Jessi Colter is, too, though nobody believes it because she's married to one of the Outlaws, Waylon Jennings. And Larry Gatlin, who wrote a song called 'Help Me.' You can always spot a Christian. Almost every name entertainer I know or have had on my program is really into Christianity. Most of them started out in their own little churches, singing gospel."

That may be one reason country artists sing with such conviction. They were raised largely on those traditional old values, and they believe in them, however far from their roots they've roamed.

Women's lives have increasingly extended beyond the provincial sphere, though, and in recent years country lyrics have come at last to reflect the change. Wells was the trailblazer, but while her "Honky-Tonk Angels" is a milestone, Wells herself is no militant. In her personal life and in the lyrics she records, she preserves the image of female domesticity. She's an unlikely pioneer: with her first hit recording, she launched a trend of musical dialogue that led ultimately to today's country candor, and yet she seems to have failed entirely to link the two in her mind. Nevertheless, sexuality —openly discussed and endorsed without shame—has become a country-music reality. We hear Sammi Smith implore her lover to hold his warm and tender body next to hers; Tanya Tucker asks frankly "Would You Lay with Me in a Field of Stone"; Loretta Lynn sings of the Pill, and Jeanne Pruett admits that "Satin Sheets" just weren't enough to keep her satisfied. We even get a look at a honky-tonk heroine in "Queen of the Silver Dollar."

But these are exceptions still.

Generally, the traditional male-female roles are endorsed

and reinforced. In most country lyrics even today, women are advised, as by Tammy Wynette, to "Stand by Your Man." And the woman who started it all would agree. She remains as conservative as the provincial milieu in which she has her roots. Kitty Wells never intended to make a career in country music, and there are those who point out that she has neither true pitch nor an inspired sense of rhythm. Even so, her nasal twang, plaintive and clear, is immediately recognizable, and she's never resorted to vocal tricks or onstage gimmicks; she sings in a dignified, restrained manner, seldom moving onstage, and when she sings people cluster 'round the stage in hushed reverence. After a quarter of a century in country music—and despite challenges from sleeker, younger stars—she remains the Queen, much revered by those who've followed in the path she cleared.

"I grew up with the Grand Ole Opry," she says. "Goin' to the Opry and watchin' different ones perform, and it never entered my mind maybe one time I'd be standin' on that stage singin'. I never once dreamed I'd be in the music business. Never did think I'd be anything other than a wife and a mother and a homemaker. 'Course I love to sing. And I always had to sing quite a bit, travelin' with my husband."

She began as a gospel singer, part-time, and before the release of "Honky-Tonk Angels" had sung for years as a member of the Tennessee Mountain Boys, the group headed by Jack Anglin and her husband, Johnny Wright. She's gracious and affable, and she still seems a bit perplexed at the turn her life has taken. Her house, peach-colored brick with lime-green trim, is comfortable but unassuming; there's a white Cadillac in the drive and an abundance of plush red carpeting inside, but otherwise there's nothing here to suggest a superstar occupies the premises. Kitty Wells was born Muriel Deason in Nashville, and considers her childhood unremarkable.

"My mother, she was a real religious-minded woman,

'course my father, he was too, but not as much as my mother. He was a railroader, he was the brakeman on the Tennessee Central. We just had a comfortable livin' and my father made sure we had plenty to eat and clothes to wear. That's mostly what everybody was interested in back then. 'Course the Depression, it was hard on everyone. But I think as long as you have a home and you know you're loved and all, that's the main thing. You might not have the finest, but you had the main things. We admired my father. We were kind of in awe of him. When he'd say something, we'd do it. But my mother, she'd reprimand us and call us down for things, and we never did mind a whippin', you know."

Music was a part of her life from the first.

"My father played the guitar and sang. My mother, she just picked a tune on the banjo. My father had one brother that played the fiddle and one that played the piano and different instruments, and I just used to sit and listen. 'Course I sung a lot of songs at church. My mother, she liked to sing the hymns, and I'd sing along with her. I'd sit and learn to sing harmony. My father played where they had the square dances, you know, with his guitar and all."

As a bride, Wells worked in a shirt factory in Nashville, and she and her husband performed in their spare time for extra change. Wright and Jack Anglin traveled through Tennessee, North Carolina, and West Virginia, playing for radio stations and rural audiences, and, most of the time, Wells went along.

Then came "Honky-Tonk Angels."

"I'd recorded previous tunes with Decca. 'Course they were religious songs, and semi-religious. Back when I first started, it was hard for a girl artist to get any records played or to sell any, you know, that amounted to anything. I never dreamed this one would make a hit. It was banned on the radio! I never could sing it on WXM, even back when it was the number-one song. A lot of NBC stations banned it. 'Course, a lot of them played it, fortunately, but some banned it and I couldn't do it on network shows. The same with 'Backstreet Affair.' Now songs like that, I really don't think they're all that bad. But they've come a long way now. They play some songs now that really *tell* it. I don't like them if they're too suggestive.

"People ask me about Willie and Waylon, you know, about their music and the change. But basically the new ones didn't change the music. They just changed in appearance. They're still country. The songs are about everyday livin'. I think that's why people buy them. People think I wrote 'It Wasn't God Who Made Honky-Tonk Angels.' I didn't write it. 'Course I've written a few songs, but not all that much. I did another song, 'Payin' for the Backstreet Affair,' which is an answer to 'Backstreet Affair.' It didn't pertain *in any way* to my way of livin', you know, either one of those songs!"

Kitty Wells cares very much what people think. And she's largely unaffected by the trappings of superstar status.

"I never thought of myself as bein' a star, you know. I'm just like my next-door neighbor. I tried not to spoil the kids. We didn't want anybody to treat them other than just normal children, 'cause that's what they are anyway. We always took them with us on the road when we could. Then after they got big enough and wanted to sing, well, we let them sing. We didn't force them to. We just let them sing if they wanted to. I don't think they missed that much. They know you love them or you wouldn't be doin' these things to make them mind and havin' a set of rules they have to go by. They may not think it just then, but when they get a little older, they respect you for it. They love you."

She's a true provincial, steeped in the provincial values. One senses she'd just as soon it have been Johnny Wright who revolutionized country music, somebody else who led the charts all these years. As much as she's able, she leads a traditional life. Like her country kin, she takes a dim view of feminist militancy and is totally disinterested in ERA legislation.

"I think they should leave it as it is. I've never felt discriminated against. I think a woman was made for man to protect and make a livin' for. 'Course, there's some women, well, we have to have exceptions to the rule. If they want to work, fine, but I think the man should be the head of the house. That's the way it's meant to be."

Today's Rhinestone Cowgirls, widening the path Wells blazed, are shrewd, complex, and talented businesswomen who've conquered a *macho* industry and made it work for them. They live in a world of flash and plenty, but they work like field hands for the privilege of enjoying the glitter: only 10 percent of the country's rhinestone-studded superstars make substantial money from recording-company royalties, and all are on the road, performing, 180 to 200 (or more) nights a year. Still, there's a lot of gold to be mined here: television, packaging Johnny Cash, Glen Campbell, and the stars of "Hee Haw," has introduced country music —at least in its sleeker watered-down form—to the urban middle class, and movies like *The Last Picture Show* and *Deliverance* use country-music soundtracks. The Country Music Association and Nashville's recording execs have worked hard to identify the music with that vague and amorphous group of citizens presumed to constitute the conservative, patriotic, virtuous middle class. At the same time, attempting to be all things to all people, they've campaigned diligently to attract younger audiences, the ones whose members don't necessarily share middle-class values. There are a few songs that protest social conditions, some that verge on advocacy, and others that imply sexual equality. Country music, like other forms of art, has to bend when social change pushes, though anti-feminist sentiment dominates.

Kinky Friedman and the Texas Jewboys advise women to "Get Your Biscuits in the Oven and Your Buns in Bed." Now, doctrinaire feminists are rare in the South. But when Friedman performs this particular number women tend to swarm the stage, hurling blunt objects and shouting or weeping hysterically. Even in the Cosmic capital, Friedman is not well loved.

Please note that songs about immoral wars, racism, doping, and exploited wet-back labor are typically performed by males. Women in country music boast repertoires with lyrics that cluster mainly toward the conservative end of the musical spectrum. Rhinestone Cowgirls make an art of their lifestyles. Even if they don't write their own songs, they choose lyrics more appropriate to the traditional view of woman, and these become part of their identity. What they're doing, of course, is telling us what we already know: what it's like to be a woman in a man's world. That's one reason we reel with sudden recognition, spinning the records and thinking, why, that's just the way *I* feel. To an extent unparalleled elsewhere, Rhinestone Cowgirls live their lyrics. They're the most conservative, the most provincial, the most traditional of Dixie's daughters. And age doesn't matter much. Helen Cornelius, a generation younger, echoes Kitty Wells' thoughts, at least when it comes to traditional sex roles.

"A Southern woman babies her man," she says. "And men need and like to be babied. Every man likes to be babied. But that's *great*, because when somebody comes and offends his woman, he'll fight the biggest man in the world to protect her! I feel very feminine, and I *love* being a woman, and I love being treated that way."

Cornelius sings both traditional and progressive country lyrics, but prefers the hard-core country songs.

"One thing that still holds true is that the world just doesn't want to hear a woman put down in a song. If a woman sings a song, she can sing about the man cheating on her. Or if *she's* done wrong herself, she can sing about wanting to make it up to him. But you don't want to sing a song that makes a woman look bad or immoral."

What about "Lucille," who cut out and left good ol' Kenny Rogers with four hungry children and a crop in the field?

"Oh, well, but there's so much compassion in that song for the *man* that you just overlook the woman. The accent's on *him.*"

And "Ruby"?

"Well, your thoughts are with him, not her. You still don't write a song that makes a woman look terrible, because men still like to uphold their women. And every woman wants to feel she *is* a lady."

You can't change her mind.

Like most other Rhinestone Cowgirls, Cornelius shares a deep conviction, rooted in her past, that the old values are the real ones. But what the new Rhinestone Cowgirls truly have in common is a background of rural poverty. Loretta Lynn, the Kentucky coal miner's daughter, grew up in a cabin so remote that there were no roads to give access, no electricity or plumbing. Tammy Wynette was a Mississippi farm girl who used to haul water from a stream and cook on a wood stove. Stella and Dolly Parton look back on a shared childhood in a wooden shack deep in the mountains near Sevierville, Tennessee, where the average annual income for a farming family is just $1500.

> *We slept five to a bed. It didn't matter none*
> *if you stopped wettin'*
> *'cause somebody else was gonna pee*
> *on you anyway.*
> —DOLLY PARTON

This is the point: country music is one of the few quick routes out of backwoods poverty. And if the odds on a rags-to-riches story in Nashville grow longer every day, there's still that chance-in-a-million to tempt women who were, after all, raised in an environment where music mattered profoundly. Those who make it stay close to their roots: country superstars are less pretentious, more accessible to their fans than celebrities in any other field.

Like Cornelius, Stella Parton—sister to the fabled Dolly and a major country artist in her own right—takes considerable pride in being a lady. Although having shared a few romps with her, I can tell you she's not unduly stiff-backed about it. She's as likely to be found shinnying up a tree after her son Timmy as tracking tapes in a recording studio, and while she can handle a French menu with breezy ease, she'd just as soon be home frying up a mess of pork chops and 'taters. Stella is 14-carat country, and independent as a hog on ice. She's a high-spirited Rhinestone Cowgirl with a bright and perceptive mind, for all her slapdash education and unpredictable grammar, and a down-home (if lively) sense of humor. She's coming up on thirty years old and appears not to mind, perhaps because from a distance of five inches she looks nineteen.

There is no freer spirit, none more candid, and few who can fire off such mile-a-minute ricocheting chatter while appearing simultaneously to be quiet, ladylike, and pensive.

"I have to tell you this funny little thing, 'cause we were raised up real religious, you know. Mama'd say the devil's gonna get you if you do so-and-so. Anyway, that carries over to your own children. The other day, Timmy was gettin' his first-aid kit ready to take out on the boat, and he had this big bottle of alcohol and this merthiolate and everything, and he had this little Bible. And I didn't know what it was there for, so I asked him. And he said, 'Well, in case everything *else* fails, we can always pray.'

Now I didn't know he thought like that."

Stella grew up in a region where theology tends to run to snake-handling, and an eighth-grade education was considered a mite extravagant. Her grandfather was pastor of the House of Prayer Church of God; Sunday attendance seldom exceeded twenty-five, and offerings ranged from seven to thirty dollars. Services were idiosyncratic, full of feeling, and exceedingly loud. Grandpa Owens may have preached hell so hot you could feel the flames, but he played a mean fiddle, and it was the music as much as the religion that drew people there and captured their souls.

"We were Pentecostal, you know. Church was more'n just Sunday. We had all these prayer meetin's and services different nights of the week. Nothin' fancy. Some people didn't even wear shoes. A lot of people brought their fiddles or banjos or tambourines. A lot of those Church of God churches, they were more reserved than us. With us, there was always lots of singin' and shoutin' and hollerin' and carryin' on. No snakes, though, not in Grandpa's church. 'Cause he was afraid of 'em. The people who handle the snakes, they're real good people, real nice, you know, they just think that's part of it.

"Like we had foot-washin's. You know what that is? A foot-washin's usually done about a week before Easter. The women are all on one side of the church with the little wash-pans and the buckets of water. And they line up between these two benches, and they sit there and wash each other's feet, and they sing.

"It's a real solemn ritual, to cast out vanity and show your love for your sister. Well, she might be your cousin or your real sister. It's just an expression. And the men are on the other side, you know, same thing. And before it's over, usually, most of the church is shoutin' and all.

"You don't question things like foot-washin's and speakin' in tongues. If your grandmother did it and your mother did it, you don't question it. You don't question washin' Aunt Leona's feet 'cause you've seen Mama do that in church.

"I feel real lucky for bein' raised in the South. People might laugh at you for the way you talk or 'cause you like to make gravy and biscuits. I'll say, 'Come on over and I'll fry us some 'taters,' and people think that's funny, but they still kinda appreciate it, I think. They really had a time with me up in Washington, D.C. I went in this little market and asked for some washin' powders, and they didn't know what I meant. They laughed at me, and I had to explain. But I figure, well, I'm different from them, but they're different from me, too, so we're really just alike."

Stella has a deep respect for the way she was raised and the values taught her. She misses east Tennessee but, like Dolly, she wouldn't go back.

"I miss bein' out in the country, but that type of life, I don't miss that at all. It's hard livin'. It was rough. I don't feel like I was deprived of anything, 'cause I didn't know then what I was missin'. One thing, though, we grew up in this real little community where the sheriff's kids and the mayor's kids and the schoolteacher's kids, they were the important ones. If your mother wasn't in the PTA—and Mama wasn't, she couldn't, she was always sick or havin' babies—well, you were looked down on. I don't need that. I'm an equal. Not just one of those Parton kids that's always barefoot."

With sisters Cassie, Dolly, and Willadeene, Stella used to build playhouses in the woods, using ground-moss for carpet. They'd pick birch or sassafras or mountain tea berries; late in the afternoon Stella's mother would bring molasses sweetbread and a teapot, and there would be high tea in the playhouse before trekking back to the house to cook supper.

"We ate soup a lot, and beans and cornbread. When Mama made baked beans, she called 'em cowboy beans to make us more interested in eatin' 'em. And stone soup: it's really just plain old vegetable soup, but Mama'd let all us kids go out and get rocks, and the one that found the prettiest rock got to put it in the soup. Mama'd just let it bubble with the soup. It didn't do nothin' but it was a way to make us willin' to eat soup again."

On clear nights the Parton family radio picked up signals from the 50,000-watt WXM station beaming the Grand Ole Opry back into the hills. Next morning, Stella and Dolly would play Opry, stringing all the other kids out along the front porch or, inside, on the stairs. There would be a broom or tobacco stalk with a tin can on top for a microphone. Dolly would thump the can to make sure the "mike" was working, then retire to a distant corner while Stella, playing Grant Turner, introduced the star of the show. Dolly would sweep graciously forward for her big number, and later, as Grant Turner herself, bring Stella onstage.

"I always got to be Minnie Pearl."

The Parton kids, yawning and squirming and singularly unimpressed, didn't make the most respectful of audiences, but then every aspiring superstar has to learn to deal with occasionally unruly crowds.

As soon as she could, Dolly fled the poverty of Sevierville County for Nashville. Stella got married.

"Don't most Southern women marry young? I married my high-school sweetheart when I was a senior. Dropped out of school the first semester and went back five months pregnant a year later so I could graduate. I was just barely seventeen when I got married. I didn't know much about anything. High-school girls get pregnant all the time now, but I was a virgin when I got married. I couldn't *not* have been. I mean, I had me some opportunities, but I was sure the devil'd get me if I done wrong. I really was."

She worked from the start.

"I'd always been singin'. I grew up singin' in church and

singin' country music at home, and I always enjoyed that. I was workin' in a club, just to make a livin', and I'd take Timmy where I was playin'. I had a playpen up in my dressin' room and I'd get somebody to watch him while I was onstage. I'd go down and sing a set and go back up and babysit and then go back down for another set. I was real young when I worked there, and I looked for the Lord to strike me dead. I felt like I was supposed to be singin' gospel. But I was real inexperienced. Then I formed a gospel group anyway, and I did that for a couple of years."

Then came the divorce and a couple of rough years. Stella quit the gospel group.

"For one thing, I just didn't think a lot of the gospel groups then were sincere. And also, 'cause of the divorce, I didn't feel like I was worthy to be in the gospel field any more than the rest of 'em. I didn't see how I could be a Christian and be divorced at the same time. Real mixed-up. But I finally got over feelin' like that. The marriage was real wrong. Everything about it was wrong. I finally realized I didn't have to prove to God how good I was, 'cause I'm His child, just like Timmy's mine. If somethin' goes wrong in my life, God's not gonna punish me for that if I can't help it, just like I'm not gonna punish Timmy for somethin' he does if he can't help it. I might punish him if he *could* help it, but I'm gonna love him just the same and forgive him.

"But I'm happy I went back to country music anyway. I can be myself more. I can do some good here. Every once in a while I meet somebody who's really down and I think, well, maybe they could really hurt themselves 'cause they're in a real bad state of mind. I say, 'Hey, look, this ain't the only day, you know, tomorrow's a new one.' I guess you gotta be down so you know how it feels to be up.

"And I think Southern women are real strong. The ones I know was raised on the farm or out in the country, and they had to work in the fields and come in and take care of three or four babies, and do all this other stuff too.

"Women in the South aren't forbidden to do things. They're real free in a lot of ways. The only thing about redneck people is this moral thing. If a girl isn't a virgin, then she's a tramp. Now I don't like that. A man can screw anybody he wants to from the time he's six years old. If he hasn't gotten to the girl next door, then he's a sissy. I never liked that, either. 'Cause I think we're all equal, or we should be. You have to think about what you want, and watch what you do if you want to be respected. It's not fair, but it's the way it is. Otherwise, you can do anything you want.

"Kitty Wells is a real good example of what female country singers should be. She's a real respectable lady. She always has been. Minnie Pearl, too. When they started out, people just assumed you were immoral if you went on the road and sang with a band. Some people still do. You just ignore it and go on actin' the way you think's right.

"I like bein' a woman. Down here we were taught that women take care of their men. 'Cause we think we're stronger. We're capable of doin' for ourselves, so we do for others, too. That's okay. I like it. But I like to be paid for what I do. Women deserve everything they work hard for. But if they want equal rights and all, they have to be willin' to take on equal responsibility. If we don't have it good, there's a reason for us not havin' it. It's either we didn't work for it, or else God didn't mean for us to have it."

There never was a Parton scared of hard work.

When Stella decided to return to country music, she set to work like Jerry Jeff Walker sets to boozing. What she didn't want were countless one-nighters in rowdy honky-tonks with fifty-cent covers and ten-drink minimums. But she didn't mind pulling herself out of bed at four A.M. to make an early-morning radio interview in some backwoods country town, or driving through the day to sing in a high-school gym in Pelion, South Carolina. Briefly, she billed herself "Stella Carroll," hoping to avoid confusion and inevitable comparison with her sister Dolly. It didn't wash: small-town emcees now brought her onstage as "Dolly Carroll" or "Stella Stevens," so she dropped the pseudonym and set about the tedious work of carving out a career in an industry notorious for gobbling up would-be superstars like buttered popcorn on Superbowl Sunday.

She's tougher than most, and damned near fearless.

Never mind the little-girl smile and doe-like eyes that suggest fragile timidity. Stella's shy, all right, and quiet and gentle-tempered. But that wispy ninety-five-pound frame of hers hides an awesome strength of will. Stella Parton's a woman who knows what she wants, works hard to get it, and reserves the right to do it *her* way. She takes her time, honing, polishing, perfecting, waiting for the best available material. Never pressing.

"Nothing moves as fast as you want it to. But I don't mind workin' hard, and I don't mind waitin'."

The patience and perfectionism have begun to pay off, and the dividends are downright handsome. After ten years of struggling to establish herself in her own right, Stella's got both head and act together. In 1975, she hit the airways hard with her "Ode to Olivia," which she wrote in response to the furor that flashed through Nashville when the Country Music Association named Olivia Newton-John the best female vocalist of 1974 over established country performers. She gained national notice with "I Want to Hold You in My Dreams Tonight." So determined was she to retain control of production on her first LP that she gambled with an unknown label; the album rocketed, earning Stella her first ASCAP Chart-Buster award and new respect in the industry. She picked up a second within months. When she wasn't singing, she was writing songs.

> *Stella's name means "star,"*
> *and Stella shines with*
> *a special light all her own.*
> —DOLLY PARTON

"I'd like to write more. I'd like to have some of my songs recorded by other people. That's probably the biggest compliment you could have. 'Course, I'd want 'em to do the songs real *good*."

There's an authentic friendliness to Stella, and it is a large part of the amazing personal contact she makes with the strangers who buy her records and attend her performances. But there's a professional friendliness, too, of the kind politicians develop—if they have any sort of luck at all. Stella gets first names right, listens thoughtfully to tedious and absurd questions from the press, recognizes hundreds of fans individually. From time to time she crosses her eyes, sticks out her tongue at photographers as if to prove she's no citified glamour-girl. She leaves the rhinestones and wigs to her sister Dolly, who likes to camp it up in gaudy glitter, elaborate Carvel curls, and flashy jumpsuits.

"Usually I wear just a little white blouse and a pair of jeans. Every once in a while I come out in a sundress or somethin', but I always do my last set in jeans. I have to be comfortable up there. I don't feel like I have to look like I'm tryin' to be a star. I want the audience to relate to Stella, not to some little country singer."

If she resents following in the peripatetic rhinestone path blazed by her flamboyant sister, she doesn't show it.

"Dolly's country. Nothin' else you can say, 'cause she's real country, real Southern, real capable too. She's the very best songwriter *anywhere*.

"But you know I've got this temper, which I have been tryin' to learn to control, and it kinda irritates me for people to come up and say, 'Boy, you sure don't *look* like Dolly!' They'll say, 'Where's your WIG?' or 'Where's your BIG BOOBS?' And I just take on this ol' mountain twang and say, *'I* don't know *where* they went!' 'cause if they're stupid enough to say somethin' like that, they deserve a stupid answer. She's my sister and we're real close, but she's still Dolly and I'm still Stella."

Yet both are able to translate the provincial experience into songs listeners relate to and understand.

"I think outsiders kinda envy the way we live. I don't mean they'd want to be poor like we used to be, but I think they'd like to be closer to the land. Land's real important down here. We have to know we can get out in the country. We have to know we can go pick an onion out of the neighbor's garden if we need one. I want Timmy to be able to do that. That's why I'm gettin' that place outside of town. I don't want him growin' up anywhere else but here. People here are always on your side. 'Cause you're part of it, part of the South. You're country."

> *A true, natural born and raised corn-fed country*
> *person will have a different feeling in their songs. There is just*
> *something in it, in country life,*
> *that comes through if you've experienced it,*
> *and won't if you haven't.*
> —DOLLY PARTON

Small-town Mamas, Up-town Grit:
The Sweet Revenge of Aunt Jemima

*It really bugs me to have
some Northerner come down here
and love me to death
'cause I'm black.*
—SYLVIA JACKSON

When they're not busy making fruit-jar whiskey or waving the rebel flag, yahoo Southern separatists are fond of bragging on Dixie's vast and varied contributions to the rest of the nation. Tobacco and rice, of course, are important exports. What would them peckerhead Yankees do without *our* Co'Cola? Our sugarcane and peanuts? And hillbilly music: why, it 'pert-near puts ol' King Cotton in the shade.

'Course, you don't hear about what really grabbed everybody's attention up north: the South's traditional mass *human* export.

By the time Reconstruction drew to a close, Southern blacks had been stomped every way but flat. When honky legislators got it into their heads to go whole hog with a slew of new Jim Crow laws, a good many right-thinking black people decided it was time to put the chairs in the wagon. And the next sound heard across the land of moonlight and magnolias was that of running feet, as thousands of backwoods blacks bolted the South in search of reasonably equal treatment and jobs that paid a living wage.

Always, black women led the way.

For every three black men to flee northward, there were five black women; they found ready employment in the urban North, usually in private households. Thousands signed with employment agents who roamed the South guaranteeing jobs and transportation north; by accepting terms of service that gave them "justice's tickets" out of Dixie, they became in effect indentured servants. Thousands more made the move on their own. A fortunate few followed relatives or friends able to arrange employment for them; most poured daily into the "hiring market" in the Bronx, where white housewives would look them over (much as in a slave market) and hire those of their choice. Typically, the work included scrubbing floors, walls, and toilets, and ironing. The pay ranged from twenty-five to seventy-five cents an hour, no lunch, no carfare, no sick-leave or vacation time provided. But if the American dream Yankee-style wasn't all it was cracked up to be, it beat what there was back home, where a firmly entrenched sharecropping system put little or no capital in black hands and a lily-white judicial system denied blacks even the right to try on clothing in department stores. No wonder so many high-tailed it north like possums up a gum stump. They kept right on hooking it north, too, till the proportion of blacks living in Dixie tumbled by half, then by half again. Between 1900 and 1940, Southern black people mounted an invasion of the North General Lee would have envied.

But the sun don't shine on the same dog's tail all the time.

And lately the trend that's caused sagging population figures in every state of the old Confederacy has been reversed. Country folks tire sooner or later of walking on concrete, especially if they're obliged to dodge bullets and muggers at the same time. The brash new prosperity of the Sunbelt economy and an obvious lessening of old racial barriers make a powerful lure for Northern blacks weary of coping with ice and snow, urban inflation, ghetto rats, and deteriorating schools. More than a few remain apprehensive about the South, recalling those segregated water fountains and Bull Conner's dogs. But many more have a need to explore the special nooks and crannies of their beginnings, and conditions in the "new" South make return feasible. For the first time in a long while, all the Southern states are gaining in population; for the first time ever, more blacks are moving in than are migrating out. As Dixie emerges from twenty years of turmoil, those who were estranged from their home and their heritage during the years of upheaval are snapping to the fact that once a few lingering sins are rooted out, the South is a place to inspire neither fear nor shame. Fifty-five million people live in the area that comprised the eleven Confederate states. Eighty percent is a mixed bag of Chicanos, Cubans, Jews, Vietnamese refugees, Cajuns, WASPs, and routine rednecks. The other twenty percent is black.

And most of these live in Dixie by choice.

Now capital-courting politicians and sloganeering journalists have been proclaiming a "new" South 'long about every second Tuesday since Henry Grady first coined the term back in Reconstruction days. And any moderate-minded lint-picker with a lick of sense can find inequities enough to prolong the cliché of the South as a land of lost causes and hidebound racism. There are white churches still that do not welcome blacks into their congregations. There are white teachers who offer third-grade children a bleached and sanitized version of the Southern past. The South still leads the nation in its percentage of residents living in poverty, in sub-standard housing, without plumbing, and with fewer than five years of schooling; and most of these residents are black. There are those who suggest that the John Birch Society has taken up where the Klan left off (and it's difficult to give credence to the notion that this is progress), but Klan members still clash with Southern blacks and chafe at the notion of racial parity. As recently as 1977, the Klan's Imperial Wizard cited the FCC's Doctrine of Fairness in demanding that ABC television grant the KKK equal time on TV to present the "other side" to "Roots," the eight-part series on the history of a Negro family; reporting the demand in the *Summit Sun,* editor Mary Cain issued a pessimistic prediction: "Would you like to bet he'll be completely ignored despite the Doctrine of Fairness?"

There remain in Dixie a few diehard rabble-rousers who persist in declaring that "nigra" blood boils at a lower temperature than "white" blood (thus explaining racial riots in the humid dog days of Southern summers). Such knee-jerk redneck racists will cling to such fantasies as this till elephants take to roosting in Georgia pines.

For the most part, though, the old allegiance to lost causes has abated, and the South is living down its immoderate past. Dixie may not yet be color-blind, but it has changed enormously. Black voter registration now lags fewer than 10 percentage points behind that for voting-age whites. The old literacy test has been banished. The number of black officials elected to public office has grown forty times over since 1960. Those who don't cotton to statistics can take a quick look down south and find graphic evidence of change. A mellowed-out Wallace grinnin' like a polecat as he crowns a black homecoming queen up on the 'Bama campus. An all-black opera company running through rehearsals over in Jackson, Mississippi. A straggly band of leathered-up cyclists out on Highway 49 out of Hattiesburg, Mississippi, staging their ebony version of the Hell's Angels—with nary a pot-bellied honky sheriff riding backdoor.

It's a long, long road that don't never turn.

And the civil-rights movement was no Yankee invention: it started in Montgomery, with the decision of a gentle but weary black lady to retain her disputed seat on a segregated bus. It was carried out by Southern blacks on Southern soil.

If Dixie's darker-skinned daughters have made greater strides than black women elsewhere (and most insist that they have), they've no one to thank but themselves. Gritty black belles banded together in 1892 in the Colored Women's League, formed the National Federation of Afro-American Women three years later, merged the two the following year to form the National Association of Colored Women, and have been battling bigotry and bias ever since. Such groups never were an excuse for tea-cakes and cookies; the threat of vigilante ropes and flaming stakes loomed then not only for black men but for their women as well.

And in the years since, it has been Southern black women who have borne the brunt of conflict in fighting the social and economic conspiracy of a system that would have the few ride the backs of the many. Dixie's black women are part and parcel of the jasmine-drenched Southern heritage. They are the only American women to enter the country by special invitation, with passage paid, then suffer the consequences of this dubious honor. The South's peculiar institution planted the black woman deep in the subsoil of the provincial culture, making her the most quintessentially Southern of all.

That may be why the old black stereotypes persisted for so long in the face of cataclysmic change.

White Southerners have a penchant for making their own perverse rules of logic. If they discover something intolerable in their midst and find that they can neither change it nor make it go away, they glorify it. And so there evolved a cast of black stereotypes agreeably suited to the white code. You'll recall, of course, the much-loved stoic black mammy, who could not rest while there was a mouth to feed or a good deed to be done; she was the one who force-fed the disgracefully hearty Scarlett before the barbecue so that she would not risk that seventeen-inch waist and feminine facade by bolting down food at Twelve Oaks. It was a mammy, too, who assumed Miss Melanie's lacteal duties since Melanie (a lady and so by Southern definition fragile) was too delicate to manage mother's milk. Mammy was a caricature right off the front of the Aunt Jemima pancake box, and as dear to the Southern heart as grits and beaten biscuits.

There was also the deliciously wicked Up-town Mama who wore black net stockings and skirts slitted to the hip. Had she been white, she'd have been dismissed as a sly piece of po' white trash; as it was, she boldly cruised black bars with a derringer in her bosom, and cast her flashy spell on men with pomaded hair (one reason, according to Southern logic, so few black men showed up for work come Monday morning).

And there was the Butterfly McQueen model patterned after Margaret Mitchell's Prissy, the shiftless young household slave who routinely spilled the milk, dropped the baby, dallied 'neath the stairs, spooked at the mention of Yankees, and made up stories tail-deep on a tall Indian.

If the casting-office mentality of the "old" South paid little homage to the black reality, the reality persisted nonetheless, and does so to this day. Poke around some down in Dixie, and you'll find an Aunt Jemima or two and maybe a few Butterfly McQueens. Mostly, though, you'll discover that the majority of tar-baby belles are working-class women who started with a racial handicap and managed, by grim determination, true grits, and sheer good luck, to come through the hard times sturdy survivors. They're logical heiresses now to the brighter side of the provincial dream, and ready to *get on* with it. They're newly aware of their African heritage, knowledgeable about the black-perspective Southern past. They understand the origins and development of those obsolete black stereotypes, and know the reasons for antebellum black heel-flinging and banjo-picking. But they're less interested in bemoaning the past than in moving on into the future.

Angela Davis, after all, springs from the same tradition that produced Aunt Jemima.

The black women of Dixie have given up bandanas and pomades. They do about as much dallying as the rest of us do, but they're no longer likely to be found doing it 'neath the stairs. For the most part, Dixie's black women find they are able now to set their own standards; if they do so within the context of the provincial heritage, it's less a matter of dressing in blackface old white values and attitudes than of pursuing their own dreams. They boast inexhaustible reservoirs of strength and staying power, and for good reason: the South's most outstanding virtue is obstinacy. To survive, despite virulent prejudices and an economy that drains working-class blacks physically and spiritually, is a full day's work.

Vestiges of the Old South (i.e., racist and reactionary) persist, and there are plenty of black women who rage at the reality of closet racism. But the majority find it more difficult to be female than to be black, and most firmly believe that their place is in the South. As realists, they do not share their Northern sisters' preoccupation with the single issue of segregation. As optimists, they are convinced that the days of ugly confrontation are over in Dixie. They've moved from blacklash to busy. They honor and admire the Angela Davises who vaulted the old barriers with torches aloft, but they see little sense now in demonstrations and protests of the sort that dragged the South, kicking and screaming, into the twentieth century. If yesterday's answer was retribution, today's is *work:* get out there and bust your ass. That's one reason that of all the tired old stereotypes, they resent most the eye-rolling, teeth-chattering, ghost-fearing, skirt-clinging, foot-shuffling, tongue-wagging, blundering *Fo'-Gawd-Miss-Scarlett-Ah-doan-know-nuthin'-'bout-birthin'-babies* Butterfly McQueen caricature. Today's brash black belles take pride in their legendary strength, stamina, and competence. Given a handle on opportunity at last, they're not about to blow it through stupidity or incompetence. They got a late start on the fabled American dream, and they're racking up mileage fast. They are, for the most part, small-town mamas with up-town grit.

Bye-bye, Butterfly.

Southern black women have caused more than a few heads to turn watching their progress. They've learned to make their voices heard without fiery oratory. They've come to know the power that comes from joining other groups with the same goals. But most work behind the scenes, doing whatever they do best with unbounded drive and unfettered zeal. They boast a high-powered, directed energy that makes them dear to the hearts of those involved in civic action, community causes, and private enterprise. They're bonded, especially in Dixie, in soul sisterhood. But it is as *individuals* that they now fix their attention on the ordinary business of life.

They know it's time to hang up the dashikis, stop raising hell, and get to work getting things done.

The foxiest true-grits black lady I know is Sylvia Jackson, who lives in Greenville, Mississippi, juggles a high-pressure job with a husband and eight children, and talks of the mellow Southern tempo while maintaining a personal pace that'd turn Wilma Rudolph green with envy. Jackson is a product of the provincial South, and she carries her heritage with her into her cluttered office as director of aging for the South Delta Planning & Development District. She's realistic, pragmatic, and serenely content to view the Delta milieu without trying to score any pretentious socially significant points. When racial issues intrude on the work that she does, she takes a quick no-nonsense view of the problem and dispatches it in practical if creative terms, leaving the dictates of black pride to others. She is not here, she says, to cram integration down the throats of the elderly.

"We're trying to *feed* these people, not integrate them. We had just one white lady, one solitary white lady, to volunteer to come across town to the nutrition site, and the blacks didn't want to eat with her. They weren't used to it, they weren't comfortable. Okay, we're not so integrated. But these people are starving. We're here to feed them. Why give them indigestion trying to integrate them?"

Old habits die hard, especially among the aged, and racial bias is a tricky problem Jackson addresses as best she can. Often, this involves imaginative maneuvers certain to enrage militant Yankee blacks less accustomed to the practicalities of Southern compromise. Jackson is a woman fanatically devoted to her job; she's maniacally pleased when she finds a way around the ribbons of red tape and threads of lingering prejudice that would hold her back. Last year she became aware of an elderly white woman who lived several miles outside the city limits; the woman was too weak to cook for herself or walk into town for food, but sufficiently strong to cart around enough racial biases to fill a half-ton pickup. She'd been notified of the district's nutrition-program dinners for the aged, and told that the district director would provide transportation for her there and back. When Jackson arrived to take the woman to dinner, however, the lady made gestures that indicated she was not real proud to see Miz Jackson.

"In her age and senility, she assumed I was going to take her to *my* house to eat. When I got there and she saw I'm black, there were a world of things she'd 'forgotten.' She couldn't go to dinner."

Jackson retreated, sending a white district employee in her place.

"The lady told Jo Ann that I was just as sweet as I could be, that I was a real pretty colored girl, but that I'd invited her to eat at my *house*, and she couldn't bring herself to do that. You know, this lady was *starving.*"

She couldn't bring herself to accept food made available to her by a black director, either.

So Jackson packed a hot dinner and trekked on back to the woman's house, hoping to pass as some sort of "nigra" underling.

"I knocked on her door and held out the food and said, 'Oh, Miz Jackson asked me to bring this back to you.' And of course she took it. As long as she thought 'Miz Jackson' was white, she'd accept the food. So I kept carrying meals out to her every day till one of the white girls in the office could get her to come to the nutrition site where there were all whites."

Pride and principles aren't worth a nickel if you can't get things done. The reduction of red tape and unintelligible guidelines to the level of inventive practicality makes good, hard-nosed common sense. Jackson is one of those small-town movers and shakers grown weary with the exhortations of kamikaze militants who crash and burn against the big guns of the white establishment. She's interested in using her authority and staying power to insure the survival of those she serves: the poor, black, and elderly.

"I think integration was a means to an end. Employment gets down to performance, now, far more often than color. If an employer is hiring because he's forced to comply with racial quotas and guidelines, then he looks for a token black; if he's hiring because he wants a willing worker, then he looks for performance. If you can perform, there are people looking for you. There was a time when a black person was sheer window-dressing. Just get some black into the office. No more.

"I might have gotten this job because I'm black. There was just one white person—the director—in the program then. I think, because he was dealing with federal dollars and looking beyond the end of his nose, he may have been looking for a black. The next person he hired was white. They sandwiched me in.

"So, theoretically at least, I was a token. But I've never felt like one. I've always been so escaterious—don't ask me how to spell that, it's a word my aunt made up—that there've been occasions when my big mouth might have been an embarrassment to my director. But he was a Southerner, and he's great. I'm a Southerner, too, and we had some adjustments to make. But it never was a serious problem, and we got along very well.

"And if I *was* a token, my performance here hasn't been window-dressing. When I became director, my raise didn't begin to compensate for the work load. They don't care what color I am, you know, they just want me to get the work done. Do it! Do it! Do it!"

It used to be that being light, bright, and almost white was the only way a Negro, male or female, could get a foot in the economic door. Jackson thinks the South has made phenomenal progress.

"There was a time when we couldn't even *apply* for certain jobs, simply because we were black. There's been an enormous improvement in recourse. If you can handle the work now you can apply just like anyone else. But then I see change in little simple things you might not notice. There was a time when many whites felt that all blacks smelled. Well, you know, now that we've been rubbing shoulders with white people for a while, we've begun to think some of you-all smell, too.

"But I used to think all whites smelled good. Why not? Even the cosmetics were better for white women. Revlon and Avon and Max Factor were providing colors intended for lighter-toned women. Now a black woman can go in and buy something that looks good on *her.* She doesn't have to look like a sideshow with this real red lipstick, this real white powder.

"Just the other day I heard a fellow downstairs argue that all this emphasis on black cosmetics is exploitation. That's because he can't see a need for it. There was a crying need for it for *us*.

"Black people didn't want to be white. It just seemed the only recourse, because white was all we saw. You had to look white, you had to act white. Straight hair was good, kinky hair was bad. Of course, there were people in my family with straight hair, and they wished to hell they had a little curl.

"But if you never had the candy, you don't know how it tastes."

Jackson and her Southern sisters have had the chance to do some sampling now, and they find the candy—chocolate *and* vanilla—downright pleasuresome.

"Everything's much better now, especially in the South. There's a blending you don't see elsewhere."

There's a certain chauvinism to her words, and it's righteous. White Southerners used to argue, usually in an effort to forestall federal attempts to integrate Dixie, that they *understood* black people far better than the Yankees did. It was a rationale that prompted visions of small children whistling as they passed the local graveyard at night. But it was a rationalization grounded largely in truth. Southern white families have always depended on blacks. Black maids and housekeepers tended their children and taught them manners; black men tilled their gardens and built their houses. Martin Luther King called the Southern experience a web of mutuality, and it's not to be found in the North, where the black is a newcomer seldom welcomed with open arms. In Dixie, though, even in the days of brutal confrontation, blacks and whites lived in close proximity. Both viewed the "other side" as a collection of flesh-and-blood people rather than as an unknown amorphous mass. This is one reason integration proceeds relatively smoothly now. Another is that race relations in the South tend to be frank and honest. If there is in that honesty an aspect of prejudiced brutality, then at least black people know where they stand.

"In the South, we always knew from the start that where there's a white person there's probably some prejudice, and where there's a black person there's probably some prejudice also. When Southern blacks and whites come together, they deal with that problem from the outset."

What infuriates Jackson is the Yankee-promulgated fantasy that Northern race relations are invariably fair, invariably tranquil.

"It's nothing but veneer. These people believe their own propaganda. And, you know, when there's any sort of ruckus in a Southern town, it's bound to be blown way out of proportion.

"I was living in Little Rock when they integrated Central, and what I saw on television had almost nothing to do with what I saw going on in town. There was some agitation, and it wasn't pleasant. But things *never* got to the extent of the bayonets the press reported. My son was in the first grade, and I heard on the radio there was rioting in his school too. I went flying over there with my butcher knife to get my baby. And when I got there, there wasn't a soul on campus making trouble. The kids were in class, everyone was happy, everything was fine."

This is not to say, of course, that the South today is a utopian democracy, where minorities share so fully in social and economic life that all feast routinely on champagne and winter strawberries, and each views the other with trusting eyes. There are a lot of blacks in Dixie, says Jackson, who are yet highly suspicious of whites, and many who remain skeptical of the promise of equality. Even so, there are personal relationships here upon which blacks and whites can build in ways not possible in Chicago, or Harlem, or Watts. Antebellum slavery took a domestic and rural form that led to particularly intimate group contacts. Southerners *know* one another—and always have—at far deeper levels than Northerners imagine or have experienced. Increasingly, Dixie's blacks and whites meet on selective terms, and such communication is voluntary, stemming from interest in common goals. The Southern sense of unity is deeper and stronger than its prejudices, and provincial homogeneity transcends, even now, conflicting interests and attitudes.

"Half the Northerners I've met have never even been around black people," says Jackson. "They're more isolated and segregated in their urban neighborhoods than we were here in the old days. In certain ways we've always been more integrated here than they've ever been. But they seem to feel superior to *all* Southerners, black and white.

"And I never know what I'm getting when I meet a Northerner. I've mingled with Northern women, but not enough to be able to separate the silver-plate from the sterling silver."

She has no trouble making the distinction at home.

Having shared a unique provincial history, the two races here have always had more in common than they've had outside the borders of Dixie. If shared losses and gains and a mutual Southern experience made for a better understanding of one another, however, members of neither race fell heir to a full understanding of their history. Whether enrolled in schools that were predominantly white or shunted off to those infamous separate-but-unequal ones, black children traditionally were taught far more white history than black; white children learned nothing at all of Afro-American history, aside from the obligatory nod toward Booker T. Washington. More recently Southern children have been tutored in tokenism: there's the black author Augusta Baker, the black singer Marian Anderson, the black dancer Janet Collins, the black tennis star Althea Gibson, the black baseball-club owner Effa Manley.

Interest in black genealogy began to surge in the sixties, but Alex Haley and ABC television achieved what two decades of black-pride slogans could not: blacks gained new insight into their heritage and whites were reminded that the roots of both races are inextricably intertwined. "Roots" became a social phenomenon with impact so staggering that black leaders judge it a major milestone in U.S. race relations.

Never mind the flaws and omissions or the widely publicized charges that Haley faked where his research failed: "Roots" is no transitory sensation. And it makes not a dime's worth of difference whether Haley's facts are straight. For more than a hundred million Americans, black and white, "Roots" is real, and this counts for more than literal truth.

It had a visceral impact on the Jackson household. Long before "Roots," Sylvia had traced her lineage back into slavery on her mother's side; data on her father, whose parents died early, is fragmentary.

"I can only tell you about my family. I find it difficult to even know how it was with others. But 'Roots' was hard on our six-year-old daughter."

Soon after the television epic, Daisy Jackson—called more often "Pooh"—came home from school with a few judicious observations of white folks.

"She said, 'Mama, white folks are slick. They ask you for all of your paper, and then when you run out and ask them for some of theirs, they don't give you any.' So I told her maybe it didn't have anything to do with color; maybe they just didn't have any paper. But in a couple of days, she came home with more questions: 'Mama, did the white people hold you up and whip you? Mama, did you have to clean up for white people?' And until then she didn't know the difference between black and white. She's too young, and we've never harped on it. It came from seeing 'Roots' on television, and it was at my indiscretion that she watched it. But it did more good than harm, I think. A lot of whites saw part of our history they never knew existed. A lot of blacks, too."

No single book or television epic can create jobs for the chronically unemployed, or provide decent housing, or feed the backroads elderly. But it may well be that Haley's book, for all its flaws, is one of the most eloquent statements for democracy yet advanced. No Southerner of any color doubts its lasting effect, and none who read or watched it was unmoved. For those who have based their biases on color came the shock of realization that the die of slavery was cast not by color but by economics. The earliest African importees shared, generally, the same rights accorded indentured English bondsmen and convict debtors, including the right to purchase their freedom through private enterprise. Many did so and became slaveholders themselves after the fashion of white landholders. But so desperately was free labor needed in the colonial South—and so available were captive Africans—that slavery soon became inescapably, indelibly black. Negroes bore the brunt of the feudal plantation system, diverting it from the backs of poorer white settlers. Black immigrants, then, did Southern whites the favor (however reluctantly) of having someone to look down on.

"You've got a lot of people who are still hanging on to that old myth. Some people are stereotyped and slotted, and there just ain't nothing you can do with them. I've always felt that those who try so hard to preserve the myth of white superiority are using blacks as an incentive. They have to be over *somebody*. They've got to be better than blacks because this is all they've got going for them. And they don't know how to deal with it when they see a black who's surpassed them."

It's said that being black and female is double jeopardy, and not just in Dixie. Yet Sylvia Jackson believes that black women enjoy an odd sort of freedom specifically because of their sex and color.

"I've always thought that a Southern black woman could go where no black man dares tread. She gets away with it either because she's black or because she's female. There've been times when she could move mountains while the black male was immobilized because of other factors, like mythological jealousies white men may have of black men."

Oh yes: there are white provincials who perpetuate the fantasy of the dangerously over-endowed black man. There are white males still who think integration begins with jumping into bed with the first black female he can get his hands on. There lingers, even now, a widespread white conviction that every black male hungers for a blond, blue-eyed bride; failing matrimony, of course, rape makes a reasonable second choice. When a Southerner hunkers down to discuss the probable perils of social equality, what he's really talking about (whether he knows it or not) is sexual parity. In the old days, that was when the hoods went on and the noose came out. Now there's no evidence that the educated, race-proud, newly enfranchised Southern black male is any more determined to marry our daughters than was his great grandpappy.

But the old fears persist.

And even the most militant of black feminists knows better than to squander precious time and energy lobbying for rationality in this most irrational of human activities. The provincial attitude toward sex is no more or less logical than the Confederate decision to start a war without possessing a single munitions factory. Jackson is relieved to see a lessening of that particular brand of down-home logic:

"People aren't so hung up on the sexual mythologies as they once were. There was a time when I'd have been afraid for my husband to stop to help a white woman who'd had a flat tire. Afraid of what someone might think, afraid of what that woman might say. I don't know what her needs are. She may need publicity. She may need attention, attention she could get easily enough by saying she'd been molested. She might become hysterical simply because it was a black man who stopped to help."

According to the old (*read:* white) folklore, black males not chronically intent on raping white women were chronically and deliberately unemployed: shiftless and irresponsible, they left it to their wives to bring home the bacon.

It's fairly easy to mistake for laziness and sloth the debilitating signs of sickle-cell anemia or hookworm or diseases that derive from dependence on polluted water. And of course shiftlessness wasn't always attributable to such hidden causes. It stemmed as frequently from the white penchant for maintaining a separate moral code for black people (so long as it didn't interfere with their work). Traditionally, dating from antebellum times, black workers were expected to steal. Large-scale larceny was never tolerated, of course, but theft within the limits of moderation and good taste was anticipated and condoned. The so-called whistler's walk that connected the kitchen (located in an outbuilding due to the danger of fire) with the main house in so many Southern plantation homes bears testimony to this unspoken cynicism: slaves carrying hot food along this well-worn path were required to whistle as they hurried to the master's table, a white strategy designed to insure against sampling of the master's cuisine before it reached his table. Slaves, like other humans, tended to live up to their billing: faced with the clear expectation that they were born thieves, they stole. Moderately, of course.

When two differing sets of morality exist side by side, everyone loses. The Southern habit of condoning pilfering by black employees, and the black habit of getting even, made for spiritual destruction neither race could afford. It was the black male, Jackson says, who suffered the greatest loss:

"Okay, you had black men who were chronically unemployed or underpaid, and black women who worked as domestics in white households. Family income was supplemented by the white family for whom the women worked. It undermined the black male's efforts to provide for his family. You know: why should he work harder to buy three pair of underwear for his girls when Miss Ann is going to buy nine pair because she knows his wife will sneak out three for the kids. Why should he work? She'll bring food home from the big house where she works. She'll bring clothes home.

"And why *should* he work harder at a low-pay job? The need wasn't there. The pride wasn't there. So the black male appeared shiftless, and many black men were. You know, there are a lot of people, black and white, who are parasitic and shiftless."

But then almost anyone would appear to be, compared with Jackson, who's done everything but lead a Virginia reel between labor pains.

"My bachelor's degree was in physical education. I've never taught physical education in my life! It took me fifteen years to finish high school because I traveled with my husband, and everywhere he went I had to change schools. I became a jack-of-all-trades and a master of nothing! I went to school between babies. I had enough credit hours for anything. When I went into the school system, they sent me in as a librarian. A physical-education major! They sent me to Ole Miss to groom me. Well, I thought I was going to have to teach music, so I started studying the piano again. But they did the reverse and sent me into library science. I dropped out after two years to work with urban renewal. Naturally, urban renewal failed: we didn't get the referendum passed. Fortunately, they needed someone here in the Aging Division. I guess as big as my mouth is, and as much as I talk, they just assumed

I could handle the work. I *really* love this job."

With her no-nonsense approach to the subtleties of race prejudice, she's uniquely qualified for the position. She understands the special problems of rural Southerners because she *is* one. And she has particular appeal to members of Greenville's white establishment: she's diligent, capable, and energetic, and she shatters all the old stereotypes. To mossback racists, she proves that blacks are not necessarily shiftless or dumb. To guilt-ridden liberals, she proves that not all blacks belabor past inequities. Jackson is shrewd enough to temper her go-go passion for performance with warm good humor, which softens the knowledge that a black female occupies a position of authority and thus has the right to demand community response to district urgencies. Besides, the local power elite—white and male—can accept Jackson, convincing themselves and one another in doing so that they are neither racist nor sexist, all in one fell swoop.

Making the transition from administrative underling to administrative director wasn't all that difficult. Having been sensitized to the needs of the poor, the black, and the elderly, she began with a keen grasp of what was needed here. And the local leadership found it feasible to support her efforts. Being black, Southern, female, and resourceful, Jackson is prime capital, not to be squandered on mere tokenism, but rather invested wisely for the resolution of the community's special social problems.

"You know, we've got special problems here. Washington decided to fund these programs in areas where there is the highest concentration of elderly folks. Well, that's fine for Washington, D.C., and Chicago. But we've got some counties down here with no more than six hundred people living in them. We don't *have* population density. So we have to angle and wiggle and decide how to get the food out to the people who need it most. When you're fragmented like this in a small rural area, your resources—like welfare and health care—are fragmented too.

"It takes so much more money to get a meal to a person who lives out in the boondocks. We've got a list, a schedule, and the feds say we have to do it exactly this way. But at the back of your head you've got voices hammering 'Why can't we have meals here?' "

A problem arises when the elderly, most of whom are rural blacks living in shotgun shacks, have no money for telephones. But Jackson's a provincial powerhouse accustomed to maneuvering around limitations.

"We've gotten a few gracious people to pay phone bills for our elderly folks. And where we can't get phones, we work out a system of signals. Our people do things like move a pot from one side of the door to the other or raise a shade or whatever—anything to keep some kind of contact with their buddies and be able to signal if they need help.

"Another problem is transportation: in the cities, where these programs are designed to work best, you've got built-in transportation. Here we have to provide it. It's a big thing to ask a person to use his own personal car to pick up someone. The folks in Washington don't think about that. They probably haven't even noticed. You know, everybody's got transportation. Most times when people come down here with their budgets and programs, they don't even include a line-item for special transportation costs. Maybe fifteen cents a trip. But a trip in *what* for fifteen cents? We ain't got no buses!"

It's not a federal giveaway.

"It's like in the old days in my culture. You know, you worked hard and you were too tired and too frustrated to be bothered with asking for what you were entitled to. So you stayed in your place. The same thing goes on with elderly people: they stay in their place.

"But, you know, we need the elderly people. Not just the

ones that we feed or we take to an office or to the doctor or to get groceries. We need the people that've been forced into retirement as a human resource. They're a human library.

"Mississippi, Arkansas, Louisiana: we've got the lowest reading level in the country, you know. Our kids can't read well. The teachers teach them fundamental whatever, but many kids just don't have anybody at home to supplement what they get in school.

"So, okay, we've got programs where elderly people can get together and chat with other elderly people. We've got programs where they can get people to comb their hair and stuff like that. Well, that's fine. But they *could* be helping the kids. You don't have to have a college degree to do that. We can get the elderly folks together with the kids so they can read with them. You know, we can't pay enough people to help the kids with their homework. But the elderly folks can do it.

"It's a lot better than spending the money on streets. Well, you know, these people have put streets in already. And you're never going to have all the streets in good shape in Greenville, Mississippi. But you could have one building for the senior citizens. And they could do a world of good."

Jackson has received considerable media attention for her work with the aged. But like other Southern women, she knows full well when people are pissing on her feet and calling it rain.

"Look here: I may just have a vested interest. My work may be interest I'm paying on my insurance. It's popular to stick old people in a home. But if we can make people aware of this resource we have in the elderly, maybe someone will see after *me* later on. Maybe with as many children as I've got they'll keep me, oh, maybe two months each and not get too tired of me. Or at least recognize the fact I'm still human when I get frail."

She'd like to change the world. Preferably, this very afternoon. Certainly not later than tonight. She's busy and she's impatient. She hasn't any time to waste:

"I'm not in that group of bonded women. We've got a lot of clubs in town, but I don't have time to go to the clubs and watch talent shows or have a fund-raising party. I've got some very good friends that I never see till I need them or they need me. *Very* good friends, and without their friendship, black and white, you cannot survive in the South."

Nor is she tied, as most of her contemporaries are, to a church.

"You're supposed to go to church every Sunday. Well, I don't. If I go to church on Sunday, it doesn't make me a better person."

If the Church played an important role in her life, says Jackson, she's yet to find it out—unless it was to foster a spirit of rebellion.

"I feel that as a child, I was *raped* with religion."

She was baptized a Catholic as an infant.

"If I had to select a religious path to follow now, Catholicism is my preference. But if I were going to be a true Catholic, I'd feel I had to be baptized again and let it be *my* decision. The decision *should* have been mine, not my mother's."

In any case, Jackson feels no need to attend weekly mass.

"If there's a person who needs my help on Sunday morning, that's where I need to be. I don't need to be sitting up in church listening to some Father regurgitating the Bible to me. I've heard that through all my years.

"I married at sixteen. And you know, it was baby, baby, baby. I'd have one baby and put him over here and then I'd have another. I thought in my younger days that I was cursed. I hadn't lived long enough. Not even twenty years old and, my God, all these babies.

"I could not understand why God would allow me to be so stupid, or give me these children not realizing what was happening to me. So I went through a lot of changes. Why was I a mother?

"I remember hearing a priest talk to my mother once. I heard him say he'd rather have been an archaeologist than a priest, but he felt that he was called to the priesthood. It was his duty to be a priest, but he'd rather have been out looking for rocks. And I said to myself, 'Listen, if he can stay in a seminary and be single and fool around trying to convert people to God, selling somebody something they can't see, you know, then I can be a mother with ease!' That was my therapy. I thought, 'My God, I'm lucky after all.' You know: suppose I had to be a *nun?*"

It was a sobering thought, and it enabled Jackson to come to terms with her life. As an adult, she considers herself a controlled rebel.

"I'm deceitful. I don't rebel with sticks and stones. I believe that if you're shrewd enough you can rebel and people will never know what happened to them. It's easier, I think, and you're more successful doing it that way. It requires a lot of deceit, of course, a lot of strategy. But I don't think you can make anybody do anything they don't want to do. The slick thing is to prod them and make them come up with the idea you want. Let them think it's their idea.

"I try very hard not to get angry because when I get angry I always let people get the best of me. It's draining. You're just running and racing and suppressing, and at night you sit up and think about it. So you try not to let the anger get to you. You try to do things reasonably, peacefully, so you can get down to what you want to do. To what you want to see accomplished."

She gets her way a good deal of the time, probably because she's serene and secure enough now to focus on true priorities, letting the smaller inequities slip on by.

Float like a butterfly, sting like a bee.

Handicapped at birth by race and sex, she permitted

neither to throw her off-stride:

"I think being black, Southern, and female has been an *advantage* for me, because I'm not all that smart. There are ten thousand others just like me in Washington, and I might get lost in the crowd there. In the South, I'm considered pretty sharp. With the little intelligence I do have, being black and female here is a definite plus for me."

Well, now, she's smart enough to know what's going on, make a living, work some tricky grass-roots magic, live a little joy, and not take herself too seriously.

And that's smarter than most folks I know.

What turns her solemn are questions that have to do with what she wants for her children. And if she had a choice of any city in the nation to raise them in, she'd opt to stay right where she is.

Greenville is a place of Southern comfort so compelling, despite its startling pockets of poverty, that people here feel obliged to try to get along. Located in the heart of the state's Delta region, it boasts very nearly an equal number of blacks and whites. It was the first town in Mississippi to agree to school desegregation without the threat of court order.

Jackson finds her hometown sufficiently small, Southern, and provincial to prepare her children for the life she envisions for them.

"I want them to be self-sustaining emotionally. I'd like for them to be economically secure. If they can achieve just those two things, I'll rest easier. Well, I won't be at rest; no mother ever is. But if they're emotionally stable and economically secure, it'd make me very happy.

"I want them raised here. Greenville's small enough. I'm just one person, and my husband's half a person because he's working so damn hard all the time to feed us. It's a real asset to live in a community this size with my eight kids. Somebody's got to help me raise them, and here there's closeness and friendship across the community.

"I'm rural by nature. I'm not geared to the fast life of the city and the insensitiveness that seems inherent there. I'd have been a failure, probably, in a large city. I might have gone unnoticed for years. I'm Southern, and I'm rural.

"The adjustment I'd have to make to the city would dilute the time and expertise I need to raise my children. I'm learning while I'm trying to teach. If I already know some things —like I do here—then I can spend more time teaching, raising, rearing, preparing my kids. I can find jobs for them here. I can give them exposure to both black and white people. They can learn how to live with people; it's easier here."

This is a woman at once consistent and contradictory. She defies typecasting. Yet, while she has nothing in common with the old magnolias-and-banjos tradition of blacks as childlike innocents, she derives directly from that heritage; she fits comfortably into the enduring stereotype of the black woman who lived and worked closely with whites and sustained in that relationship that fabled web of mutuality. Her presence and her power are rooted firmly in her explicit refutation of that image. As Sylvia Jackson plays out her high-spirited, idiosyncratically competent Southern role, the ghost of Aunt Jemima rises up, rolling pin aloft, to assume the lead in the provincial parade. Jackson is part and parcel not only of the past but of the future as well. As Southern women have a way of doing, she marches in two directions at once, and to the drummer of her choice.

True grits in blackface, with up-town dash.

Tough Hides, Tender Hearts:
The Happy Decline of Derivative Glory

*Maybe it's been necessary
to have some women hollering
and screaming and burning their bras,
but I think what they're doing
is winning the argument
and losing the customer.*
—BETTY TALMADGE

Having Betty Talmadge on your side is roughly equivalent to having Henry the K run interference for you in Peking.

Only better.

Betty, recently divorced from Senator Herman Talmadge, taught the nation a lesson in good old-fashioned Southern-style loyalty when she threw a luncheon for Pat Nixon in the Senate Dining Room while—just a few doors away—the Senator and his Watergate colleagues were grilling John Ehrlichman. When reporters quizzed her later on the political implications of the luncheon and demanded to know what was said about Watergate, she gave *them* a quick lesson in form. She breathed a little down-home fire in their direction and pronounced the questions rude, crude, and inconsiderate.

That's what I like about the South.

Betty's known in Washington (and nearly everywhere else) for having a quick wit and a word for every occasion, and she is renowned for her business skills. When her ham company merged with Cagle, Inc., in 1969, the Washington *Star* reported that she'd been earning $3 million annually.

Betty penned a quick correction: that was her company's *gross,* not net. "However," she wrote, "if you plan a retraction, please let it be a small one, for this certainly brightened my financial and social standing."

If the South is on the rise again, it is precisely because of women like Talmadge. An aristocratic lady with a bit of tar and turpentine on her heels, she knows the difference between style and substance, and opts for both. Heavy odds don't faze her: she has learned (the hard way) to fight her own battles, and she makes a point of winning when winning counts:

"I won't take a back seat to anybody when it comes to moving when I have to and getting a job done. But that's not the way I really function best. I like a little slower pace."

She finds that pace at Talmadge Farms in Lovejoy, Georgia.

"Herman's father bought this place and this old house. It was an old washed-away cotton farm. When Herman came home from the war, his father gave us this old house and a thousand acres of land. Even though I didn't actually build this structure, in a sense I did. I planted every shrub out there, laid every brick by hand. Inside, I selected every color, every light fixture, every rug. I built it. I buried my son over here back of the house. There's grief there, but a lot of love and a lot of peace, too. When I'm keyed up, I come home and put on an old pair of shoes and just walk the land. Slowing down. There's something here I can't walk away from.

"And you know I love to walk!"

Almost always, she's on the move: to Atlanta, fifteen miles north, for lunch with Faith Brunson and an autograph party for her new cookbook, *How to Cook a Pig;* to Texas, to visit Lady Bird Johnson; to New York, to Plains, or any of a hundred towns across the country where she's in constant demand on the lecture circuit, speaking on any subject from pig-picking to women's rights. Always, she circles back to the white-columned antebellum home on the outskirts of Lovejoy. It's a gentle house, lovingly restored, solid but not pretentious: a place where comfort, the needs of children and friends take precedence—a place where Betty Talmadge walks, adjusts her pace, mends her psyche.

She's had a rough few years.

In 1975, her son Robert died in a holiday accident at Lake Lanier. In 1977, six days after their thirty-fifth wedding anniversary, her husband Herman filed suit for divorce. He didn't get around to telling her: she heard the news first on television in the den, while the Senator lingered in the breakfast room.

Now *that's* bad form.

There followed a pressure-cooker year of tension and legal entanglement. Betty did a good deal of walking and a good deal of thinking. She emerged from the hard times, as Southern women tend to do, a survivor with a clear new notion of what she is. She looks soft in her pink lipstick and Ultrasuede and a cloud of Givenchy III. But the "outgoing wife" of Senator Talmadge, as she so breezily referred to herself that anxious and interminable year, found out that she is strong as morning-glory vine, tougher than pig-iron.

True grits.

She is, she says, "more Betty Talmadge now than I've ever been in my life."

She was finished with derivative glory several years back.

"I've always been in business, you know, ever since I married. I sort of looked at the men and felt, well, I'm capable of rubbing the hams and doing the minor things, but when the big decisions came along, I turned to a man for help. It finally occurred to me that I knew more about my business than they did, or at least as much, and I wouldn't take anything for that ability to believe in myself. And I got that with the help of a psychiatrist.

"He didn't tell me things. Sometimes I thought all he did

was grump. But somehow I got the message. Now, my life has been rough for several years, and it's rough right now. Don't misunderstand me. But you can live without everything but self-respect. If you haven't got that, there ain't no way you can have any happiness in your life."

You get that by declining derivative glory. You don't have to steal anybody else's thunder; you just have to have your own.

It was something Talmadge had to learn for herself.

"I wasn't competitive when I was young. I didn't have the self-confidence to be. Now, you've got to survive well or you don't survive at all, but I wasn't competitive. What I wanted then was male approval. You know, we were taught that if we're pretty and sweet and behave ourselves, then we're going to be loved; some man is going to come along and look after us, worship us, take care of us.

"My mother used to say, 'Oh, you'll be a lovely complement to Herman.' This was my role in life: to be a lovely complement. And I *bought* that!

"But you've got to mind your own store. There comes a time when you have to quit looking for a father. Grow up. Look after yourself. This is what the psychiatrist hit me with. And I believe in this very much: by going to a psychiatrist and getting this out, it gets you to the point where you can see you have to get up off your ass."

Everything she has accomplished in life, Talmadge says, was because she had to do it.

"The ox was in the ditch, and I had to get it out. I remember I felt very put-upon: raising children, running this house, running the Governor's mansion, running the ham business, and politicking, too, you know. I hated sitting here balancing books alone.

"But now I just thank God I had to do it, because of the turn my life has taken. What would I do if I hadn't had some business interests that not only helped me financially but also kept me involved? I've seen too many women whose whole being is tied entirely to their husbands' lives."

She never put much market value on being a successful Washington hostess, and she wasn't "temperamentally suited" to serve as an ornament on Herman's arm.

"It's hard on your ego if all you have is reflected glory. When you get into your fifties and sixties and lose that glory, you're no longer marketable. You have to prepare for the fact that it can happen to you: this man may die or leave you.

"And I've also seen a lot of wives my age whose husbands are busy. They're lost when the children leave. You can't lead your children's lives. I'm a member of that club: I tried to. You must have *some* work. You must make your own way."

Talmadge backed into business, she says, in the fifties, when Herman succeeded his father as Governor. They'd started with just 1500 hams to process in a tiny concrete block-house with a small refrigeration room. After two or three months, the Governor was too busy to tend the business, and short of working capital as well. Betty had a few stocks and bonds, which she sold and invested the money in Talmadge Farms.

"And I took charge of it, because everything I had was invested in it."

She traveled all over the country to find original formulas for curing ham, and reached into the past for methods used by her grandfather. She enrolled in Washington's American University in order to learn accounting and corporation finance. She "didn't know a debit from a credit" when she started, but she was a quick study; between presiding at political teas and shaking hands in receiving lines, she managed to build the business until she sold $3,000,000 worth of corn-fed hams yearly. She found, oddly enough, that being female was a help rather than a hindrance.

"It's perfectly acceptable for me to say I don't know when I don't. A man is *supposed* to know, and that makes for constant pressure. If he doesn't know, then he's really not very successful; if he doesn't make a million dollars, then he's really not successful. And that's a bunch of crap. Women have it a little better. There's no pressure on us to know everything and to be what we were expected to be. We get a lot of extra credit when we succeed in business because success isn't expected of us.

"And I got a lot of credit for eccentricity, too. When I started, I was sort of an oddity. I was the wife of a governor and I was a woman out there in the ham business. I was an oddity, and I realized that, and it was a great help to me.

"But that doesn't make you successful.

"They'll be nice and sweet to you, but they're not going to buy unless you've got a product or a service they want or need. But it helps in getting started."

It must, though clearly Talmadge is exceptionally gifted and committed to the notion that what's worth doing at all is worth doing exceedingly well. Her success does not derive from luck, for it seems she's had little of that. The sale of Talmadge Farms was for stock in a booming poultry firm, which promptly ran aground, having over-expanded. Talmadge went back to work. One of the firm's prime products, chicken hot dogs, was in need of a market; Talmadge thought the surplus wieners might appeal to the Japanese, who tend to buy high-protein foods whenever available at reasonable prices. Sure as a cat's got climbing gear, she found that inferior-quality beef wieners were selling in inflation-ridden Tokyo for something like three dollars a pound; she could (and did) deliver chicken hot dogs at good quality for less than a dollar a pound. Right now, she's wondering what might come of exporting pregnant cows to Iran.

Back in the United States, she has banded with partner Richard Peck to form Betty Talmadge Associates, Inc., a meat brokerage firm with offices in Atlanta. She makes it a point to personally visit the larger clients four times a year, though she can usually find an excuse to drop in on the smaller ones as well; friends who accompany her when she travels to lecture, promote her cookbook, or socialize generally find themselves cooling their heels in the car while Talmadge pops in on a client—or a potential one. She is a born saleswoman, likes to keep a close eye on her business interests, and finds that the personal touch pays handsome dividends. The firm's slogan, ever mindful of the consequences of failing to mind one's store, is "sell it or smell it," a typical Talmadge touch.

It's more than enough to keep her busy, but she's a woman determined to avoid the trap of home-hugging.

"Women who sit at home and feel sorry for themselves simply destroy themselves. It's the most devastating thing. I *have* to be busy."

Southern women always have kept to this tradition, partly through economic necessity. Talmadge was raised in Ashburn, Georgia, and her father died when she was nine.

"My mother was left with four children and an income of a hundred and twenty-five dollars a month. And we were among the more affluent. It was during the Depression, and seeing her struggle to make ends meet really made an impression on me."

She has believed, always, that women must make lives for themselves outside the home, not only for financial security but for ego reinforcement as well. Her own unexpected divorce during her fifties reaffirmed that conviction.

"Where would I be now without Betty Talmadge Associates?"

Her book, *How to Cook a Pig and Other Back to the Farm Recipes*, published by Simon and Schuster, is packed with good advice on how to cook Sally Lunn bread, sausage pinwheels, and grits soufflé. But it's filled too with Talmadge wit, reminiscence, and admonitions on the importance of feminine self-reliance. Talmadge is one of the few Southern women who have come out openly for the feminist movement and for the passage of the Equal Rights Amendment.

"I'm very much for ERA. The best lawyers I know say that they can defend women in case of sex-discrimination suits far more effectively if the Amendment passes. I'm not a lawyer, but this makes sense to me. It's getting to the point where most women *have* to work, whether they're supporting themselves or carrying the responsibility for providing for an entire family. Now, I've hired women for less money simply because I could get them for less, and that's still being done today. But these women must get equal pay if they do equal work. Their children get just as hungry, want an education just as badly, as a man's children.

"I know that the feminist movement has become some kind of a threat to housewives. They're feeling left out and demeaned, as if they're not really in there unless they work outside the home. Well, if they're happy with the traditional role, then I think it's wonderful. But I *will* point out that they can go along for years and suddenly find that because of death or divorce, they're without resources. We spend a third of our lives alone; if our husbands protect us as child-like individuals, we don't know what to do when they die or leave us.

"Now, waiting on men doesn't bother me. We were raised that way, you know, and they like being waited on, and it's not an imposition to get up and fetch somebody a drink or a cup of coffee. I like doing that. But when I see women who've got to go into the job market to work and they're hungry and want clothes and yearn for a house just as much as anybody else, and they're paid almost nothing, then I *do* get upset. People tell me that women can't get credit for what they do. My answer is that men get too much credit. That doesn't bother me. Just give me equal pay for equal work. Give me equal opportunity.

"Somehow, too, we've got to place some value on the work women do at home, a dollar value. I don't say you actually have to transfer dollars, but just, by golly, say *this* is of *this* value in dollars and cents. Society thinks of housework as *fun*. It *is* fun baking bread. But when you've got to do it free three times a day and meet those schedules, it's not play anymore. We need to admit that, and put some value on what women do in the home."

Talmadge admits militant tactics might be necessary, but abhors them ("women see them as unladylike strategies").

"It's necessary to get what you want. But this is what I'm trying to say to the women's movement: *Cool it some.* You can't take people any faster than they want to go. Now, if we can stop and say, look here, your work *is* important, and not only for somebody else, then we'll get somewhere. The housewife has *got* to value the work she does, because if *she* doesn't, I assure you no one else will.

"I don't know how we'll ever get it across to them, but I think men will be so much happier when they accept their wives as partners rather than domestic servants or chattel. You know: you just be sweet and proper, barefoot and pregnant, and I'll look out for you. I've got a little daughter-in-law whose father always had an expression: 'act pretty.' That means 'don't cause me any problems.' And he's one of the dearest men I know. But this is what most men want: they want all their daughters to be pretty, and find some man to put them on a pedestal. 'Course, you can't be had unless you let yourself be had."

She's a woman who'd appear to be more at home on the magnolia-scented veranda of an antebellum mansion, or in the kitchen of a plush plantation home, than at the forefront of a feminist rally. If there's anything more satisfying than to sit with her near the fire in her Lovejoy kitchen, munching sausage pinwheels and cheese grits soufflé while listening to her talk, in mellowed tones, of hemlines and puff pastry, I haven't experienced it yet. There is no more feminine woman, no creature better suited for the traditional role.

Yet she throbs with the need to convey her message to those who rely solely on derivative glory. Talmadge is the best of the provincial South: she mixes practical business flair with sensual seductiveness, lively humor with feminine grace, candlelit elegance with denim verve. While younger women are blow-drying their long straight locks, Talmadge crops hers short, Hemingway-sexy, and streaks it rich; while the strident militants disdain perfume as a sexist sell-out, Talmadge walks in a satisfying cloud of expensive, aphrodisiacal fragrances, and manages to capture the attention of every man in the room. If she's made of the stuff that suggests a good bosom in a simple silk shirt and great legs glimpsed through the slit of a slithery skirt, she also has more than a smidgen of Jacksonian gut and grit. She may well be the only feasible Southern spokeswoman capable of advocating feminist practicality: she does not threaten so much as she inspires.

Spend half an hour with Talmadge and you come away convinced that once you put your hand to the plough, it's unconscionable to take it away till you reach the end of the row.

For the most part, Southern women view women's lib with all the enthusiasm usually reserved for hookworm or rabid bats. For one thing, militant feminism is, well, *impolite*. And, as you know, a Southern woman is unfailingly polite until she's angry enough to put a 12-gauge to your temple or pour sugar into your gas-tank. For another, feminism implies change; and an agricultural society (or an industrial one that continues to think of itself as rural) is resistant to change by outside forces, and enslaved by patriarchal traditions. Third, Southern women know a good thing when they see it. They'd rather take their chances this way than see the end of a system that permits them the best of both traditional and contemporary worlds. Why not stay on the pedestal, enjoying all the perks and privileges that come with Southern womanhood, while reaping as well the freedom attainable through that informal loophole of provincial eccentricity?

A good many Southern women wouldn't vote to repeal the Code of Hammurabi, with its institutionalized view of woman as male property, if you carted them to the polls in golden coaches.

And they will tell you, asked or not, that they've already got more freedom than they need, citing the achievements in every field made by Southern women who broke free from the passive provincial stereotypes to make a difference in the varied institutions of Southern life. There are, in fact, more than a few daring and independent Southern spirits who've found fame and fortune in the absence of sexual parity. Sarah Caldwell, the Divine Sarah, was an Arkansas fiddler who became the first woman ever to conduct at the Metropolitan Opera. Birmingham's Angela Davis became a symbol of black rebellion while still in her twenties. Frances Wright established a commune in the 1820s where Tennessee slaves could earn their freedom. Wilma Rudolph, unable to walk normally till the age of eleven, shattered world records as a sprinter in the Olympics. Alabama's Helen Keller put the blind and deaf in touch with something beyond themselves. Florida's Ma Barker proved that the family that slays together stays together. Susie Marshall Sharp of North Carolina served with distinction as the first woman to be popularly elected chief justice of a state supreme court. Carol Sutton, the first woman to become managing editor of a major U. S. newspaper, guarded the Louisville *Courier-Journal*'s reputation as one of the nation's best dailies. Isabella Walton Cannon, who at age seventy-three insists she's "not the book-club type," got herself elected mayor of Raleigh, North Carolina.

Birmingham's Marie Jemison sees these feminist coups as trappings of power in a powerless world. And it's true that, like blacks, Southern women have made their greatest political gains at the lower levels: as members of mayors' councils, city councils, boards and commissions, lower-echelon elected officials. Although, like Talmadge, Jemison dislikes militant feminist tactics ("you pay too much"), she's passionate in her commitment to the movement—and pessimistic about its chances in the South.

"Southern women are tough—they've *had* to be—but I don't know if they're tough enough to break the mold. The men have so much vested interest in the status quo that it's difficult for women to break out, to have new experiences and new ideas."

Despite the Southern tradition of self-sustaining women and the widespread conviction that in this provincial society women wield considerable power, Jemison sees women as an oppressed majority. The power they have, she says, is illusory:

"I make a lot of decisions. I decide where we're going on trips, where the children will go to school, what kind of car I want. I decide more and more often how I'm going to spend my time. But I really don't make any major decisions. For example, I can't decide what my inheritance is going to be or what I'm going to do with the money I inherit. The way the tax structure is set up, whatever I inherit will be mine for my lifetime, and then it goes to my children. *I* don't have any say-so. To me, that's an important decision, and I don't have the power to make it.

"I'd like to see women have more power, more economic power and more political power, and more control over their lives. I think the old-white-boys club that runs the world needs shaking up. But I don't see it happening."

One reason, says Jemison, is that women have failed to learn the techniques of gaining and wielding power:

"I was talking last night with a woman who'd just graduated from law school. She wouldn't admit it, she's too timid, but she indicated that she's interested in corporate law. But she's going into family law instead. I don't see many women going into corporate law, and that's where the power is.

"I look around and see women with ambition, women who want to get to the top but who are not willing to use the necessary strategy to do that. They don't attach themselves to mentors the way men always have, so they can't rise with those mentors to the top. It seems to me that we just don't seem to be catching on to how the system works."

Because Jemison's orientation is primarily political, she's particularly concerned that Southern women seem disinterested in politics.

"It may have to do with role models. We've never had any female role models in politics. We've had just five women, one at a time, in the state legislature. We've never had two women in the legislature simultaneously. There's a great deal of talk about Alabama having more women in elective office than any other state, about how women have been elected secretary of state, state auditor, state treasurer. But those are jobs that are virtually powerless. Ever since the forties, jobs like that have been turned over between women. Men don't even run for those positions, so you *know* there's no power connected with them. The legislature's where the real power is. Women have been running for legislative office in great numbers for the past few years—but have won no elections."

Nor do they campaign, she says, on women's issues.

"They act as if they're not women. I don't mean they play down their femininity, but they use their initials rather than their names on the ballot so they won't be recognized as women. They're careful not to talk about ERA or abortion or anything that has to do with feminist goals."

You'd think Marie Jemison would be content to sit back and coast on her aristocratic credentials. She's rich, white, beautiful, well educated, and descended from one of the oldest, most prominent families in Alabama. Her home, set in a rolling glade of sun-dappled dogwood, would send the haughtiest *Town & Country* editor into ecstasy. Her husband is successful, charismatic, and attentive. Her children have perfect white teeth and flawless manners. Marie turns a pair of faded jeans into couturier fashion, and has the style to run a household in a way that looks at least effortless, holding a light rein in a well-manicured hand. Even her maid makes magic, silently materializing with garnished drinks on a silver tray at the first syllable of a whispered request (mine, if she can be found at all, usually shouts back that she'll get to it in a little while, seein' as how I've left her eight weeks of laundry to do in an hour, then ambles in with sloshing jelly-jar glasses and plops down to join in the gossip). Evangelist Louise Mohr, who's no slouch herself, says Jemison is one of the most delightful people she knows, adding that for her money, any woman who at the age of fifty-six can wear see-through lounging pajamas has *got* to have something on the ball.

I'd figured Marie Stokes Jemison to be, oh, about thirty-six.

But being a nice, proper, well-bred, soft-spoken Southern matron isn't enough for Jemison, nor would it be for the majority of Southern women. Historically, the nature of Southern industrialization, coupled with the traditional employment of black women as domestic and agricultural laborers, has carried an exceedingly high percentage of Southern women, black and white, into the work force. But the economic contributions of these women go far beyond mere wage labor. Southern women have always worked, though few admit it; even when their labor involves staying at home, taking in laundry, tending eight children and ten boarders, and doing a little pin-money sewing on the side, they maintain almost to a number that they "don't work." Because of inflation and the low wage scale of non-unionized industry in Dixie, many work because their husbands simply can't earn enough to make ends meet; very few labor for no other reason than a desire to pursue a career. Almost all carry woman's traditional double burden, simultaneously helping to bring home the bacon and providing the caretaking services that insure the continued survival of the family.

Those who don't take salaried jobs seem compelled to work like field-hands anyway. Southern women are master builders of an astounding network of voluntary organizations that are the very glue of the community. Although survival is their forte, they do far more than survive; a few are fierce and angry warriors who battle the status quo in highly creative ways. If most of these fail to gain national prominence, they provide nonetheless the grass-roots leadership necessary for implementing social change. Southern women are accustomed to pitting themselves against tough odds; if many cling still to the traditional role, there is, nevertheless, in every Southern community at least one feisty militant female willing to speak out and catch hell, having already caught more than her share of it. Whatever limitations come with the Southern pedestal, the women of Dixie have always used their strength and wit and freeing eccentricity to do, not what they were taught to do (which, mostly, was to dimple prettily, tuck in the children, heat up the grits, and keep the home fires burning), but what they have it in themselves to do.

This is the case with Marie Jemison.

Jemison was born into an aristocratic family and enjoyed a privileged, sheltered childhood. She was, she says with some embarrassment, a "typical Southern belle, interested in exactly what everybody else was interested in," except that she excelled academically and wanted a good education. She wanted to go to Vassar and was registered there when her parents decided it wasn't quite suitable.

"There was a family conference at the last minute. They must have heard something—maybe there were mixed dormitories, I don't know—but I was told they wanted me to go to a girls' school that was, ah, more *supervised.* So I went to the Finch Junior College in New York, and regretted it every day of my life."

She did, however, enchant the Yankee males, who clustered around and made much of her accent and winning ways.

"Why wouldn't they? I was a *belle.* I had a lot of dates, a lot of attention. I think they looked down on me, though, for being frivolous. That was the stereotype then. They teased me and it was fun, but I imagine now that they were really making fun of me."

There was no family pressure on Jemison to involve herself with substantive issues ("custom told me that my role was to please men"), and female involvement in politics was hardly a family tradition.

"I had an uncle who was a state senator and an uncle who ran for governor, and I was taken around on the stump, but the women in my family were social rather than political. The men were always talking politics, but the women didn't join in."

In retrospect, though, Jemison sees that the seeds for her adult political orientation were sown in girlhood by her mother.

"She didn't want me to be too independent—not to the point that I could choose to go to Vassar, where I might get pregnant or otherwise get myself talked about—but she wanted me to make my own judgments. I don't remember her ever telling me directly what I should or shouldn't do. It was always very fuzzy, and there was never anything overt, but I believe she may have been very liberal on race."

Jemison was driven to school by a black chauffeur. One day, when she was ten or eleven years old, the driver was stopped for speeding; he panicked and ran from police, who chased him. He was captured, arrested, and badly beaten. It was a "milestone" in Jemison's life, though she hadn't thought about it till recent years.

"This was in the late thirties, when lynching was big in the South. When the police found out who owned the car, of course, they were afraid he'd tell about the beating. So that night they went to his house to threaten him. He saw them coming and ran out the back door. My mother hid him in our basement till his trial came up. I remember going down there to take food to him."

There was no philosophical discussion of the incident. But when the chauffeur came to trial, Jemison was taken out of school so that she could accompany her mother to the court-room.

"My mother testified for him. I don't remember her testimony—it was too long ago—but I remember that it was important, and that two policemen were dismissed from the force because of it. Certainly she had a reason for taking me there."

Southern women have never been quite as loyal to the ideology of segregation as Southern men. They've put the welfare of a single individual above the collective welfare, and many of them have been betraying the tenets of white supremacy since they took their first wobbly steps in infancy, almost always without being able to articulate their reasons for doing so. It took Jemison years to link the chauffeur episode with the abhorrence she felt as an adult toward racial inequity. But she has now an inexhaustible reservoir of energy available for combating threats to racial parity.

"We've had Wallace in the state now for a decade, and, well, when he first stepped out from under his rock, he was my personal enemy. I'm probably the most knowledgeable Wallace-watcher in the world. When he ran this last time, or started to run, a friend and I were talking about how, *oh, God,* we had to go through all this again with him. How could we, you know, kill him off politically?

"We decided that people don't read anymore; they look at pictures. So we decided to do a photographic essay on Wallace. We found a photographer who's crazy and a genius besides. We used Wallace's own words, taken from his speeches, and juxtaposed them with photographs showing the real condition. We got it together in record time, working day and night for three months, traveling all over the state, and took it to New York."

Numerous publishers were interested, many highly enthusiastic; many New York editors still talk of the potential Jemison's project had.

"But by that time—I think it was around the time of the Pennsylvania primary—it was obvious Wallace was dead politically."

To the dismay of the publishing houses, Jemison set the project aside. Why fight to destroy a benign tumor? By that time she'd discovered a different malignancy.

"It all melded together for me when I testified for the Equal Rights Amendment in the legislature in Montgomery, as did many women, pro and con. It was my first realization of just how sexist the legislature is. The buffoonery that went on made me livid. I came away furious and frustrated beyond reason. I could not believe that people I knew, people I'd grown up with and lived around all my life, could be that way."

She went immediately to the library to prepare herself for a new fray.

"I'd never been interested at all in my history, but I wanted to see whether any similar arguments had been advanced against suffrage. It was the same all down the line.

But I also found in the library some scrapbooks that belonged to the four leading suffragettes around the turn of the century, and one of them—Bosie Hunley O'Brien—happened to be my grandmother's first cousin. I sat there in the library with tears running down my face: here was my own relative who'd put up with all this derision and demeaning attitudes and was still willing to go on and on all her life."

It turned her into an ardent feminist, a species rare in the provincial South. If the daughters of Dixie have been comet-ladies whose paths have blazed across varied skies, they've seldom ignited much fire in the political arena.

They do, however, make remarkable political wives, mothers, and daughters. Even the fiercest opponents to Lyndon Johnson had compliments for Lady Bird. Rosalynn Carter was said to be the mightiest weapon in Jimmy's campaign arsenal. Until her divorce, Betty Talmadge never acted in any way—politically or privately—without stopping to consider the political impact of her actions, a habit that must have challenged the self-discipline of such a freewheeling spirit. Joy Baker, herself a determined free spirit, has made it a point to do all she can to advance and reinforce Senator Baker's causes. Even the uninhibited Lillian Carter confines her bluntspoken candor within the bounds of provincially defined idiosyncrasy. If such women boast fierce drives and tough hides, they possess tender hearts as well, and they know that tradition would have them play the backstage role of human catalyst, being defined by the results of bringing others together in the well-tended nest.

It's a role played with absolute authenticity by Mrs. Allethea Smith, Rosalynn Carter's mother.

Left with four children when her husband, Edgar, a mechanic, died in 1940 of leukemia, she worked at the school cafeteria, sewed for Plains, Georgia, neighbors, and clerked at a small grocery before finding a job in the local post office, where she worked for nearly thirty years before retiring at the age of seventy. Even now she works part-time at a flower shop (less than a block from her home), and puts in a fair share of time at the Plains railroad depot, now a souvenir stand, facing the Instamatic assault of tourists. She's a woman whose day-to-day decisions about how to spend her time reflect a deep-held commitment to family and community.

"My children always kept me going. I had to keep going and push for them. Until my husband died, I'd never paid a bill. I didn't know how. I didn't know anything about business. But it doesn't take long to learn when you have to."

She's a shy woman, quiet and unobtrusive, with a down-to-earth conviction that the small-town values have currency yet. Like most daughters of Dixie, she takes pride in her staying power and in her ability to survive the hard times.

"I had a pretty tough time for a while when the children were young. I sewed for the public. And my children worked as soon as they got big enough to do anything. Some of the boys ran errands for the store or delivered groceries or clerked. Rosalynn helped out in a beauty parlor, ran errands and washed hair. That was just for their spending money.

"You know, my mother died twenty-two days after my husband, and my daddy came to live with us and help us out. And I managed to send all my children to college. Both of the boys have two degrees. The girls went to Georgia Southwestern. It's just a two-year college. Then one of my daughters got a job in the bank, and Rosalynn got married."

Allie Smith "can hardly believe" she ended up the mother-in-law of a president, and she found it, from the first, a mixed blessing.

"It's good and bad. I enjoy talking to the tourists. They still come in from the other states and all. But sometimes it gets so crowded in Plains you can't find a parking place. I go uptown and get *parking tickets!"*

I asked her what the most important things in life were. What she said was, keeping close contact with one's children.

"It's just one of the *most* important things. And raising them right and having faith. Just doing what's right and working."

She realizes that non-Southerners tend to view Dixie with some condescension. But she doesn't let it bother her much.

"I know one time they made fun of me, and it embarrassed me so. In Georgia, you know. They make fun of Georgia, too. I was going to Kentucky on a train. I don't know how it came up, but these people were talking about radios. And this man asked me, 'Do you have a battery radio?' And I said, 'No, electric.' And then something was said about lights, and he said, 'Do you have lamps?' And I said, 'No, I have electricity.' They all thought I came from 'way back in the sticks, sure enough."

But she was born and raised in the South.

"And I wouldn't want to live anywhere except right here."

We talked quite a while. The subject of feminism never came up. Allie Smith doesn't need feminist rights.

Apparently, few other women here think they do either. The twenty-four words of the Equal Rights Amendment add up to nothing more threatening than a simple statement that equality of rights shall not be denied on the basis of sex. And yet if the Amendment fails to pass in enough states to insure ratification, it will be because the Southern states, which still proclaim the romantic ideal of womanhood, resolutely refuse to support passage. Feminist leaders maintain that Southern conservatism is now the major obstacle to passage of ERA.

And it's not only those chauvinist good ol' boys opposed to the measure: however they argue for equal pay, Southern women are for the most part quick to deny their support of sexual parity.

Many are impressed by the viewpoint espoused in the roadshow tactics of Phyllis Schlafly, a conspicuously liberated Yankee housewife whose right-wing politics lead her to travel the country, gathering bands of housewives willing to don long skirts and STOP ERA buttons. Schlafly, who believes that women already enjoy superior rights, recently announced that her followers will boycott Girl Scout cookies in protest of the national Girl Scout endorsement of ERA. Schlafly and her cohorts have specialized in misleading rhetoric designed to stop the measure, and they've found fervent support among Southern women. Everywhere in Dixie there are women convinced that sexual parity by constitutional amendment will lead to homosexual marriage, loss of alimony, and coeducational toilets. The argument that we've all utilized the latter on airplanes carries no clout in the provincial South, where conservatives equate ERA with the unhappy image of teenaged women slogging through foreign rice paddies with M-16 rifles on their arms.

Such logic is a Southern trail that leads nowhere.

And if you're deluding yourself that the old knee-jerk Southern conservatism is gone with the wind, perhaps you'd better meet Mary Cain.

Cain is editor of the *Summit Sun,* a weekly newspaper in rural Mississippi and, says Gordon Cotton, a "ball of fire" at age seventy-three. She was the first woman to run for governor in the state and didn't do too badly, either. She's a rugged individualist. According to Cotton, Cain decided in 1951 that she wasn't going to pay any social security taxes, maintaining that they're unconstitutional and amount to government-forced insurance. She sold her newspaper to a relative, the story goes, and leased it back; she relieved her husband of all his financial obligations, got rid of all her property, did away with her bank account, and notified the government that she was refusing to pay for forced insurance she neither wanted nor needed. There was nothing for the government to confiscate except Mary Cain herself. Government officials locked the newspaper office while Cain was home in bed recuperating from the flu. When she heard that the office had been padlocked, says Cotton, she raced over in her housecoat, fetched a hacksaw, and opened her office, adding a prominent sign that warns NO TRESPASSING BY ANY FEDERAL EMPLOYEE.

A quarter of a century later, the sign remains in the window.

No one knows exactly how Cain and the government came to terms, and she's not telling. Rumor has it, though, that she writes the Social Security Administration annually, communicating her displeasure with their activities, insisting she has no social security number, and refusing to accept one.

She refused initially to enter the gubernatorial race in 1951, but thought better of it:

"And so I did, and got my feet wet, and I thoroughly enjoyed it. I scared them to death 'cause it was the first time a woman ever ran; they didn't know what to make of it. And I got wonderful crowds. I was the only candidate getting any crowds. I made about eight speeches a day, and everywhere I told people, 'Now this literature is expensive, so if you're not really interested, don't take it.' Well, they took it, and I just thought, 'Well, we're on *fire,* we're just going to keep going.' But it didn't work out that way."

She believes she had an effect, however, in that other state politicians acted on some of the issues she raised.

"For example, this business of consolidating schools, that was my idea. I said 'A sound educational program based largely on consolidation of the two thousand nine hundred thirty-two one-, two-, and three-teacher schools.' But I never dreamed they'd make it compulsory."

She works seven days a week.

"On Sunday morning, John and I are in the church office, and that afternoon we have to handle the church money, and it's quite a little chore. We're First Baptists, of course; that's part of the Southern Baptist Convention. And while we have a few liberals among us at the top, they're not authorized to speak for us. We have local autonomy, and that's important to me. Where would we be without organized religion?

"I *wish* I didn't have so many irons in the fire. In addition to the three papers, I have the Congress of Freedom. I'm treasurer of that and the awards chairman. We give these awards to people who we think have done a good job for constitutional government, trying to see that we get back to some basic common sense. I wish we could. It couldn't possibly get worse. It's sad, but it's gone so far. I told them when I ran for governor I felt there was some hope, that we could bounce back.

"But not anymore. I wouldn't *be* governor today.

"We're so imbedded in federal policy that no one seems to think of anything except federal money and how they can get it. Of course, I'm much opposed to that. I feel like every state should stand on its own feet. We here in Mississippi were getting so much more from the federal government than we were paying in it was ridiculous. Now New York has had problems; New York is big, but New York pays so much in taxes. They could *keep* what they're paying in, and they might be able to swing out of it.

"Reduce taxes. Refuse any federal grands and aids. You'd be surprised the number of people who tell me now they just wish they'd listened."

Her campaign literature, now slightly yellow with age, calls for a "sound public health program but within the bounds of state and county aid only," with "no federal funds" accepted; for "opposition to all New Deal socialism, which includes subsidies for farmers, unemployment compensation, federal aid to education, socialized medicine and compulsory health insurance, arbitrary wage and hour regulations, public housing," and others; for "purging of state mental institutions of all except those who are genuinely ill"; for purging "present welfare department rolls," repudiating "further federal aid," and ascertaining that "only absolutely destitute people are aided"; and for "jury service for women who wish to serve." In the matter of the latter, Cain added a parenthetical notation: "all women are not yet ready for this."

To say that she opposes the Equal Rights Amendment is to suggest that Scarlett O'Hara was a bit of a belle.

"It will simply open the door to lawsuit after lawsuit, and the courts are already so heavily burdened that they cannot take care of it. Women can make their own way. I didn't need any ERA to launch out into my campaign. It's a dangerous, *dangerous* thing! We'll be in constant wrangles, and it destroys states' rights *forever.* We've already had enough states' rights taken away."

I allowed as how I'd like to talk a bit about states' rights, and Miz Cain spoke carefully, enunciating clearly, as if I were a retarded child.

"The states *created* the United States."

So there.

"Listen, I *revel* in being a woman. Why, I wouldn't be a man for anything on earth! Oh, pshaw. I used to tell people when they'd present me with a corsage at a club, I'd say, 'Now wouldn't a man look silly with one of these on?'

"The one thing that we did not have in Mississippi was jury service for women. We had every other right and privilege that the men had. And we got *that.* So in my mind, we're finished with that issue. But the Business and Professional Women's clubs are all on record in favor of ERA. So I resigned from the national and state federations in protest. *I don't want any part of this ERA deal!* I love sound Christian women wherever they are, but I despise these things that profess to speak for womankind. *They don't speak for me!* Some of them are just horrible, just utterly horrible! To *me.*

"Of course, to me the whole world has gone crazy on the subject of sex. The women's magazines are loaded with it. I've gotten to the place where I hate to open one of them. We have a television in the bedroom, but Johnny Carson is all we ever get to see because he comes on about the time we get home. And he is so filthy-mouthed."

Cain is also editor of the *Woman Constitutionalist,* a monthly newspaper published by the Women for Constitutional Government. In the February, 1977, issue, one Father Robert E. Burns, C.S.P., dismisses ERA and Howard K. Smith as a "snow job," while Cain takes on James Whitmore in her own column:

"I have heard some filthy language in my time but nothing to equal the obscenities in 'Give 'em Hell, Harry' via TV. The whole thing was a disgrace to America and to TV. How they got by with it passes my comprehension. We had to turn it off, it was so vile."

I mentioned the Southern sense of belonging, of roots, and it reminded Cain of the book.

"I have a wonderful review here. This man says, 'Roots,' or 'Hate,' as I prefer to call it, 'has been manufactured by Manhattan's moneymongers for the American market.' The thing that disturbs me most is that people will say we are racists if we are opposed to all this mess, but they can be anything they *please,* and it's not racist.

"I don't think there's much racism in the South. You see things you never dreamed you'd ever see. *I'm* frankly racist because, ah, I feel that every person is what God made him, and he ought to be proud of it. I don't like people that try to break down color lines. I just don't."

What about black pride?

"But this is what disturbs me. Here we have given them this civilization, and it *is* civilization, and today what do we find? Bushy hair just like they're out of a jungle! It just *does* something to me!"

Perhaps if we'd put real money into separate but *truly* equal schools?

"But we were doing our best. All the schools in Mississippi, the money was all going to Negro schools to benefit them. Our white schools were suffering."

Such women, I think, aren't completely self-created racists. Most grew up in homes that subscribed to the social mores of the time. They were taught and they believed that separation of the races was best for both worlds. They never learned the last names of their mothers' maids. And while many of us came to understand a measure of the Southern guilt, if only for the romanticism that comes with an anguished liberal consciousness, others did not. It may be that it's better not to know. Being called racist when one knows in the marrow and in the dirty backroads of the mind that one *is* racist is paralytically painful; being called racist when one's mind is shut like a clam against the reality inflicts no wound at all. That's why, I think, so many Southern racists are so likeable and charming; lacking the need to defend and rationalize, they're free to develop other, more agreeable traits.

I do not, of course, refer to conservatism, though it remains a favored Southern state of mind—or, in its more outrageous manifestations, hallucination.

Mrs. Dizzy Dean lives in tiny Wiggins, Mississippi, on the acreage she roamed in childhood. Twenty acres surround her, giving her the space she needs for the time she needs, like others, to be alone.

"It may be selfish, but everyone needs to be alone at certain times. Still, every one of us here knows each other. If somebody needs help, we're here. Southern people aren't ashamed of emotion. Country kissing and all that. They love to show their love. It's part of their makeup.

"And we *have loved.* We did not hate. Just like I had a colored girl that cleaned for me for twenty-three years. She moved to Dallas and to Phoenix with me, and when I came back here she came here with me and at first she was *scared,* she had visions of hanging from limbs and all. But she called me today, and I'm going to help her replace her old car. We love one another. That's love.

"She said she could be an individual here. She says that the people in the South are the only people that know how to treat blacks. Now we have some of the finest doctors in the United States right here in Forest General Hospital, and nobody thinks of them as being black. They're people. We don't think of them as being black. They're our friends and neighbors. We grew up with them, we know them, and they know us. And in time of need, somebody is going to take care of them. I believe in equal rights. All people are your neighbors. But there's been a wall thrown up. There's a wall between us now, between the blacks and the whites, and it's sad.

"There are so many restrictions now about what you can do and what you can't do. We have too much government, not only in the rural areas but throughout the entire nation. There's too much policing. We're not a free people anymore. Washington was originally set up as a clearing house of arguments between states. They had no governing power there. The Constitution doesn't need any governing power. But there've been so many amendments to the Constitution that it's destroyed the real meaning, and now we have centralized government, which is bad business.

"We're going to have to do it that way, because force is going to have us do it their way. One thing—it's a small thing, but it's something I just went into arms about—we are not allowed to use our rebel flag at the University of Mississippi. And the rebel flag has always stood for Ole Miss. That was their emblem. Our cheerleaders would run across the field and the band would come out with a great big flag that would almost cover the field, the big rebel flag.

"I live my life by the Bible. It's so easy to love. If you give love you're going to get love. And love is the all-powerful force because God so loved the world that he gave his only begotten son. He loved the world, He didn't hate the world. And He created the world. If people would just stop and think, a little love goes a long way.

"You know, my mother was a nurse, and I have seen her get up at night in pouring-down rain and go deliver a Negro baby. Because they didn't have enough money to have a private doctor, and they'd go after the country doctor, and he'd say he'd come in the morning. They'd come to my mother, and she'd get her starched white apron on. And my father would say, 'Rachel, *please.*' And she'd say, 'Sam, I've got seven children and I know how she's suffering. Her flesh is just like mine, and it will tear, and if I can give her relief, I'm going.' And I'd see her go out at twelve or one or two o'clock in the morning in driving rain and never turn anybody down."

Mrs. Dean is energetic, too. She's had two cancer operations, she says, open-heart surgery, and two arterial bypasses. Yet she tends the Dizzy Dean Museum and serves as state chairman for the Easter Seal drive. She's deeply involved, too, in politics, but tends toward the pessimistic end of the spectrum.

"You see, everything now is controlled at the federal level. First you have to accept their guidelines. You really have no choice. Our nation is going downhill. I don't like to sound like a pessimistic type, but I can see the lack of pride going day to day. It used to be year to year. The great white father will provide.

"And where are the federal dollars coming from? One-half of the population, the working population in the U.S. They're carrying the freight and the other half are sitting on their behinds and doing nothing. I could not get *anybody* to mow this yard last year, and I pay a hundred dollars every time it's mowed, and I furnish the riding mower and the gasoline. They'd say, 'Miss Jean, I can't do that, I'll be cut off my welfare, I'll be cut off my food stamps.' If I paid them by cash, and I wouldn't do that, I still couldn't get them on this yard. I have to give them a check because I want a record for my own files. I could not get it mowed.

"Here in the U.S., we've lost our pride as individuals, lost our pride in individual accomplishment.

"You come closer to God, to nature itself in the South. We're not so distracted. Southern people don't aspire to a great deal of the material. It's easy-come, easy-go. It's a marvelous way of life. But we're coming to the end of our time.

"It's just running downhill. The falling away of the churches. We're not immoral, we're becoming unmoral. You know, when I was growing up, you pulled your skirts away from a girl that lived with a man without marriage. Now it's an everyday thing. The level of standard education, not only in the South but also in the Northern states, is being lowered too. You can't fail students now. But the teacher doesn't have anything to do with it; it's the guidelines that are laid out. We're wasting minds because the students that want to learn are being wasted. Those that don't want to learn are being wasted also, because all students are not college material. We need a lot of Indians as well as a lot of chiefs. I'd say that at least fifty percent of the students in college today are not college material.

"And all the ERA is doing is emasculating the men, and we're losing our top spot. I like to be a woman. I like to have a man open the door for me. I like to have a man pull out the chair for me when I sit down, to light my cigarette, to hold my coat for me when I put it on.

"You know God tells us, and it plainly states in the Bible, that man is the head of the house. If we'd just stop and think, man was not created for the woman. Woman was created for the man. Adam came first and God took his rib and made Eve."

In more than one way, this culture is trapped like a fly in honey in the mellowed past with its lush woods, descendants of slaves, courtly and protective men, belle-like ladies still breathing the rarified air of the "old" South. There remains in Dixie an astonishing emphasis on beauty, an awesome infatuation with beauty contests and rhinestone-studded crowns. Of the past twenty-six winners of the Miss America pageant, nine were Southern, two in a row from muddy Mississippi. (I personally did not know such heady fame, but I *was* Miss Watermelon Thump for 1961, a glory for which my Southern daddy damn near disinherited me.) It is possible to capture the Little Miss Dixie crown at the tender age of five; no one over five, in fact, is eligible to don those hoop skirts, ruffles, and grown-up airs and trot lustily (if lispingly) across the stage before the judges while mothers in bouffant wigs coach from the wings. And when a Southern state legislature is debating the issue of sexual parity, hordes of prim ladies clad in pink gingham invade the capitol, bearing loaves of homemade bread with which to ply their elected representatives. God forbid they vote to make women like men!

The provincial insistence of Southern women on holding their space on the pedestal but re-plastering the column as well has less to do with feminist sellout, I think, than Yankee feminist arrogance. The movement made a few tactical errors in the beginning, posing a problem of image, and seems disinclined to correct its strategy. Fair or not, when it attacked marriage and family and other institutions traditionally oppressive to women, Southern women (and their sisters elsewhere) took the attack personally: if you've devoted a lifetime to housework that has no value, is your life negated in full? If the sleek new role models are all free-wheeling career women, urban and ambitious, is there no honor left in tending the home fires? To a woman who's just spent all day wiping noses, washing dishes, changing diapers, scrubbing toilets, and taking her shift at the Mom-&-Pop store, *what do you do?* is a question certain to incite a troubled mix of shame and fury.

"Well, first I scrub toilets and then I get to the breakfast dishes. I wipe noses a lot, but my real specialty is removing fecal material from downy-soft cotton diapers. You know how important it is, of course, to use a water softener. . . ."

When a woman busts ass in the traditional role, she gets a little riled when she's told she could be out there starting a bank or driving a truck. The new emphasis on feminine fulfillment outside the home seems to suggest that women who opt for the traditional role are intellectually incapable of decisions more complex or sophisticated than choosing Cheer over Brand X. And because Southern women have been killing their own snakes for more than a century, such implications amount to feminist arrogance.

And that's not all, either.

They don't see Yankee females faring much better, particularly in the political realm. They've counted only twenty woman senators from across the nation since 1920, and they have the sense to know these women obtained their party's nomination through derivative glory: for the most part, they were widows of successful officeholders, swept to political success on a tide of nostalgia and gratitude to their late husbands. Back home, they let out a collective whoop and heehaw when Lurleen Wallace is cited as a female governor: they know full well Lurleen was a puppet stand-in for George, who was ineligible to stand for office. Say *politics* to most Southern women, and you see their lips purse automatically as if confronted with a sea of postal glue; they've been doin' the lickin' and stampin' all along while the men did the more prestigious work of plotting strategy.

You don't need to be a registered voter to wield a hoe.

You don't need a political office to charm and enchant, Southern-style. Southern women know their men and the feelings they, as good ol' down-to-earth free-thinkers, have about the womenfolk: of course they got the right to be independent, but they need protection too, don't-you-know. This may be why some Southern women devote far more time to simulating convulsive mirth ("oh, Billy Don, I declare, you're just the wittiest old thing") than to simulating ruthless ambition. The South awards so many points for devastating feminine helplessness that it's no wonder the sight of a fire-breathing Yankee feminist, advocating new-style self-reliance, sends them rushing into bookstores for manuals that instruct them in the finer technicalities of dimpling, cooing, and generally making everyone around them feel relaxed and important (e.g., what they've been taught to do from girlhood), and storming their state legislatures to implore their representatives not to make them (please, God) *equal.*

They tired long ago of Yankee interference. And they've had independence all along.

Some fiery few use it today just like those shrill Yankee feminists do; most are appalled at the notion of feminine militancy. There aren't many Talmadges around to carry the banner 'neath a decorous demeanor and in terms acceptable to conditioned Southern thinking (ladylike and eccentric). The great majority openly denigrate feminist goals while making their own freeing adjustments at home in small subtle ways, without confronting the system head-on. More than a few slip through that legendary hidden loophole that is down-home eccentricity to lead Technicolor lives.

Creativity, subversion, and such survival skills as tough hides and tender hearts all are part of the Southern woman's legacy.

Drugs may be a crutch for people who can't handle reality, but nobody ever OD'd on derivative glory when she had a little something of her own going for her at the same time.

As always, there are a saving few who make a reassuring bridge to link the way we will be with the way we once were. And they're the truest belles of the South, these honky-tonk heroines who cherish the old ways and implement the new.

Southern Comfort:
  Honky-Tonk Heroines & Rebel Queens

I wouldn't know how to just do nothin'.
I'd have to pick up somethin'
to do or I'd be the dumbest
old woman till the sun don't shine.
—GUSTA STREET

When Robert Graves wrote that man *does*, while woman *is*, he hadn't gotten 'round to visiting Dixie. Leave it to the menfolk to sit around swapping tales of their latest coon hunts, shouting their arguments over hog-waller politics and enjoying their amiable discussions of lost crops, hard times, good whiskey, slow horses, and fast women. Leave it to others, too, to debate the finer ethical implications of solutions designed to alleviate such hard-core problems as unemployment, race discrimination, sexism, poverty, pollution, urban decay, and socialized medicine.

When it's time to go to the well, the provincial daughters of Dixie don't stop to hold a committee meeting.

They never put much stock in theoretical solutions. They never had much use for philosophical musings. They're far less romantic, for all their canopied beds and moonlit verandas, than Southern men. This may have to do with their long familiarity with age-old burdens like washing diapers, administering enemas, and laying out the dead.

Such chores don't inspire debate: they just need doing.

If Southern women fear change, and question occasionally

the emptiness of contemporary life, they respond as they always have: by clinging to the known, by continuing to value time-honored traditions followed by their Southern grandmothers. It's not a matter of taking a principled stand against cultural disintegration; Southern women simply do what they have it in them to do, addressing the needs that confront them. Often, the traditional methods are known now only by strong-willed country women steeped in the pioneer ways.

A few ply the old provincial crafts.

At age eighty-one, Gusta Street has cured the aches and ills of three generations with wild roots, homegrown herbs, home remedies, and blunt talk. Ginseng, asphidity, wild onion, squaw weed, and snake root grow around the faded frame house she helped build on Lookout Mountain, near Collinsville, Alabama; these are but a few of the substances she has used for years to offer a measure of Southern comfort and good health to her family and neighbors.

This is the first year she has not tended the garden on the edge of her seventy-seven acres. She's frail now herself, and finds no herbal medicines that will alleviate the symptoms of advancing age. During her most recent hospitalization, she pitted her garden-variety remedies against the miracles of modern medicine, and emerged a clear winner.

"This nurse had a grandbaby that like to choked to death the night before. I told her it could have been the croup. She said all they did was rock the baby. And I said, 'Get you a teaspoon full of honey, and put some lemon and a little bit of table salt in it and give it to her, and in a little bit, give her another.' I had one kid that had diphtheria and one that had Memphis croup, and I told this nurse I just mopped the throat out good with peroxide. And she said was that all right. And I told her I didn't have no doctor book, but I did it, and it cured them. And then I remembered you put some powdered alum in with the honey and salt. That nurse's grandbaby, her throat had gathered up that croup, you know, and she vomited it up, and that cured her.

"Ginseng is good for the liver. I reckon. I had an aunt that would take ginseng and put it in whiskey."

They say in Collinsville that Gusta Street is stronger than steel. She's a true-grits mountain lady for sure.

"When I was up there in the hospital there was one of them men nurses, and I asked him, 'Now how are you going to get rid of me?' And he said he couldn't imagine. And I said I'd tell him. I said, 'You're going to have to get the biggest, richest pine knot ever and hit me in the head with it!' And he said he believed it.

"But I like it better here on Lookout Mountain. I sure do. I've got to have somethin' I can look at, and when I've got to have somethin' done, I pay someone if I've got somethin' to pay 'em with. It ain't like it used to be here. Sometimes it seems too quiet. But I have to have it quiet now. The quieter things are, the better off you be.

"My husband, he's a help. Last time I came home from the hospital he said I need somebody here to stay with me. I said I ain't going to do it. I said he can wait on me, or down the road he goes! If he don't want to do it, he can pack his clothes and down the road he gets and don't come back, much as I've waited on him around here. And he said he can't do what women can do, and I said we'll see about that. Well, he can cook better than I can now.

"I raised up seven kids and a bunch of grandkids. I doctored 'em pretty well.

"When there's somethin' that needs doin', I do it."

It's a philosophy that has served her well. Eta Nichols hasn't done too badly by it, either.

Granny Nichols is a midwife, and has been for forty-eight years.

"My dad was a doctor and my granddad was a doctor, and I just took it up and went at it. I'm not gonna stop, I guess, till my toes are sticking up. When I started delivering babies it wasn't for money, just to help out. I never thought about doing it for money till I went over to a neighbor's house. They sent for the doctor but he was busy with somebody else and he didn't come, so they come after me. When I went over, the baby was already borned. The second time I was asked the baby got there before me that time too, so I cut the cord and took care of the mother. Then the next time was over at this woman's place, up above us. Well, my husband was working on the road up on the mountain, and I couldn't leave the children by themselves. So I said I'd come later. I got supper ready and took the baby with me and went on up there, and I checked the mother. I might not have knowed too much about it, but I checked her anyway, and I delivered her baby and her next one, too. Then when we went out to bury the afterbirth, her mother said to me, 'Now you'll be going places from this one on!'

"Well, for the first fifteen or twenty years I didn't deliver too many babies. There were so many more midwives and doctors went out then, so I didn't get near the practice I got now. I've not counted up since nineteen seventy. By nineteen seventy, I had one thousand seventy-eight I think, and I haven't counted up since then. Don't have time to get them together, but I will some of these times.

"I used to go to their houses. I done that for I guess about twenty, twenty-five years. Then my mother fell and broke her hip, and I couldn't leave her at home by herself. But then my husband's mother broke her hip too and there was nobody wanted to take her but me, so I had to take her too. So I had her and Mama both and I brought them up here. So I had to let the women come in here and have their babies. I got a room where I let them have their babies in. I got two beds back in that room, and I've delivered two in there at once and had one in this room too."

At eighty, Granny Nichols lives with her husband, James,

eighty-one, on some twenty-odd acres off a gravel road somewhere past Del Rio, Tennessee, in the southern Appalachians. There is no address, and the place is impossible to find unless you luck into Vi Smith and her husband, Hugh, who works as the regular rural mail carrier; the Smiths know everybody on the mountain, and, if you can get past their dog, they'll take you where you want to go. Directions are meaningless in this forested clime. You can spot the Nicholses' house by the battered plank bridge that spans the stream that fronts their acreage. Beans, beets, tomatoes, carrots, corn, peas, squash, cucumbers, watermelon, turnips, okra, mustard, kale, sweet chard, collard, and rhubarb grow in wild profusion; the porch is littered, but the interior is spotlessly cleaned. Like they say, you could eat off the floors of the birthing rooms.

"Generally the women stay overnight and the next day, and some stay three days. Whatever they want. If I can't keep them no longer, I don't. Some of the husbands come along, and some of them don't. If they have work to do at home, or children they have to look after, they go back. Sometimes their mamas come along. Some brings their mamas, and some don't."

Whatever the duration of labor and birth, Granny Nichols charges fifteen dollars.

"If they got it, they pay me. I know how it is to need things where you couldn't get them, and there's so many of them that just don't have the money, and I never have asked nobody if they had the money when they speaked to me about having the baby. I never mentioned it. Sometimes I get it, and sometimes I don't get nothing. I delivered a whole bunch of kids and never got a penny for it. But I never said a word. I never turn them down or anything. I just go ahead and deliver them. I wouldn't turn nobody down, not even no black person.

"Some of them trade. I generally got enough eggs of my

own, but there's been people who let me have honey and stuff like that. Our substitute mail carrier, he let me have two gallon of honey for pulling their baby. Closest hospital is at Newport, but they charge so much. I don't hardly know what makes them charge so much."

She knew her husband in childhood, and has been married sixty-two years.

"We always lived around here, except when we were over at Virginia at the coal mines when our first baby was little. James didn't work in the mines. He worked at the tipple. I don't hardly know what all he done, but he didn't have to go underground. So many of them get caught down in there, and some gets killed. Terrible thing to think about getting trapped down there.

"We moved back over here in this house—let's see, Bill was nine and we moved in January, he's forty-eight—so it's thirty-eight years.

"I never had too much trouble with the birthing. I learned from my dad, and then he told me a whole lot, but I never could remember half of what he told me. He give me one of his books and I read some in it. But what you learn from experience, you don't forget it. It'll come back to you.

"Daddy's been dead for a long, long time.

"I delivered lots of breech-births and I always had good luck with them. Some come feet first and some, they're breech, you know, and then other ways. I know it wouldn't do me no good for people to just tell me things. I'd forget it. Best way is you have to go at it and learn yourself. I delivered some black babies, babies and mothers just fine. I never have lost a mother. Hope I never do."

Well, there was one.

"She got shot about a year afterward. I think she had too many boyfriends. I think there were three besides the one that shot her.

"No abortions, though. Somebody called me, well, I guess

it's been a year or so, and wanted to know if I'd do an abortion, and I said no, and she hung up. She didn't give me time to tell her what I had to say. I was going to tell her I weren't no murderer!

"Some girls now, they get pregnant in high school. Their parents send them away for a while, and they don't come back with no baby. I think if they get that way they should have to take care of them and not destroy them."

She does a good deal of repeat business.

"This one woman has eleven, and I delivered every one of hers. One has seven, and I did all of hers. And there've been different ones had just as many with me. A lot of them would rather have their babies in a home than in a hospital. They say they had their first baby in the hospital and they wish they'd knowed about me, and they always come back."

She handles crises of her own with equal serenity. She underwent major surgery eleven years ago for breast cancer.

"I felt uneasy going right then. My mother was sick. But this doctor, he said he wanted me to go that week. I said, well, if I had to go then I wanted the best doctor that can be got. I knowed we'd have to borrow some money, we didn't have quite enough to foot the bill. So we did, and fixed the papers, and I went to the hospital and he operated on me. He got it out. My blood was all right, and I didn't have to take no treatments, never had a thing. Went back there every three months for a check-up, and then I went every six months, and now I just go once a year.

"It didn't slow me down much. I just stayed there a week, and the nurse told me, she said to use that arm every bit I can, so I just did them exercises."

Thirteen days after a radical mastectomy, say her neighbors, Granny Nichols was out hanging wash on the line.

"Sometimes somebody says I need to retire. If I live till the nineteenth of this month, I'll be eighty-one years old. I say I'm not gonna retire till I need to.

"I don't know much about other women because I stayed put here. I'm happy to stay here all my life. I don't guess I'd be satisfied anywhere else."

There's just one thing in her life she'd change:

"If I had my life to live over, I'd live it just the same, except I guess I'd start delivering babies a whole lot sooner."

Other Southern women, lacking the old provincial skills and specialized crafts, invent crafts of their own.

In Belzoni, Mississippi, just north of Yazoo City, Mrs. Ethel Mohamed works over tapestries she calls "memory pictures." Her work is documentary in nature, recounting the saga of her own family and community. Doris Bowman, curator of the Smithsonian's Division of Textiles, calls Mrs. Mohamed "a real artist with stitches," and adds that Mohamed has an "extraordinary sense of color, a deeply creative use of stitchery, and a rich use of humor in her work." She's internationally known now for her tapestries; her charm is in the fact that she cannot understand why. Busloads of tourists file into Belzoni to see her work, and she's amazed.

But delighted.

"I feel like Cinderella. Because my work seems so little and so common till I think maybe these people just can't see good. I think maybe they just want to be nice. After the first year, though, I've never been ashamed of it."

Born in Fame (near Eupora), Mississippi, which she describes as "about the size of a bird's nest," Ethel Mohamed learned to stitch embroidered pictures created by her mother, Nina Ramsey Wright.

"I didn't really know what I was doing. But when little girls get too noisy, they have to sit down and do a little handwork."

She was courted "old-style" by Hassan Mohamed, a Lebanese dry-goods merchant, in 1923, and married him a year later. Their marriage of forty-one years produced eight children and a raft of memories. When Hassan died in 1965, "Mama" Mohamed floundered badly, she says, "like a ship without a rudder." She knew only that she wanted to keep the family dry-goods store in Belzoni.

"It would keep me busy during the day, and I wanted to prove to myself I could do it. I didn't have to prove it to anyone else. It was a great thrill. You know, to manage the store and keep it going and do well with it. I bought the building next door and paid for that. I did a lot of things. I was thrilled and proud of myself. At night when you go home you think of little small successes. Success makes you *feel* successful, you know."

But it didn't take care of the nights.

"I was like a big old ship floating around without any reason or any purpose. But one thing I had was a lot of beautiful memories. I wished I could live my life over, but of course I couldn't do that. I thought if I could write, I'd write a book. I didn't think I could write, so I thought I'd try to paint some, and I started off and had fun doing that. But my grandchildren—I have nineteen grandchildren—they'd come in and say, 'Oh, your little people look funny,' and they'd get in my paints and leave the lids off. So I had a lot of trouble with my painting. So I said, well, I believe I'll stitch a while, and I got my needle out. And it was *just the thing!* The children didn't bother my needle."

She didn't cotton to patterns or kits.

"I'd see something simple and beautiful, and I wanted to try it out to see how it'd look in materials and threads. I made one and then another, adding a few things of my own as I went along.

"When I first started doing this embroidery, I was kind of ashamed of it. So I didn't show it to anyone except the children. I'd never seen anything like this before. I was afraid folks would think I was just way out or goofy or something. Well, we had an open house one New Year's.

And one of my daughters-in-law just loved my work and she got out something I was working on at the time and showed it to a few artists who were at the house. I held my breath. I didn't know hardly how they were going to take this. I really didn't know if I was all right myself, you know.

"But they didn't laugh or anything. And I thought, well, that's not the best thing I've done, so I brought out my other stuff and gave them just the whole stack to look at. One of them looked at another and said, 'You know, she's found her thing.' So they took some of it and put it up on display."

Her first "memory picture" recaptured the excitement of her wedding day. Her second work recreated the family setting when Carol, her eighth child, was born. Since these initial efforts, Mrs. Mohamed has executed more than a hundred tapestries. Her work was discovered by a team of art scouts from the Smithsonian Institution and found enthusiastic acceptance by the thousands of visitors to the 1974 Festival of American Folklore in Washington, D.C. A year later, she was commissioned to create a tapestry to represent the Bicentennial Festival. She blocked out the design on a six-foot section of butcher paper and stitched steadily for six months. She was honored to do so, but there was a catch: the Smithsonian insisted on a national theme rather than a regional one.

She got around that by stitching in a small catfish, representing Belzoni and the Yazoo River.

Her work has been exhibited also at the Mississippi Arts Festival, the State Historical Museum in the Old Capitol Restoration, the Renwick Gallery in Washington, and in the new Mississippi governor's mansion. A problem arose when she was asked to sell four "memory pictures" to the Smithsonian.

"I realized it was an honor, a great honor. But I don't sell my pictures. I said, well, could I loan them? I think the young man was angry with me in a way. He said they'd have to go through two committees. I said, oh, well, mine would never pass the first one. He had his camera and he took some photographs, and I just knew I'd never hear from him again, though I was honored to death that he'd look at my work. So in about two weeks this man from the Smithsonian called me and said can you come up here to our festival and bring every one of them? I said, oh, I think I can. He said I'd get some papers in the mail in a few days, and I said fine. And he asked me if I was afraid of people. He asked me a lot of questions, trying to find out about me. And I told the children about it, and they teased me, but of course they believed me, finally."

Her needlework is elaborately detailed, recreating scenes from her marriage and from the Southern past. Some are interpretations of traditional activities like sacred harp singing, housewarmings, barn-raisings, and baptisms. Most, though, tell her personal history. One, "My Pot of Gold," depicts Ethel Mohamed and her husband, Hassan, riding the bluebird of happiness in search of the pot of gold at the end of the rainbow.

"When we found it, it was full of children, not gold!"

Another, called "Buddy Getting the Figs Picked," recreates a day in the life of her youngest son.

"He was the baby, and he played a lot. He had nothing to do but just play all day long. It was during the Depression days, and I said I'd pay him fifty cents to pick every fig on the tree. I wanted him to know he'd have to work for a living, and that hard work wouldn't hurt him. It was a hot day, but this would be Buddy's job, and he said he'd do it. He was a good little old boy. So in the afternoon I still had Buddy on my mind, so I went on home to check on him. And I expected to find him just wet with sweat—it was the hottest day in the world—but when I got there he was laying on the ground and he had a little colored boy in the tree picking the figs. I said, 'Buddy, I told *you* to pick those figs!'

And he said, 'Now, wait, he's going to pick every fig, and I'm going to give him a quarter, and we're both going to the show after.' "

Buddy's first sub-contracting project is immortalized in stitchery.

Ethel Mohamed, known in art circles as a primitive genius to rival Grandma Moses, keeps her needles of various sizes in a roll of paper towels. She traces her patterns on anything handy: a grocery bag, the back of a letter, a shopping list. She pays no attention whatsoever to stitch type, and she chooses colors by instinct, at random, because "this'll do" or "that seems about right to me." *Never* will she pull out a stitch once she's put it in:

"Once in a while one of my little people will be ugly in the face, but I just tell him, 'I'm not going to pull you out: you were born that way, and that's the way you're going to stay!' "

She couldn't have anticipated the artistic furor that greeted her work.

"It was just a thing I wanted to do. I didn't do it for any reason except just the pleasure of doing it. To get the little memories down so that I could look at them, relive them, you know. I never dreamed that anyone would ever see them. If I had, I think I would've made them so much nicer."

She continues to run the dry-goods store in Belzoni with the help of Virginia, a gentle black lady who takes a proprietory interest in Ethel Mohamed.

"Virginia's been helping me for years and years. She's just a joy. I mean, she's really fine. She can't read and she can't write. She never tries to sell a dress because she can't tell the size. But she's got plenty of sense. On days when I'm busy cashing checks, she'll stand right here and see if I'm putting the check in the drawer or see if I'm giving the right change. I guess she's been here twenty years. Sometimes I tell her to take a day off, but she wouldn't do it for the world. I think she has two or three sisters but they live away from here. She doesn't have any people here. She told one lady she can't quit because I can't get along without her. Well, that's right. I can't."

At age seventy, Ethel Mohamed can't decide just where she stands on this business of ERA.

"I want to see women get equal pay. But I don't hardly know where all this should begin and where it should stop. Now if a woman's qualified to be president of the bank, she should be president of the bank.

"A lot of women have more sense than men, you know.

"But all this time on my own, I never liked going to the bank or dealing where there were men. I don't know how I felt about that: I just didn't like to go. I didn't like to go pay my taxes, and I didn't like to go to the bank. I send Virginia. I never go out. I don't understand this about myself. I don't enjoy going out and competing with men. I know I'm doing as well as they're doing. But to go out and talk and maybe go to a meeting, well, that's their territory. I belong to the Chamber of Commerce, but I don't take any part in their meetings. I can't explain how I feel about it.

"But I know this tendency Southern women have, to give men credit when they've actually done the work, stretches way back. If you do something great, you want your husband to have the honor. You want to help build up the family name. I think a wife should add to her husband as much as she can. Now, Northern women aren't like us. They're beautiful. They're sweet and kind and gracious, but there's a certain charm they don't have. You can't relax up there. Southern women are, well, they're *Southern*. Real free.

"Oh, yes, we're *real* free. I know I can do anything I want to do. But I don't hardly know how to explain it."

She knows how to enjoy it, though, and (like most Southern women) how to spread that joy around, how to make other people feel relaxed and comfortable and quite important indeed. It is just this sort of specialized Southern knowledge that makes Dixie as pleasant as it is.

Ethel Mohamed lives alone in a great Victorian house encircled with hydrangeas, lush trees and shrubs that push against the house as if to support it. Upstairs, there's an attic specifically designed for the pleasure of grandchildren: toys and cribs, nooks and crannies, old photographs, and other childish treasures beg for exploration. Downstairs, Mohamed's bedroom is all white and ruffled, and memory pictures hang on every wall. High-ceilinged rooms are filled with Victorian furniture plusher and more comfortable than was common for that strait-laced era. Toward the front of the house is a room once occupied by Sunshine, one of her daughters; there's a fireplace and a soaring canopied bed, and a small bathroom off to the side with a clawfoot tub.

Do you know the joy of being pampered by a woman like this? Of being tucked into that tall goosedown mattress and served muffins and eggs, of listening, warm and drowsy, as she rocks and talks at the foot of the bed?

More than anything else, visiting with Ethel Mohamed is like going home.

If Ethel Mohamed is guardian of a unique family tradition acclaimed for its impact on Southern folk-craft, Katherine Grafton Miller is guardian of a town—and of a way of life symbolized by antebellum beauty and grace. Miller was awarded the Silver Trophy in 1932 from the City of Natchez for civic progressiveness; the Amy Angell Collier Montague Medal from the Garden Club of America for Civic Achievement; the "Missy" Award, given by the University of Mississippi and the First Federal of Jackson Foundation for "vision, determination, and ceaseless endeavor"; the National Council of State Garden Clubs Presidential Citation for "meritorious service"; and the Order of the First Families of Mississippi Award of Merit for Miller's "services in the preservation of Mississippi history." The mayor of Natchez proclaimed an annual Katherine Grafton Miller Day in 1970, and, out on the levee overlooking the Mississippi River, a bandstand has been erected in her honor for "contributions throughout the years toward the cultural well-being of the city of Natchez."

You thought I'd never get around to the garden-clubbers, didn't you?

But she's more than that: Natchez *National Democrat* editor James W. Lambert—drawling, courtly, and exceedingly Southern—says frankly that Katherine Miller *saved* Natchez. And I think he just may be right.

It's a city with a rich and romantic history. The bluffs of Natchez, standing two hundred feet above the rampaging whims of the Mississippi, have long been a magnet to men and women who saw promise in the Delta soil. Natchez Indians worshipped here. LaSalle insisted that whoever claimed this site could control the river. Unfortunately for the Natchez, France, Britain and Spain spent the next century or so proving him right.

When the Revolution ended, Americans swarmed into the region, and by 1798, the elegant Spanish dons of Natchez abandoned the bluffs forever. The Natchez Trace was opened in 1801 by treaty with surviving Indian tribes, paving the way for wagon travel and mail service. Ten years later the first steamboat docked at the wharves "Under the Hill," ushering in the era when cotton was king. For five decades the aristocrats of Natchez rode the crest of unbelievable prosperity: by 1830, the city boasted more native millionaires than any in the United States except New York. Even during civil conflict Natchez was blessed; occupied early in the War Between the States by federal troops, the city was safe—except for a single episode when the Yankee gunboat *Essex* briefly shelled the town—from the ravages of war. With Appomattox, Natchez knew some hardship: many of the men did not return. But river trade enabled the town to scramble to its feet. Natchez-Under-the-Hill continued to flourish as a center of prostitution and gambling; on the heights, the city recovered to serve for twenty years as a trade center. Boats loaded with goods—especially cotton—crowded the wharves, and the aristocracy maintained the imposing plantation estates they had founded during the South's brief idyllic age.

At the turn of the century, though, river traffic began to decline, and with it the city's economy. The boll weevil brought devastating losses to the region's cotton planters; the railroad swept the great steamboats from the river and left Natchez stranded, high and dry, in a world of ruptured fortunes and weed-choked fields. And when the rest of the nation found that happy days were here again, the good times bypassed Natchez. The antebellum mansions fell into disrepair, the great gardens were neglected for lack of funds. When prosperity came again, it would be brought by dowager queens intent on preserving the Southern heritage and restoring the city's antebellum prestige. Dismiss these women as violet-growing little old ladies if you will, but you'd do well to keep in mind that these ladies, busting ass, succeeded where the town's shrewdest businessmen turned tail and ran like twenty hells. If such high-styled rebel queens seem inordinately fond of the jasmine-blossom, antebellum past, you might recollect too that the time since Appomattox is but an instant in folk history.

Especially for the folks who were on the losing side.

The rebel queens aren't all blue-haired and liver-spotted; I can't think of one, in fact, who is. Pilgrimage ladies and Southern garden-clubbers constitute a freewheeling army with an arsenal of winning weapons; feminine soldiers range from sleek and sexy to plump and aristocratically formidable.

Katherine Grafton Miller reigns supreme among them.

At eighty-three, she has the satisfaction of knowing she's

a high-spirited benefactor in the provincial tradition, broken free from the passive aristocratic role to make a substantive difference in the economy of her region. She's an enchanting mix of dowager and belle. If arthritis has robbed her of the pleasure of waltzing, Southern-style, in Natchez' dazzling antebellum ballrooms, time has failed to diminish the curl-tossing, foot-stamping, eyes-flashing mannerisms she mastered in girlhood.

"The thing about Southern women," she says, "is that they really are *capable.* They love to cook, and they love parties, of course, and they're very active.

"Northern people think Southern women are so helpless and fragile. They don't know! But Southern women are very natural, you know.

"And I've used my Southernness. Forty years ago when I organized the first Pilgrimage, I had to travel all across the country giving lectures. It was my Southernness that helped so much; it interested people, especially the men. I'd tell them about Natchez and they'd be *moved.* One man said, 'Oh, Miz Miller, you make it sound so pathetic.' And I said, 'But it's so sweet and darling.' I used my Southernness, and it *worked.*"

She's got the eye of the antebellum dreamer, the optimism of an aristocrat who has never had to worry where the next ham would be coming from, and the down-home practicality that transforms voluntary organizations into lucrative, high-powered enterprises. Virtually all the Southern pilgrimage societies, constituting now a gold-mine industrial bonanza, date from 1930, when Miller was invited to join the first garden club in Natchez. The following year, she was elected president of the club; that year, too, the state Garden Club selected Natchez as the site of its first annual convention. Miller was asked to arrange four garden tours for the entertainment of delegates to the state convention. But the gardens of Natchez, so long neglected, were so disreputable that she suggested the town's grandest antebellum mansions be shown instead. Simultaneously, she lobbied to get the town's gardens back in shape before visitors descended on Natchez. At her instigation, crepe myrtle trees were planted along the roads, flower exchanges established, efforts made to beautify the bluffs, and Miller took up where organized efforts left off.

"I said we ought to give away free seeds, and we did. Plants and shrubs were brought in and sold at cost to beautify the city. This was during the worst Depression years, and people had very little money for anything but the necessities of life. But we did it. During the convention, camellias, japonicas, spiraea, and others were in full bloom, and wisteria vines as well. Their perfume permeated the whole city. I shall never forget it."

Mrs. Lalie Adams arranged for the placement of prominent visitors in local cars for touring purposes. As club president, Miller should have escorted the ranking state officers.

"But Mrs. Beltzhoover and I considered the situation and thought it'd be much better for her to escort them. She had a fine new car, and I had only an old Chevrolet."

This rebel queen from Natchez knows full well the importance of form, but she doesn't write off substance, either.

"Now you have to have money. Money is everything. It takes hard work *and* money. If you've got that, you can do anything."

The Garden Club had no funds to publicize the first Pilgrimage, but Miller flooded the nation with letters telling of the event and asking for help. Newspapers in thirty-seven states responded, printing Miller's submitted articles without charge. Tourists filed into Natchez from every direction, and that first Pilgrimage was so successful that extra tour transportation had to be arranged at the last minute—and the houses had to be kept open an extra day to accommodate the crowds. Members of the local Chamber of Commerce, dazzled by the new flood of tourist dollars, asked Miller to travel outside the state, giving slide-illustrated lectures to promote the next annual Pilgrimage. She'd never seen a photographic slide, but she thought it was a cunning notion.

"I decided to wear a hoop skirt."

That may sound a bit hokey, but it worked, largely because Katherine Miller looks as if she were born to such fashions. She traveled constantly, contacting every news medium, using every imaginable means of free publicity.

"If no representatives of the press appeared when I spoke, I visited the local newspaper and invited people to come to Natchez. They helped us not only by writing about my lectures but also by printing Natchez stories for their papers and magazines. Automobile associations, railroad agencies, travel bureaus, bus lines, and a lot of women's clubs promoted the Pilgrimage."

Since then, Natchez has reaped millions of dollars in free publicity, with the city emerging as a site as well known as Williamsburg or any other national shrine. Miller and her garden-clubbing, rebel-queen colleagues set a precedent for the thirteen other cities in Mississippi that schedule annual pilgrimages. As a result, azaleas and white-columned mansions are big business in the Delta.

And it's the belle-like Mrs. Miller who started it all.

"If a Southern woman cares, she can accomplish anything. Southern women are very strong, you know." But she's aware of her special advantages:

"I remember my grandmother Rose. I had these crystal fingerbowls; they were so pretty. Grandmother and Mother were talking one time about my fingerbowls. And my mother said, 'Oh, my mother never took care of anything.' And my grandmother Rose said, 'Well, of course, I was busy working my fingers to the bone to keep you all, and I didn't have time for crystal!' She was still independent at the age of ninety. It takes money, you know. You have to have money."

She does. Married for more than sixty years to J. Balfour Miller, she occupies a home that dates back to the days when the Union Jack floated over the city. Hope Farm was built in two parts: the first, or rear wing, was constructed in 1775, the front added fourteen years later. Because both Millers trace their own lineages back to colonial times, many of the furnishings they brought to Hope Farm were family heirlooms; so many other fine pieces were added over the years that Hope Farm enjoys a national reputation as a connoisseur's delight. In addition, it boasts the best-equipped pioneer kitchen in the region. It's a lordly structure that represents a faded era, but even in her eighties, Katherine Miller makes it throb with activity. She opens the estate during the annual four-week Pilgrimage in the spring, coaxing lovely young locals into hoop skirts and ruffles and hostessing duties. When she's not actively involved in Pilgrimage activities ("I'd like to turn all that over to the younger girls now, but there's always something—like that seventeen-thousand-dollar copper roof for Stanton Hall—to get done"), she's entertaining visitors from Washington. Miller was prominent in work on behalf of the Eisenhower administration, is active in women's issues supported by the Republican party, and was named a member of UNESCO by past Secretary of State John Foster Dulles. And she lavishes a good deal of time on her husband:

"I decided I was going to marry him *long* before he knew it. I've always *adored* him. He's just the cutest thing in the world!"

The feeling is mutual.

Mr. Miller, courtly and attentive, paid me elaborate compliments during my stay in Natchez in the way Southern men have, but his eyes always were on his wife: at eighty-five, he is very much in love.

"Do you know what that little monkey said about me at our fiftieth anniversary party? Somebody asked her why she stayed married to me, and she said, well, she just didn't want anybody else to have me. Isn't that just like a Southern woman?"

When I told him she'd called him adorable, his eyes misted over.

All this makes you want to go out and save a city, Southern-style, and it makes you wonder whether the traditional belle-like role, soft and feminine, might not remain at a premium. Miller, of course, is a *grande dame* of the first order, and freed by the provincial script that would have her blend saucy femininity with aristocratic eccentricity. In Louisiana, St. Francisville's Elisabeth K. Dart shares in that freedom, but offers an updated version of the traditional role. She is president of the historical society there, and breezily unpretentious. What she conveys is total self-confidence; she was born to soaring columns, too. But she has pondered the social issues she deems relevant and admits to more than a few self-doubts. She believes in economic parity for women ("equal pay for equal work") but isn't "a woman's libber" and doesn't think ERA is "essential." She was an only child born late in her parents' lives.

"My father was forty-six; he'd been a bachelor till two years before. He took me everywhere with him, but I went on his terms. I was expected to be the best I could be. It wasn't a matter of being sexist, not a matter of being the best a *woman* or a *girl* could be, but being the best I could be as a human being. He expected me to live up to my capabilities. Daddy left me with the feeling that we were privileged. Not materially, but privileged in knowing who we were.

"He also left me with an obligation to be a bloody do-gooder. I've used every wile, every trick to get things done. I don't simper, but I cajole, I beg, I plead and wheedle. I see other women doing this in the South. I have a friend who wanted to save a cemetery. She used every feminine wile. And she saved the cemetery, every stone and every tree.

"I find myself role-playing to get the Society's work done. For example, I am excessively polite to older people. I don't think it's a matter of being false or selling out. I'm aware of what I'm doing. But it works. I never felt crippled by femininity."

She did, for a while, feel crippled by the Southern past.

"Paul Hemphill said to a college audience that he's found he doesn't need to be embarrassed about the South any longer. He's no longer embarrassed by his origins. The college students looked puzzled; they don't remember a time when one felt a bit ashamed to be Southern.

"I tried very hard once to shed my Southern accent. And when I did I felt a deep sense of loss. We always felt here that we lived on top of our dung heap. But we've felt too that we have a sense of identity, a sense of place, you don't see outside the South."

On the other hand:

"How are you going to keep a sense of place and identity when you've got people here who can't get FHA financing to buy a trailer home?"

To love the South is to love it all, blemishes and blossoms, and find ways to leave things better than they were when you found them. For a non-activist, Elisabeth Dart is astonishingly aware, energetically committed. Southern women don't need consciousness-raising sessions: they have a keen perception from birth of what needs to be done. Like others, Dart is a product of her provincial past: her feminist awareness (and she has that, if she won't accept the label) clashes constantly with her conditioning. She likes homemaking, for example, but not housework.

"*Nobody* likes housework. I like the nestbuilding. I have a fairly large house now. My children are both gone, and I've been blessed: I've had wonderful help. When I'm at home, though, I'm plagued by this tyranny of *things.*"

The more things you have, the more there are to keep clean, dust, water, wipe, wash, polish, scrub, repair, maintain.

"I have a one-room cabin in the woods. No heat, no electricity. There's a portable generator so I can use the vacuum cleaner, and butane for heating water. No other conveniences, on purpose. I bought the cabin with my inheritance, and it's my great escape."

Always, in the provincial fashion, her husband comes first:

"It's my society, and it is in my bones. I'll walk on eggshells if he's brought home his anxiety.

"It's not fair: I shouldn't have to walk on eggshells because he brings problems home from the office. But it's my conditioning. But I think when I married, I assumed a certain responsibility. I keep the house, provide those three squares. It's not fifty-fifty, but no marriage ever is."

Dart grew up, she says, with "an absolute horror of women who do nothing but play bridge." Like other Southern women, she juggles varied interests; the most important, outside her unwavering commitment to family and home, are her interest in eighteenth- and nineteenth-century history, and the work she does for the St. Francisville Historical Society.

"I want to involve everybody in every walk of life: black and white, rich and poor."

Southern women, she thinks, have an ability, born of economic necessity, to work well in tandem.

"The bulk of the work in the Society is done by women. We've never had the first quarrel. Now, there're many people who doubt our worth, but not our sincerity. And Southern women are enormously competent. I've friends from the North who can work circles around me, of course, but I think Southern women stand stress better. They've had to.

The women of the rural South have always been extremely capable."

If there's charm in such true-grits community heroines as Miller and Dart, there's an equal measure in tar-and-turpentine women who inspire awe nonetheless for the cohesiveness they lend. This is a land of Mom-and-Pop stores, of family enterprise, and even in the city, Southerners cling to the notion that you don't take to the road without hauling your family with you. Most of the employees at Nashville's House of Cash, owned by June Carter and Johnny Cash, are related; those who aren't are treated as family. Sue Hensley moved to Nashville to manage the shop.

"I don't feel like the House of Cash people have titles. Everybody does their certain jobs. John's got an executive secretary, Irene Gibbs, and she does all of his correspondence. Reba, his sister, is the general manager of the House. There's Kathy, she's his daughter. When I started here, I was promoting John's records, but, you know, downstairs we've got a souvenir shop and this was important to him, too, so I took over management of that, which I still don't know beans about. There aren't as many extended families living together as there once were, but there's still more drawing in of family members than anywhere else. The House of Cash is a family venture, in a sense at least. John considers his employees his family just as he does his own. He gets close to them. Like every family, we have problems occasionally, but it's really a very nice atmosphere."

Hensley was born in Poor Valley.

"It was called Mesa Springs, Virginia. Then they took our post office out, so it went to Hiltons, Virginia. But the people there call it Poor Valley. That's where the original Carter family was from. All the Carters are still there.

"Being from the family, we didn't pay any attention to the name. Everybody in the Valley is either a Carter or related to a Carter, or a Hensley. They were just part of the Valley, one of the few that sang. Naturally, June and them—the original Carter Family—traveled, and then when their girls came up, they started traveling, too. But her father and my grandfather and those Carters died in the Valley."

Mother Maybelle Carter kept the family going.

"When Uncle Doc and Aunt Sarah separated, it kind of split the whole group. They worked together till nineteen forty or something, but then the family more or less split up. So Aunt May and the girls took over from there, and they've been recording every year—*every* year—since then. You know, just working. You should see the Valley. Go meet Jeanette Kelley. She was A. P. Carter's daughter. She has a show on Saturday nights, a Bluegrass type thing. People from the mountains come in, and you get these eighty- and ninety-year-old women who still do the buck dance. Our Valley's ten years behind times, and I wouldn't want it any other way.

"But, you know, I don't like farming. Not this tobacco farming. When we were small, the family moved to Cleveland, and then all of a sudden Dad said we were going to go back and work the land. We were going to raise our own stuff, raise tobacco, and so he threw us out in the field. We'd had experience over the years, coming back and working with my grandfather, but never really taking full responsibility. Blisters. Soreness all over your body, and working for nothing, hardly: at the end of the year, you were lucky to get a thousand dollars for the whole crop.

"You don't pick tobacco, you cut it. You have to get in there and cut the stalk from the bottom; you just hit it real hard, and it cuts the tobacco right off. You have a spear on a wood stick, and you have to take that spear to the tobacco and hit it, and it goes down, and you do this on every one of them. That's where the blisters come from. Then you hang the stalks on a vine to cure, then take them back off, tie them, cut them in half and send them to market.

"I like to work with my hands. Just give me a paintbrush or a hammer and I'm happy. But that tobacco farming: they can give that back to the Indians. It's unreal.

"Southern women are capable of doing anything. One thing about them is that they're determined. They'll fight knowing they have no chance to win. They'll still give it everything they've got. And the hardest job of all is farming. But Southern women just aren't going to leave that farm."

Today, corporate entities buy up all available parcels of farmland, increasingly crowding out the small farmer. Hensley says that won't happen in Poor Valley.

"The place I grew up in, you can't do that. Because these people own their own farms, they've been in the family for years and years, and nobody's going to leave. But you cannot make a living on the land that you work anymore."

She left Poor Valley a second time, in 1969, to come to Nashville and work for June and John. But she retains a strong pride in the Carter/Hensley tradition of knowing at first hand the special ambiguities of working near the soil.

"The family makes it different. You live so close together, and you rely on one another to *live.* And the church holds people together, too. You don't have to be radical about religion. You don't have to have a Bible in your hand or preach twenty-four hours a day. My grandfather used to say you can sit in the first seat in the church fifty years and not be saved. The important thing is love: the love you show with your family is love you'll show outside.

"The funny thing about my family—and nobody believes this—is that the Carters are very religious. And the Hensleys are old good-for-nothing people. I had a mixture of the two. Over a period of years, the Hensleys somehow got the reputation for being the roughnecks, the loudmouths, the drunks, and the Carters were always in churches. I like that. I like being part of both."

Feminism has not fared too well in Poor Valley.

"Five years ago, I'd go home and they'd say, well, Sue will find somebody to marry. Now I go home and it's poor-old-Sue, she's not married, she didn't get a man. That's what a woman is supposed to do. It used to bother me. They never thought about the career atmosphere I like or that I'm making it on my own or that I enjoy being on my own. I don't think you can have both family and career. You have to cheat some. You can't give a hundred percent both ways.

"But I was taught that you could do anything you want to do. You're allowed to make mistakes. I think people should do what they feel like doing. They shouldn't have to hide their individuality."

Few Southern women do. They're backwoods heroines who specialize in what they do best. For many, it is survival itself that matters. Redneck mothers, good ol' girls, and other Southern belles needn't rescue their communities from bankruptcy or practice the old crafts to warrant notice: if for no other reason, they are spectacular for their survival skills.

Peggy Presley knew the realities of hard living from the start. Her father hoboed to Birmingham from a tiny town in rural Alabama to find work.

"He hoboed in where the old train station is, and he found a job in a flour mill and went back to get my mother. Eventually they bought some land; they had to clear it, cut down all the trees. I helped as I got older, cutting firewood and clearing the bushes. I helped, I always helped. That's a Southern tradition. We were a real close family. My dad worked real hard: I remember he'd leave before daylight and come in after dark. There were seven children. I was the oldest girl, so I had the most responsibility. If my daddy needed any help, he called on us, either my two older brothers or me, and he made each one of us feel needed. Now, my mother ruled the roost; he went along with her in whatever she said. There wasn't very much money, but if I did something special to help, my daddy'd slip me a fifty-cent piece or something. And I worked and saved up money, and he'd take me into town with the little money I had, and we'd stay in town all afternoon.

"My daddy was always trying to make a little extra. He'd get odd jobs, like he bought an old truck and he'd go miles to get a truck-load of coal to sell. Or he'd fish on the river, and sell what he caught. He raised chickens. We had our own eggs, and every Saturday we'd collect the eggs and he'd take them to town to sell. I'd go along and for a reward I'd get a snow-cone."

If Presley's mother ruled the roost, she didn't let it show in front of other people.

"I never heard her correct my daddy in front of others. But he deferred to her. He'd tell us, 'Go ask your mother.' She always managed the money. He'd bring it home to her and she stretched it and she saved what she could. Southern women are tougher. They have what it takes to make it."

Hard times make for unbreakable bonds: provincial families stay close.

"My daddy ended up blind. He worked hard all his life, and before he retired from the flour mill he ordered books and read them. He'd gone through the second grade and had to quit to go to work and help his mother. My mother taught him how to write his name and also a lot about reading. He ordered these books about televisions and radios and he got thousands of parts. He could take a radio or TV apart and put it back together. He did that for a long time, but it got to where he couldn't see. So then if they went on a trip somewhere, I'd drive them. When I was at home, I was the maid. I didn't have to be told. If it needed to be done, I just did it. I haven't met a fragile Southern belle yet. I think we just have what it takes."

Widowed now, Peggy Presley works at the Egg-A-Day store on 72nd Street in Birmingham. She has no complaints:

just a quiet pride in her ability to survive.

It may just be that survival is the most heroic act of all, even in the absence of extreme hardship and adversity. The provincial tradition demands it: the Southern woman is obliged to be tough, to win out over all odds, real *and* imagined. This is the reason, I think, that it is the aristocracy as often as the determined poor who opt for the chance to blaze a trail, easing the way for those who follow.

In the provincial South, almost all women are activists. But a spectacular few have a special wisdom: they know how to help without imposing their own values and attitudes on the people they serve. Near Maryville, Tennessee, Brenda Bell works as a social worker, "not particularly because I've wanted to be, but because I've had to make a living." She grew up in Kentucky, Virginia, and Tennessee; her father is a minister in the Disciples of Christ Church ("Lyndon Johnson's church—that's about the only way some people recognize it"); she graduated from Transylvania College in Lexington, Kentucky, majoring in sociology:

"I took my first social-work class in college, and I knew instinctively that was not the way to go about helping people have better lives. But here I am doing it.

"I think it has to do with being a woman, being geared towards helping other people."

"I had some pretty strong ideas that I would *not* get married, just on general principle. My grandmother was a person who didn't marry till she was twenty-nine. She did a lot of things like teach school, go to college, go to nursing school, work in an office as a secretary. You know, she's very proud of those times. She also raised a very large family, has umpteen grandchildren. But she was a model in some ways for me, though I didn't think about her like that as I was growing up. When I was about twenty-five, I'd visit her and she'd say, 'Oh, don't listen to everybody else saying settle down.' But Joe and I ended up getting married, because we didn't want to hurt our families any more than we already had.

"I didn't change my name. And when I had to go to court, which was a real trip in a rural setting where folks aren't used to going to court—I had to swear before the judge that I wanted to keep my name for non-malicious reasons, and Joe had to take the stand to say it was okay with him. I had to say I was doing it for professional reasons, and at the time, I was working in the sewing factory. I think the judge probably wondered why I needed to keep my name for professional reasons working there.

"I have a daughter; she'll be three in July. Her name is Laura, after my grandmother. She's an important person to me, and she's a neat little kid, very energetic. We try to let her explore and be and do as much as she wants to do, and I don't know what that means about how she'll grow up in terms of being a girl. She's around Joe a lot. We try to share things pretty much around the house, the cooking and the household chores. We try to do things fifty-fifty. Sometimes he does more than his share, sometimes I do more than my half. Our situation is complicated by the fact that we live out in the country. We live in a house that doesn't have a bathroom. We heat by wood. We're trying to work on our house, build, work the land, farm, all this stuff. In reality, when you have a young child and a husband who has carpentry skills, plumbing skills, that sort of thing, the most efficient way to get things done is a fairly traditional division of labor, although we really try to work it out."

Despite the ideal of social conformity, Bell agrees that Southern women are freer than women elsewhere.

"You're free to do what you want to do, but you can't divorce that from the kind of background you come from.

"I don't know if I've had any experience to know whether women elsewhere endure as well or how they get along, because I've almost always lived here. I was in the Peace Corps for about a year in Senegal, and I spent a little time traveling around. I've spent time with a few female friends, talking about growing up in the South, and about what got us involved in civil rights. I mainly see us as having a lot of problems that are shared by women everywhere.

"My mother was a traditional housewife and mother and minister's wife, which is a full-time job if you decide you're going to do that. She married right after college, had me within a year, but now that everybody's gone she's in the process of rediscovering who she is, what her capabilities are.

"I don't think she'd mind me saying this. I remember growing up we'd be sitting around after dinner, talking about some problem, some magazine article or current event, and Mother would defer, saying she couldn't really comment because she didn't have time to read and she wasn't very smart anyway.

"You should see her now! That's not who she is, and maybe that's not who she *was*. Now she's very active in church things. She's national vice-president of the denominational organization. She has a lot of speaking engagements and goes to workshops and conferences. She's got a lot of skills and talents, which we've always known, but now she's finding a way to put these to use that's separate in some ways from what my father is doing. She's got a lot of self-confidence now."

Bell is a grass-roots activist devoted to the principle of selective acculturation.

"I think Southern folks have to resist people who come in and try to change patterns of living. We have to figure it out ourselves: how we want to live and what things need to be preserved, and, at the same time, we have to change living conditions, have to improve wages, work to have more control over our lives in all different kinds of ways.

"Specifically, I'm thinking of southern Appalachia, where there are a lot of attempts to change the complexion of the land, physically and otherwise, by industry coming in, and community colleges popping up—to serve the needs of the community, supposedly—but really just churning out folks to fit into the labor force that's moving in. What does that do to the patterns already established there? The folks who go to college and come back home have learned some middle-class ways of doing things, ideas about how they're going to work in their communities to change things. They want to help, but they don't listen to what the folks around them are saying, what everyday people think is important in their lives. I don't see myself trying to change the way things are. I've been involved lately with pre-natal care. We've been working on setting up some discussion groups for expectant couples, trying to figure out ways to dispense good information and yet provide a way for folks to get together to talk."

> *Band-Aids are needed sometimes. People's lives are at stake. You can't just refuse to do something because it doesn't bring total change to our social system.*
> —BRENDA BELL

She enjoyed a traditional girlhood, but became incensed by "things I saw around me." She spent two summers, for example, during college, working with a group called Appalachian Volunteers:

"We worked in communities in east Tennessee and West Virginia, helping remodel and rebuild school buildings, being involved with what was going on in these communities. We learned a lot about how government programs work, what happens when people get a little piece of the action, feel a little power. One summer I was living with a family in a very isolated situation in Kentucky, a three-room house with a family of five.

"We were moving a kitchen cabinet, and the walls were

papered with newspapers—it was the *Lexington Herald*—and when we pushed the cabinet away from the wall, there was my picture staring at me: I'd been an attendant to Miss Transylvania, in my long white dress, and I *clutched.* They were tickled, and we all laughed about it, but I was really chagrined. It's something that's stuck with me. There was a family I was living with, who I respected. They had a lot of talent, a lot of ability, but I was the one who'd be able to go out to pick and choose. It affected me in terms of how I view things. Till then, I saw things that were wrong, but I didn't associate them with the system.

"I think I know who and where I am far better now. I've got a college education, I can get up in front of people and talk, I can put together a magazine article if I have to, I can help people fight their way through the maze of social services. But I don't think I'm any better than anybody else because I have all that.

"I think it's always better anyway if people can help themselves, if they can gain a sense of 'we've done it!' I'm sort of down on federal money, but not because I'm in a right-wing way of thinking on states' rights or local control. I'm thinking of local control in terms of wanting to know which people have a say in what goes on. Those services need to be there, but they need to be there for everybody."

The worst thing about Southern women, says Bell, is that they have some "real dependencies, not necessarily of their own doing," that too often lead them into falling back into ineffectual femininity, "selling out."

The best, she says, is their "openness, their genuine concern for other folks."

Helping out, making do: Southern comfort—and the quiet dignity of choice.

Homegrown & Grafted Hybrids:
Bumper Crops from Yesterday's Gardens

*We're able here to combine both worlds,
having our freedom and yet
remaining gentle little Southern ladies.*
—GINNIE RAYMOND

People in Memphis keep telling Dianne Vaughn to go out and find herself a new husband.

Look here, they say, you're divorced. You've got five kids to support. You're not trained for any sort of job. The banks won't lend you any money. The toilet in your hall bathroom is overflowing, and you don't know a float from a plunger. The dishwasher's broken, too. You'd better find yourself some nice guy who'll marry and take care of you —and the sooner, the better.

Vaughn, at twenty-eight the survivor of two disastrous marriages, finds this advice faulty.

"Oh, for the first few months, I was totally hysterical. I'd always had a man to take care of me—either a father or a husband—and I didn't think I could make it alone. So at first I listened to friends who told me to go out and find a new man.

"I *do* have a bad habit of getting married. I'm sure I will again someday."

But after being on her own now for two years, she's become adept at keeping a lot of balls in the air. Not only can she manage alone, she says, but she's doing all right by her children as well, thanks. So certain is she now that women can function independently that she has founded, with a friend, an organization designed to rally divorcées, widows, and other single women with children around this very notion.

The group is called WHEN?—a word that reflects the perpetual dilemma of divorced, separated, widowed, and abandoned women everywhere.

"Women alone are always asking *when*. When will the child-support check come? When will the lawyer call? When will the depression lift? When will things get better?"

She has asked all those questions herself, and found precious few answers.

"I couldn't even find anyone to talk to. Specifically, I couldn't find anyone who could tell me what to do when there was no money in the house and the kids were hungry. I was in a constant rage. I just kept beating my head against different walls."

Vaughn is a high-key romantic charmer who asks little of life, she says, except joy, security, and lasting happiness. If physical appearance guaranteed these, she'd have no problems: she is anatomically constructed so as to make dumb men talk, blind men see. Neither feminist nor revolutionary, Vaughn didn't look forward to bucking the system.

"But the system doesn't work for people in extraordinary circumstances. It's not responsive.

"Say the support check doesn't come. You call your lawyer, only he's in court all day. So you wait. When he finally returns your call, he says he'll call your husband's attorney. So you wait some more. Then the other lawyer has to get in touch with your husband. If you're lucky, you get an answer in a week or so. But what do you do in the meantime?"

Food stamps?

"One month the child support was late and I knew we couldn't make it without food stamps. But I didn't have sixty dollars to buy them, and the food-stamp office said they couldn't give the stamps to me. I said I had five kids and no food in the house, and they said they didn't know how to advise me."

She followed a tangled trail of red tape through various welfare agencies, and wound up borrowing money from her church.

"There simply is no effective agency. Each acts as a clearing house, sending you to other agencies.

"I hated the idea of going to my church for money. I thought you really should be living in a ghetto in order to have the church aid society bring you money for food, and I was afraid they'd think of me as a real rip-off artist."

It was the only option she had.

"I'd looked for work. I answered ads in the paper. I haunted the employment office. I couldn't find a job of any kind. I couldn't get a baby-sitter. The child-support check was always late, from one to six weeks. Never late enough for me to collect in court, but late enough to run up some new legal bills and mess up my budget and wreck my credit rating. My husband moves around a lot, too, which makes it harder for me to get the child support from him. Every time I get his new address, he moves again."

She worked her way through several attorneys who were unable to hasten the wheels of justice. She bombarded congressmen and senators with letters and telegrams. In desperation, she started taking her children to weddings and funerals mentioned in the local newspaper.

"It was a way to feed the kids."

Nothing worked.

"My husband is a hospital administrator. It's a very elite doctor's hospital in the very best section of a very prosperous Southern city. The only thing left to do was organize a protest march on the hospital. I went so far as to plan it. Looking into permits and all that.

"The city refused to issue a permit, of course. I was informed I'd be jailed if I tried to march there. I was afraid my lawyer wouldn't get me out; he might have left me sitting there for years.

"Besides, I didn't *want* to march!"

Southern women aren't too enthusiastic about militant tactics. What they excel at is pulling stumps out of local lakes. It's no coincidence, I think, that when Dianne Vaughn decided to shake up the system, she did so on a grass-roots level and in a typically provincial manner.

"I'd started talking to other divorced women when I planned that protest march, and I found out every woman was having the same problems. Like we'd heard so much about welfare rip-offs—I used to talk that way myself—yet a family of four on welfare gets a hundred and forty dollars a month to live on, to pay for rent and food and everything else."

That was the start of WHEN?

"I called Mary Sawyer, a woman I'd met doing volunteer political work a while back. She's about thirty, black, divorced with no children, and she's not afraid of causing commotion because she's spent years doing that. She went to law school and went through the hard years as a civil-rights worker in Mississippi."

Vaughn and Sawyer printed up about 300 WHEN? circulars with Vaughn's telephone number at the top, and posted them on public bulletin boards and in women's restrooms around Memphis.

"We made it a point to put them up in restrooms in the city's singles bars, where a couple of hundred women pass through every evening."

The circulars described the goals of the organization and encouraged women to call in to discuss their problems. Vaughn is convinced that if single women with children organize they can form a powerful pressure group capable of lobbying successfully for women's rights without resorting to militant strategies.

"A group like WHEN? could boycott businesses that tend to take advantage of women—plumbers and mechanics are the most difficult for women to deal with—and we could favor businesses that treat women fairly."

She has come a long way since she began facing her problems alone.

"I was conditioned to be a traditional wife. It's all I ever wanted. I wanted—this was my ideal, I think—to marry an Italian who happened to be rich, Catholic, and Southern, and who'd let me have eight children. I was going to stay home, have babies, bake cookies, be a good Catholic wife and mother, and keep my mouth shut.

"What happened was that I ran off and got married when I was fifteen. My first husband was eighteen when we eloped. He joined the Navy, so he was gone, and I didn't learn any reality in that marriage. I lived with my mother, had a baby, and she proceeded to raise it for the next four years. My son was a toy. I dressed him up in John-John Kennedy suits and put him in a John-John haircut. I was going to school, and once a week I'd parade around with my toy son. All my girlfriends envied me because they thought I had the most exciting life. And my mother wouldn't let me stay up past ten o'clock at night.

"I ended up getting divorced a year and a half later."

Four years after that, Vaughn met her second husband ("he was a wrong number on the telephone"), and married him within the year. She played the traditional role she had been taught was appropriate.

That was when she learned about reality.

"I went through the whole thing, including natural childbirth and breast-feeding. I never *was* able to pull it off, because I am incapable of keeping a clean house. I cannot get a floor clean: four hours on my knees, scrubbing, and the floor is still dirty. If I cook a full meal from scratch, I'm a nervous wreck for two days. But I couldn't accept that about myself, and I kept trying to measure up to my ideal of what a woman was supposed to be. I stayed at home and had babies and baked bread. I made friends with the wives of my husband's business associates, and I'd have these great discussions with them on the virtues of broccoli. I didn't know what else to do. My husband was from Illinois, and he convinced me eventually that I was inferior intellectually—that I was really *stupid*—because I was from the South and had a Southern accent."

As Lenny Bruce used to say, it doesn't matter how bright a Southerner is: if Albert Einstein tawked lahk thayat, theah wouldn't never be no bomb.

"I still resent that. About three years ago, I took an I.Q. test and found out my I.Q. is nearly ten points higher than his. I exploded. I came home and threw everything in the house at him. He said the test administrator must have made a mistake.

"The whole marriage can be summed up in something else my ex-husband said about five years ago. He told me once that his idea of a perfect Saturday was sleeping late, lying in bed listening to me clean house. I've never forgotten that. I didn't realize then that not everyone is cut out to be a perfect housewife. So I kept trying and failing and feeling stupid. I was determined to live up to his ideal of what my life should be, when I *should* have been trying to figure out what *my* ideal really was."

Too bad she didn't run into Betty Talmadge, who would have advised her to develop some skills of her own. As it was, Dianne Vaughn learned some difficult lessons the hard way.

"It was really rough at first, but I've learned that there are real advantages in raising children alone. You know, husbands take up a great deal of time. I used to get up at six every morning, lay out his clothes, start his bath, and fix his breakfast. Then I worked all day to try to get the house clean and have dinner ready when he came home. Now I have all this time to spend with my children. I feel closer to them, too, and I think they feel closer to me. It's like the domino principle: he used to yell at me, so I'd yell at them, and they'd yell at each other. Those tensions are gone now."

Better yet, she has a paying job now, one built on the foundations of the organization she founded. Dianne Vaughn may tawk lahk thayat, but she's another Southern woman whose cracker-barrel determination and high energy carry her through the hard times.

WHEN? started small, with those circulars posted on rest-room walls. Vaughn and Sawyer contacted every social agency they could find, asking help when it was available and referrals to WHEN? when it was not.

"We got a lot of attention because most people don't expect a white woman and a black woman our ages to go barging around asking for donations. People would see us when they wouldn't see anyone else. And when we *really* wanted to make an impression, we took this really nice nun with us. It shocked people so that they'd have to hear us out just to find out what the hell we were up to.

"We put up our little signs. We asked everyone in town for help. At first, there were maybe twenty calls a week. But word got around, and within four months we were getting a hundred or more calls a day. Most were women with financial problems; ex-husbands who either don't pay court-awarded child support at all, or who make late or partial payments. Some called to complain about lawyers who charge exorbitantly or don't keep in touch with their clients. Some lawyers don't want to take the time to explain the law, and some are simply inept. And a lot of women called WHEN? in panic, looking for someone to talk to because they can't make ends meet. They can't find jobs. They don't know what community services are available. If they do know, they've exhausted these resources, because most of these agencies often are unable to provide practical help or advice. Many women don't have money for buses, for telephone bills, for deposits on utilities, for baby-sitters to care for the kids so they can go out and look for work."

Initially, WHEN? survived on private donations.

"People who can't—or won't—give us money often give us goods or services. We were having garage sales every weekend just to keep going. One company donated sets of brand-new vinyl window shades. Often, we contacted people not for donations but to ask that they work with us. Like Parents Without Partners. Pretty soon every social agency that's supposed to be helping people—but can't or won't—was coming to us for help, and of course we had almost no money. But we were able to help some people. And we got ripped off beautifully by a very few women who are professionals at milking agencies and organizations. We'd give them things out of our own houses when we had almost nothing ourselves. Sheets. Blankets. Food. You learn quickly that you can't take things out of your own house.

"But many of the women we helped started helping us, going after donations or helping to man the phones."

Vaughn, Sawyer, and a handful of volunteers took turns fielding incoming calls on Vaughn's single home telephone line daily, from six A.M. till after midnight ("whenever I realized I was too exhausted to pick up the receiver one more time"). They offered emergency baby-sitting service, information on various social agencies, news bulletins on any sales or bargains around town, and a sympathetic ear to the special problems of women who suddenly find themselves in the role of head of the household.

"It hit me one day that I was functioning on my own, and doing pretty well. I'd been doing it for a year, and nothing really terrible had happened. The roof hadn't fallen in, my son wasn't in reform school, the smaller children hadn't starved to death."

A discovery.

"I realized I was getting a few things accomplished. I no longer felt helpless. I felt really good about myself. And I'd even been able to help a couple of women who were going through what I'd been through."

And, finally, she and Sawyer were able to obtain federal funding for WHEN? operations through H.E.W.

"The money covered rent on an office, minimum furnishings, utilities, and salaries for a staff of six."

Vaughn came into a paying job, then, as director of social services, and Sawyer as executive director. The funding was for one year only: the co-founders of WHEN? are beating the Southern bushes right now for additional capital. In the meantime, they're putting to good use lessons learned the hard way.

"We had a call yesterday from one mother who was living with her children in a thirty-thousand-dollar home, and the children had had no food at all for three days. Young mothers may not have family members living in the area to whom they can turn for help, or they may be too proud to ask, or they may be afraid to admit that their marriages have failed.

"Many of these women *can't* go to work. A major obstacle is finding a baby-sitter, so we're searching out low-cost day-care centers with fees scaled to income. Remember that *I* tried to work to supplement the child support, but the only job I found in all that time paid so poorly that I'd have ended up with exactly seven dollars a week after paying my baby-sitter.

"We're trying to develop some employment programs. There are state programs offering grants or stipends for people who want vocational training and we've ferreted out some public-service jobs, too.

"You can't imagine how many women need help. The thing that still shocks us most is that men who earn forty or fifty thousand a year will go through any number of court battles to keep from paying two thousand a year in child support. Some skip out on child support because it's one way to punish an ex-wife. Others have taken on second families; they're spreading their income too thin, and they resent the money that goes to their first families. The average child-support payment we hear about in WHEN? is two hundred dollars a month, no matter how many children are involved.

"And we're talking child support, not alimony. On a nationwide basis, fewer than four percent of divorced women are awarded alimony, and fewer than two percent actually manage to collect it. Each payment is harder to collect than the one before. After five years, the number of women still receiving court-awarded child-support payments drops drastically.

"That's why we've got to keep WHEN? going somehow."

Dianne Vaughn has a right to feel good about herself: she is one more in a long line of heroic and imaginative Southern belles who recognize stereotypic discord when they hear it, toss the old score away, and proceed to improvise new harmonies.

While traditional values prevail in Dixie, they are not in themselves restrictive: this is a place where tradition has always been tempered with individuality. It's a mix that makes for community involvement and grass-roots action, a blend that tends to match the South's abused reservoir of human resources with the skills and guidance needed to make full use of them. It makes good sense for those with hard-earned expertise in a particular field to take the lead. Tradition dictates that community problems be addressed; conditioned individualism encourages novel or innovative solutions.

Redneck Mothers, Good Ol' Girls, and other Southern Belles trust dirt over concrete: life grows there, and so does variety. In a culture ostensibly rooted in the soil of social conformity, Dixie's native daughters have insisted all along on their right to be non-conformists. Having rejected outside notions of what they *ought* to be, they're free to be what they *are*.

Even if what they are seems contradictory to non-Southern eyes.

So they emphatically denounce feminist militancy (too rowdy, too shrill, and unladylike, besides), while calmly conducting their own highly independent lives. They are freed rather than hampered by the provincial script. And if a good many of them choose to hide their personal freedom behind a facade of practiced femininity, they come by the habit honestly. Digging in their mothers' gardens, they've unearthed a heady truth: femininity played Southern-style makes a handy survival tool and a powerful weapon for self-defense.

You can still catch more flies with honeyed tones than with fiery feminist rhetoric.

The old-style Southern belle knew the wisdom of this cliché. So does Betty Talmadge, which is what makes her the South's most effective feminist leader. Redneck Mothers, Good Ol' Girls, and other new-style Belles with consciousness raised know it too. They're the women, in fact, who harvest the best of both worlds.

Blanche Terry has taken the time to ponder past and present—and to compare her life with that of her daughter. Terry is a fifty-seven-year-old housewife who lives and works in Vicksburg, Mississippi. She never finished high school, but she is one of the most intelligent women I know, and she has done some hard thinking on the Southern experience.

"My father lived here all his life. His father lived here all his, and his father's father came in as an Irish immigrant. When you talk Southern, you're talking about roots. My roots are here, and it's hard for me to imagine living outside."

With roots, of course, come duty and, often, an intimate knowledge of work that is grindingly hard. Married at age sixteen, Terry went to work in a factory.

"That type of life is very hard. But I had some good friends in the factory. With people like that, you don't really realize how hard the work is. I worked there for ten years, and the women did all the work. The men were the chiefs, and the women were the Indians. Years later, I came to resent that, remembering how the women worked while the men walked around talking. At the time, I never thought about equal rights."

Two years after her marriage, Terry's mother died: Terry was obliged, in the provincial tradition, to assume the management of her father's home. It didn't occur to her to complain or to demand help from her sisters. It didn't occur to her, in fact, that she carried a huge burden: running the household, tending the needs of husband and father, working at a full-time job as well. No one ever told Blanche Terry she might find emotional reinforcement or fulfillment in her work. She worked out of economic necessity, for the paycheck that would purchase the education she wanted for her children.

"I was a Catholic, and Ray was not. He'd never even met a Catholic till he was eighteen years old; he thought they had horns and tails. I wanted the children to be Catholics and go to Catholic schools, because I felt that they provided a superior education. My husband was set against it. So I went out and got a job to pay the tuition.

"But I'd sat them down from the first and told them that I worked to send them to school, to allow them to have better clothes and some spending money. I told them I *could* stay at home, but if I did, they'd go to public school and do without the rest. So they made the choice themselves.

They'd come in and help clean the house."

Terry followed the provincial pattern in her marriage, unthinkingly accepting the major responsibility.

"I spoiled Ray so early. I never realized it till the children pointed it out to me. I still do it. If he's watching a ballgame on TV and he wants a sandwich, I get him a sandwich. I thought about that this morning when I got up to fix breakfast for him and fix his lunch, and then I still had to finish and get ready. I'm always in a time-trap. And when he comes in in the evening, he watches TV while I fix supper. He'd never think of starting supper for me.

"My children are different. Not long ago, my son asked his daughter how he'd go about getting a malt. And she told him, 'Well, Daddy, you go back there and get the milk and the malt and the ice cream and put them together, and you make it.' My daugther-in-law says this is women's lib. They don't wait on him.

"I really like to do for Ray. You do out of love for your husband and your children, but there are times when you resent having so much to do.

"I see my children with *their* children, and the men are tending the children more than my husband ever did. Ray was the authority, but tending the children was *my* job. It's different now. My son was in this morning, and he'd been to a soccer game with his little boy. He spends just as much time with his little girl. I don't credit the feminist movement. I believe that the colleges and universities have instilled this new sense of family. Each of my children feels that marriage is a matter of *sharing* responsibility."

It is a marital innovation that delights and amazes her. Blanche Terry was bred to the notion that a wife properly subordinates her own desires to those of her husband and children; if it is necessary for her to work at a full-time job as well, then she does so, without expecting help with her household work. It is only over the past few years that she discovered salaried employment could be joyful. She works full-time now as assistant to the director of the Old Courthouse Museum. If the Museum did not pay her, one suspects, Terry would be happy to pay the Museum to permit her to work there. She's a happy Southern lady who has found her perfect niche. And if she's newly aware that the odds were stacked against her all along, she's convinced that it is different for her daughter.

"I think this new idea they have about family life is *great.* Things are so different now."

But are they?

Terry's daughter, Ginnie Raymond, is a social worker in Tuscaloosa, Alabama. She rivals her mother for common sense and down-to-earth charm, but she's a bit more pensive and more analytical. She has a daughter of her own and has given more than a little thought to her role as wife and mother.

"Jim and I talked this morning about what made the difference in our marriage. I said it was the university experience, knowing couples who were accustomed to seeing a husband as a student and a wife as a breadwinner, supporting him through school. But Jim pointed out that the difference predated graduate school.

"He feels that the difference comes from the fact that I've worked since before we were married. He just naturally thought of helping; not all husbands would.

"Maybe it's just the times. We married in sixty-eight, when people were beginning to be more conscious of sexual equality. The feminist movement had started then, but it had no tremendous validity, particularly in the Deep South. Then I think back, and I realize that I was raised by a mother who worked full-time but who also maintained a home.

"She never faulted my father to me. She never said for me not to marry someone like him. *Never.* But in some ways I felt she implied to me that one makes choices in life, that one can make a different choice. My father implied that too. Not that he expressed it in terms of finding a husband who helped around the house, but he implied somehow that there was a better way for me.

"My father makes it all up through the grandchildren. He loves them. He gives them the sort of attention and patience he really never could give us. That's Southern, saying things through actions."

Southerners, says Ginnie Raymond, are pleasingly indirect.

"I have a friend from New York who lives here now. She's articulate, intelligent, cosmopolitan. Yet she's missing something. You get the feeling she hasn't the subtlety that's Southern. What we do is use indirect methods of telling people things. We use humor, sometimes, and a very gentle way. When we have something negative to say to someone, we don't do it directly; we tell someone else who will tell that person. Maybe it comes out more in the Southern woman because she uses it in such a positive way. But it's the whole image, an image of feminine gentleness."

There are special advantages in being a Southern woman now, and Ginnie Raymond knows it. Feminism maintains a low profile in Dixie, but it has had a powerful impact.

"Outside the South, where the women's movement has been strong for a long time, women find it an all-or-nothing thing. We don't, which is very nice. We can have our cake and eat it too.

"I know my world sounds very idyllic. It isn't, of course.

"If I want to express it in negative terms, I could say that I have more responsibility here at home than Jim does. But I like that, and I choose it. My husband often mentions getting a maid; I can't bring myself to do that. It would be hard for me to give orders to somebody to clean up *my* dirty mess. Besides, I don't want somebody else in my territory. I think a maid won't do this work as well as I do it. And if she did it as well, that would mean somebody can replace me in a job I've excelled in.

"It definitely isn't fifty-fifty. But Jim accepts so much more responsibility at home than my father did that my marriage is *amazing* to my mother."

When Ginnie Raymond talks of household division of labor, she refers to Jim's "helping out," not to his tendency to "do his share." It's more than a matter of semantics. However supportive of his wife, Jim Raymond has one job, and Ginnie has two.

"So, really, it's my *job* that helps out. I play a traditional role even though I work. That's my choice."

She has always got an option: if she quits her job, she gets credit for staying at home and being a "good" mother. If she chooses to remain in her salaried job, she gets credit for working while shouldering the bulk of the burden at home.

"It's the best of both worlds. If my job gets to me, I can quit. I can say I want to stay home to spend more time with my child. But if there's a good job to go to, I don't have to say I'm going back to work because I'm tired of cooking and going to PTA meetings. These aren't very impressive reasons to fail your child. But your work can be made to appear important. Meanwhile, Jim carries a tremendous psychological burden that I do not: I can quit my job at any time, and he can't."

This is not to suggest that her work is unimportant to her. Ginnie Raymond trained for her career and derives immense satisfaction from it. Still, given the best of two worlds, she finds herself rooted more solidly in the one she knew first. Her work gives her status and fulfillment. Her husband shares the responsibility for tending home fires to an extent that astonishes her parents. Her personal freedom is almost boundless. Yet Ginnie Raymond, like her mother before her, defers to the male she has married. She is submissive, by choice.

Which makes Ginnie Raymond crazy like a Southern fox.

Only Dixie's native daughters admit with such soul-sustaining candor that they buy only the parts of contemporary feminism that suit their purposes, leaving the rest. Only they get away so freely with living by feminist tenets when it is profitable to do so, and abandoning those tenets when it is not. Outside the boundaries of the old Confederacy, behavior like this is labeled "hypocrisy" or "sellout." In the lower right-hand corner of the United States, it is considered sound logic.

Now, it verges on blasphemy to dissect the sublime, and Southern logic is about as easy to get a handle on as a greased pig at a county fair. But it is logic shaped wholly by the past. Like a special garden seed planted and cultivated for its special qualities year after year, then passed to new generations of gardeners, the cult of Southern womanhood persists, spawning spectacular new bumper crops in the midst of yesterday's gardens.

There are those who credit St. Paul with the development of this special strain. Now, Paul (he was a good ol' boy) claimed that the reasonable way of handling things was for women to submit to their husbands as unto the Lord. The hard-drinking, coon-hunting, bodice-tugging Southern chauvinists of colonial times insisted on a literal interpretation of the Scriptures. Southern women, currying favor, turned an obedient cheek, and *macho* males consolidated their gains. The logical result was that Dixie's daughters found it profitable to gain indirectly the objectives they couldn't attain otherwise. There are a few peckerhead Yankees determined to view this situation as an unjust feminine handicap, but don't pay them no never-mind: Southern women not only thrived on their pedestals, but managed cannily to turn them to their own special uses.

In antebellum times, cotton gained supremacy, and so did the fabled code of Southern chivalry, by which provincial males were obliged to assume a protective stance toward women. Southern men are so fiercely protective, in fact, that one wonders if there might not be another side to this masculine coin: if women are so helpless that they must be protected, might it not also be true that they are so strong that they must be feared?

The suspicion must have gnawed at more than one male mind.

The idyllic age of cotton and cavaliers was brief, though, and Southern chauvinists were distracted by the need to deal with a major crisis. The rebels had only to hold the territory in the states that had seceded in order to emerge triumphant in civil conflict; unfortunately for them, they were handicapped by the fact that they had gotten those bloody Yankees churned up before they got around to building any cannon factories. They had their hands full, all right. But what gallantry, pride and free-style individualism got them into in 1860, sturdy Celtic heritage (and iron-butterfly women) got some of them out of a few years later.

Those who survived had an even greater need to honor the old Southern code and cult of femininity.

Though Dixie's daughters had managed for the sake of form and male pride to live with the myth of fragile femininity, the War Between the States, with its attendant horrors, threatened to dispel the fiction. It was even *more* important now for Southern women to mask their strength of will and staying power behind a cloak of practiced feminine helplessness, and it wasn't all that difficult, either. The women of the South had survived the rigors of settlement and war, defeat and poverty; they had shouldered, too, the knowledge that the Southern experience not only provided for the safeguarding of individual rights and Christian principles, but also demanded the mass enslavement of millions of Southerners whose sole mistake was to be born black.

Feminine fragility was a piece of Sally Lunn cake.

Just as the women of Sevierville County pretend so valiantly that stone soup and cornbread make a decent supper, the South pretends that its women constitute the weaker sex. Southern belles of every variety, accustomed to paradox and passionate insanities, have little trouble responding within the provincial code. They have never been taken by surprise. And a measure of their commitment to the Southern experience is to be found in the extent to which they honor the old code today. Far from feeling shame in their enactment of the traditional feminine role, they tend to look down their noses at the barbaric ways of Yankee feminists. Militant tactics are unladylike (no getting around that). And those who reject militancy are acting less from a need to legitimize kittenish tricks than from a heritage that stresses the importance of good form.

Burning bras is, well, *tacky*.

And tacky, as you know, is pink flamingos done up in papier-mâché and Day-Glo pinfeathers on one's front lawn.

A Southern woman is anything but tacky, even when she's dodging stray cattle in her high-chromed pickup. She knows the code, and it demands that she greet the world daily with good manners, a modicum of form, and a sunny smile. Good breeding, said Mark Twain, was a matter of concealing how much we think of ourselves and how little we think of others, and even the hard-driving, rip-roaring, bad-ass, new-style backroads provincials honor that particular principle. They are outspoken, for sure, giving belligerent voice to all the secret biases the rest of us hide; but on a one-to-one basis, they revert invariably to *polite.* However free, they know that their point has always been to turn upon the points of other people's lives. Southern women are Dixie's most proficient stage managers, catalysts, prop directors, ego massagers. You're not going to catch *them* going around breaking fragile male balls: a Redneck Mother, in a fit of frenzied fury (or on a whim), may plant a skillet upside her old man's head, especially if he's the one who got her riled. But not in front of company.

The better part of power is a keen sense of timing. A Southern woman knows full well when to clean up her act and play the lady. There are times when she wouldn't say *shit* if she had a mouth full of it.

There are times too, of course, when it's best to give her wide berth. She can swear, fight, storm, shout, plunder, raise cain, give down the devil, turn on a dime, and meet you coming back for change.

We call her *mercurial,* don't-you-know, because that sounds pleasantly high-strung, like the thoroughbred the word describes.

Living in a male-dominated society, when you know (because your very own mother told you) you're along about ten times smarter than the ego that it is your lot to massage, makes things a tad tense, and it accelerates the competition. Provincial society concedes to women the right to remain unmarried, but it awards nonetheless a staggering number of points to belle-like beauties who succeed in capturing the choicest males. If Dixie's darlings take a notion that someone is poaching on their preserve, they can be downright treacherous. Poaching, of course, is common and great sport besides.

Just don't get caught at it.

Yet despite the dedicated competition for available males, the habit of feminine bonding is deeply ingrained. Let feminists outside the borders of Dixie crow over their newfound and joyous woman-to-woman communication; Southern women have known the benefits of bonding all through their common history. They may be cat-like in their devotion to honing their ritualistic courtship skills, but they are reasonably cautious about where they flex their claws. They have a vested interest in the feminine bond. They've always maintained heartening networks that provide emotional, psychological, and political support on a scale unparalleled outside the South.

Shared losses, shared gains, shared efforts and defeats are forces far more unifying than a string of common victories. Southern women band together in secret sisterhood to trade experiences and pass on feminine skills. Often, knowledge passes from generation to generation by means of feminine humor. Feminine irreverence in Dixie can be rough and raw and exceedingly personal: the thin-skinned, gentle, or unwary immigrant can suffer genuine psychic damage. Usually, though, the region's closet comics vent any accumulated rage on the male, in whose absence such humor is repeated. The code prohibits deliberate efforts to diminish the masculine ego; bawdy backroads humor, hidden in gleeful kitchen whispers, makes it possible (in private, at least) to take a sardonic swipe at the men who have power over them. A woman's first bawdy stories come to her before the end of her potty training; generally, they come from her mother or grandmother or aunts and focus on the consequences of confusing Vaseline with glue by sexually-untutored newlyweds. The repertoire expands with advancing age. A specialized sexual knowledge is acquired along with the traditional Southern lore of cooking, canning, quilting. Eventually, one learns that penises can be called *tallywackers,* belittling them and so diminishing the fear and awe they inspire in female adolescence. Knocking the role of sex as a wifely duty, ladies refer at times to female genitals as chore-girls (or so I hear: my great-grandmother called them wooly-boogers).

Trashy talk and closet humor: they serve as more than afternoon delights. Have you ever stopped to consider the extent of sex education contained in the one about the traveling salesman and the farmer's daughter? And, looking back, I can't recall a single joke told by the conclave of women in my mother's kitchen that made a female the butt of the joke: better to find a choicer victim, like a man or a Yankee or a Baptist preacher. This is closet humor with a special twist, poking fun at provincial institutions, serving up social comment with the grits and gravy.

Southern women laugh, too, at the exorbitant demands made on them in the roles they traditionally play. They are relentlessly busy, and there is no limit to the trouble they'll go to in order to *make things nice.* At the same time, if they hold to the code, they'll walk barefoot through a nest of copperheads before admitting they went to any bother. The Southern woman may be psychotically inclined toward over-achievement, but tradition requires that she make her handiwork appear effortless. Do you know the special exhilaration that comes with watching your mother clean, scrub, vacuum, polish, dust, scour, and bake through the night, agonize over the shape of carrot curls in mid-morning, primp and tailor through the afternoon, only to greet her dinner guests in lounging pajamas of electric-blue chiffon and an expression of confused dismay? How scatter-brained she is! What a shame they must take pot-luck! How terrible that she had no time anyway to tend the dinner.

But she'll rustle up something simple in a flash.

Had she learned minutes earlier that her eight-year-old is dealing dope, her mother in police custody for shoplifting, her husband anticipating a new heir courtesy of his twenty-year-old secretary, she'd have passed the evening in silky serenity, at least till the door closed behind the last departing guest; her life might be coming apart at the seams, but she'd never let *that* ruin a perfectly good dinner or cause her guests a moment's discomfort. Her role is to make everyone around her feel relaxed and happy. It is this feminine conspiracy after all that makes the South such a legendary pleasure.

One wonders if this might not be the only sensible way to live.

The South may be microscopic in its world view, resplendent in its traditional flaws. Pockets of paralyzing poverty remain, relics of a disastrous economic past. Rightism, repression, and racism remain scattered across the landscape. When the shifty old-style rednecks line up, fear and suspicion gleaming in their eyes, hate pounding at their hearts, every Southern woman flinches at an inner realization that a tiny part of herself lines up with them. She knows that her Junior League is still considering surrendering its tax-exempt status rather than be forced to admit "undesirable" elements. She springs from a tradition that judges sixty dollars a month in welfare sufficient for a hungry family of four. Though her love for the land may be genuine, she's often done little enough to improve it. But it's easy to seek one's identity in native flaws and regional narcissisms; whatever reservations our critics have about our virtues, they've never been timid about conceding us our vices. And if we provincial daughters have paid less heed than we might to the exigencies of social and economic progress, we have managed to avoid in the process a number of contemporary blemishes. We don't consult as many psychiatrists, file as many divorce petitions, consume as many lethal overdoses, attend as many costume parties dressed as oversize Quaaludes, or participate as freely in what the sophisticates among us call "open marriage" (the rest of us call it "messing around") as women whose roots are located elsewhere in the nation. I am not convinced that this last-noted distinction stems from the persistence of the unwritten Southern law which permits a betrayed spouse to avenge himself by blasting away with a Browning over-and-under. Personally, I prefer to think of it as a consequence of moral scruples.

The first feminist demand advanced in my memory, though, originated with a few equal-rights ladies from east Texas who journeyed to the state capital to lobby for parity in shooting rights. The husbandly right to safeguard his home by dispatching an unfaithful wife or her lover (one or the other but not both, unless, as in one case, the defense successfully argues that the death of the second party accidentally resulted from bullets that passed through the body of the first) is *not* unwritten in the Lone Star state. A bill to grant betrayed wives homicidal parity was introduced in the Texas legislature in 1967, but was handily defeated by male legislators sufficiently equipped to recognize a bird's nest on the ground when they stumbled across one.

Ours is a difficult time in which to be a woman. Feminist concepts have penetrated every region of the nation, reaching even into the rural outposts, maturing from ideology to a bold new phase of general if (often) unconscious acceptance. Acceptance, though, brings the impetus for change, and in the land of moonshine and country music, change has about as much appeal as a pit viper.

One does not tamper lightly with social roles well played and consistently rewarded, nor with sexual identities inculcated and refined since birth.

This is as true north of the Maxon-Dixon line as south of it. The seismic changes demanded by the feminist movement create as many problems as they solve, if not more. Few new role models have emerged to replace the obsolete old ones; there is no booklet of guidelines to tell how to proceed into an unknown future. Little wonder that Marabel Morgan packs such wallop when she advises women to retreat back into the known bag of kittenish tricks, smiling and cooing and listening well and stroking the male ego with soothing feminine balm. Yet once one wakes the sleeping dog of awareness, the pup stays close at heel. There are a good many women now who grapple with the admittedly exorbitant demands of feminist freedom, and with the conflicts (real and imagined) of a new, unfamiliar, non-sexist order. Some hurdle the larger obstacles with relative ease only to stumble over the smallest starting blocks. Far too many hesitate in bewildered displacement over the trappings and accoutrements of womanhood. Catherine Calvert writes of her own ambivalence and her near-obsessive fear of appearing traditionally feminine in an age of sexual parity: "Why do I wince if someone calls me sweet?" And she worries that it is impossible now for enlightened women to enjoy what once gave them untarnished pleasure: a swish of a skirt, a scent, a compliment, without feeling they betray their principles.

Yankee fears, peckerhead problems.

There is in fact a commonality to feminism: women everywhere face a need to reconcile new awareness with old behavior patterns.

But to falter over the trappings?

The Southern woman is not likely to mistake so readily style for substance. She knows the difference, learning early, before she masters the intricacies of her toilet training. This is why she has managed to strike such a rare and remarkable balance between lifelong conditioning and expanded personal and political freedom. It's a tricky emotional balance, paradoxically made possible by her unique cultural past.

It has to do in part with the fact that she is derived from a matriarchal society. Now, it has been suggested (with some validity) that woman-worship was instituted by Southern men for political purposes; there's a price tag that comes with the right to occupy the pedestal, and the cost is great. Even so, woman's high status in the South gives her a decided edge over women elsewhere in achieving parity with men. For she is not unaccustomed to the uses of power and authority: she has only to learn to exercise these openly, and in her own name. Louisiana's Lindy Boggs, like others before her, rode into the U.S. Congress on her late husband's coattails, yet I think it no accident that it took her less than three years to become, on her own merits, the first woman ever to chair a national political convention.

Southern woman springs, too, from a tradition that prizes

high-styled individuality over routine conformity. Now, she might have to endure half a dozen condescending male "now, ma'ams" daily, as Betty Talmadge did in business until she proved her grits, but she is freer by far than her Northern sisters to display the full range of her personality and so, presumably, seek fulfillment, if she chooses, in non-traditional (even "masculine") ways. She may in fact make full use of informally sanctioned regional stereotypes to be as "masculine" as she likes without fear of social censure: while feminine allure and "ladylike" demeanor still carry considerable weight in the South, it is central to the Southern myth that strength and stamina, initiative and contradiction are seen as traditional "feminine" virtues, and eccentricity an honorable female prerogative. When Kathy Speakman became the first NASCAR-licensed stock-car driver in the nation, and Sheila Dunnivant the first woman driver to represent any branch of the military in stock-car racing, both these Alabama belles took a giant step away from the traditional role. And while they were simply pursuing their own interests, giving little thought to role politics, each must have known that she did so with relative immunity from social censure; they acted as eccentrics, but within the provincial context. In a region where male/female differences are lifted to the level of art, and ritualized courtship games are played around the clock, Speakman and Dunnivant emerged as pop-cult superstars: they are judged acceptably eccentric and awarded bonus points for spunk and gritty professionalism.

Then, too, Southern women share a special closeness: they are, after all, the only American women who once stood alone together to face an invading army. Bonding, long held to be a social phenomenon exclusively masculine, is in Dixie a favored feminine tradition. It hasn't made for a militant feminist lobby within the Southern Rim, but it has long enabled women here to draw reassurance and emotional sustenance from supportive female friendships that serve in turn to enhance their individual spheres of personal freedom.

The Southern woman has something else going for her that distinguishes her from all others and lands her in the seat of honor among the newer national folk heroines: she is heiress to a cultural legacy that grants her the right to display the full range of her personality and potential. Only here can women express such yahoo readiness to break with convention, such spirited candor, exuberant irreverence, and open-option independence. Why?

There is only one answer, and it's so foot-stompingly simple it's embarrassing.

Only in this Technicolor world of moonlight and madness is a woman applauded for mastering the knack of down-home craziness. The operative aim here is to wear one's psychosis on one's most prominent sleeve. The Southern woman embraces this regional tradition with constancy and enthusiasm and turns it to her own advantage. Unequivocal eccentricity makes a multi-purpose social loophole through which Southern women can chase their own goals or duck unwanted challenges. It is a direct route to expansive feminine freedom. It is paid admission to a game where each participant sets her own rules and competes on her own terms.

Elective eccentricity? You bet your honeysuckle bottom. As often as not, it is a conscious decision. Nashville's Sarah Colley Cannon remembers her first few months at Ward-Belmont, a fashionable local college for women.

"It was during the Depression, and where I came from, everybody was broke."

She didn't mind.

"Our old house was full of laughter and fun and foolishness. But at Ward-Belmont, I quickly realized that I couldn't compete with the other girls. I just couldn't compete with their clothes, their spending accounts, and their know-how.

I was so *country*. I had to find a place. I realized I was not going to be able to play it straight. I knew I was going to have to do something."

What she did was become Cousin Minnie Pearl, the name by which she's better known.

Now *that's* creative eccentricity.

Outside the borders of Dixie, craziness is a dread malady, feared more than leprosy. Americans who talk so persuasively of their longing for individuality shrink, nonetheless, from non-conformity. The fear of being *different* without being Southern as well reaches paralytic proportions; it is a valid fear, too, for there is no room in the regimentation of contemporary life for the enjoyable little absurdities and insanities so common in the provincial South.

I have heard that those peckerhead Yankees lock *their* crazies up!

There are, of course, a good many ways of being human, and each culture selects from an infinite number a few specific ways of behaving and elaborates on these. The whole is complex and amorphous, and exceptionally hard to figure, yet if you look at a given society just right, examining small, manageable parts, what you will find is that each is consistent with the whole and with that culture's primary themes. What truly matters is how each culture provides for its *abnormal* individuals. "Normal" is a narrow concept, and there are a considerable number of people everywhere who cannot or will not live out society's major themes. Southern provincial society provides acceptable roles and niches for those who can't or won't conform. Because provisions are made for those who march to drummers of their own, abnormality here is both tolerable and tolerated. Society supports the atypical in their furthest aberrations. Eccentricity is viewed here with special affection and esteem: it is a quaint, not-of-this-world, cobwebby semi-virtue, desirable in that it sets the family apart from the crowd, making it special. Eccentrics are given free license, which they may exploit relentlessly, gaining as a by-product the freedom to do as they please.

Not that they need it.

For Southern women fall heiresses to at least two special advantages over their sisters outside the borders of Dixie. First, they find role models in the high-styled provincial stereotypes that enjoy such faddish popularity today. Few fit exactly any one of that superstar cast, but all borrow freely from each. Redneck Mothers, Good Ol' Girls, and other Southern Belles are myths personified, and myths galvanize people, directing their pursuits; they are projections of collective hopes, fears, anxieties, and goals.

Second, Southern women see no contradiction in mixing strength with gentleness. It gives them a noticeable edge over non-Southern women, who habitually view these as conflicting traits.

Dixie's various belles are remarkably diverse for a group conditioned to commonality. But all are heroic in their determination to keep what is good of the Old South while reaching for what is worthwhile in the New. These are women who have the good sense to act from a position of strength: to undertake new risks in known and familiar ways. For many Southern women (and for many of their Northern contemporaries as well), open defiance of the traditional system is an unsettling prospect, and one filled with peril. Most recoil at the thought of open rebellion, of challenging outright the dictates of life-long cultural conditioning and tossing aside all the benefits derived from old-style femininity. They're dismayed by unruly public demonstrations, appalled at the notion of clamoring for raw new feminist rights, and unresponsive to militant feminist demands that they dismantle and restructure their lives overnight. They're shrewd enough to know that tedious nine-to-five jobs greatly outnumber excitingly creative career positions.

They've no intention whatever of surrendering what they already *have* for what they are told they *can be*. There are Southern exceptions, to be sure, like Texas representative Barbara Jordan, women who measure the past and find it lacking and so leap full-fury into the fray to seize a piece of the action.

Far more women, valuing form as well as substance, are keenly aware of the heavy investments they've made in the old sexist system. They hedge their bets. They make their own freeing adjustments within the context of their social, sexual, and cultural past.

They're bumper crops harvested in yesterday's gardens.

And it may just be that oblique is better. The women who people the pages of this book have taken, for the most part, that approach. They've seized creatively on the idiosyncrasies of the Southern experience and turned these to oblique advantage. They live fully and well, and they are winners in a world ostensibly dominated by males. They pride themselves on their regional quirks and minor insanities, and exploit both fully. They have only to play it as it lays: gritty mistresses of irony, they choose to play (and win) by the very rules that limited them in the provincial past. Little wonder that they appear now as pop-cult heroines: they suggest, simply by their changeless presence, that there may be, after all, a few traditions and conventions that one can rely on in a pinch—or challenge when the need for challenge is clear. They've played it both ways, often simultaneously, and they've emerged with the best of both worlds, as Southern women tend to do. They know full well that being strong is not the antithesis of being gentle, but has everything to do with living one's life and viewing one's self as if both are good enough reasons for being human.

True grits, grafted hybrids.

If you don't want their peaches, don't shake their tree.

Epilogue

Even for those of us who have peeled back the wrapper and analyzed the contents, the South comes to mind in symbols. Some are gentle, others harsh, but all are vivid shorthand for the unique heritage and ongoing tradition that is Dixie. Moonlight and magnolias. Broken tombstones. Lightnin' bugs and chinaberry trees. Bull Conner's dogs straining at their leashes, and crowds of angry blacks falling under the force of water that explodes from the firehoses. Decaying mansions, ancient oaks bowing with the weight of gray matted moss, and yellowing crinolines. College football, that crazed collage of high-breasted pom-pom girls shrieking their bloodlust and uniformed players turning their sleek smooth fannies toward the crowd, and bands that rise up and play "Dixie" at relentless five-minute intervals. Debris from a blast that ripped open the belly of a church, and body bags for the remains of four small girls dressed that day in Sunday best. Faded Bull Durham signs, Cousin Minnie Pearl in a store-bought hat with price tag dangling, and sweet country creeks banked high with scuppernong and voracious kudzu. Five old men, all in a row, whittling wood on the courthouse steps. Azalea queens with gingham hoop skirts and Farrah Fawcett smiles. Moon Pies, collard greens, and Arr-Cee Cola. Scarlett O'Hara, always.

Check one of the above.

Check none.

Or check them all.

Whatever else it may be, the South is multiple-choice. All choices are images, all images symbols. No symbol is "false," none entirely "true." There are numerous Dixies from which to choose, and the real one is the one *you* perceive, based on the symbols you find most credible. All coalesce into an ever-expanding mystique about a complex and contradictory region which, while very much a part of the United States, persists, at least symbolically, as a separate subnation.

The most powerful symbols of all are the larger-than-life stereotypes that serve to represent the inhabitants of this colorful land of country music, moonshine, and high-powered preaching. Some fifty-five million men and women, 20 percent of them black, make their homes within the territorial limits of the old Confederacy. Among them are women who form an inexhaustible reservoir of super-charged energy, cracker-barrel courage, and stylized eccentricity. Redneck Mothers. Good Ol' Girls. Assorted Southern Belles, and Honky-Tonk Heroines of every variety.

Some are so blatant in their courage that they make better grist for the novelist's mill than for that of the reporter. Imagine a heroine, black and poor, born sixteenth in a family of nineteen children; she is sickly from birth, her left leg is paralyzed, and she is forced to wear cumbersome braces and special orthopedic shoes till the age of eleven. But she *is*, remember, a heroine, and she boasts a tremendous strength of will and determination. A decade after she tosses aside those hated shoes, she emerges as the world's most celebrated female athlete. She journeys to Rome in 1960 and returns with three gold Olympic medals. She picks up as well America's Sullivan Award. Associated Press names her tops in sports for two years running, and UPI votes her athlete of the year over world-wide competition, male and female. You're not really going to buy this rags-to-riches cliché, are you?

But it's Wilma Rudolph's story, unembellished.

Southern women have a way of squaring off and beating the odds. Take Joan Perry: five years ago, she was Birmingham's highest-paid woman in the male-dominated field of advertising. She turned down an offer to work for another agency—for fifty percent of the firm's profits and a few spectacular fringe benefits; instead, with partner Janet Hoyle, she established her own agency, a risky venture judged doomed to failure by the city's business community.

"It didn't make any sense, really, except to me and to Janet. Even now, people find it hard to believe that there are two *women* running this business, literally managing and operating it after starting it from scratch. We started with no accounts and very little capital. But out of every five calls we made, we got one account. We didn't worry about what size it was; we just worried about getting it. We've doubled our business every year, and we'll do it again this year."

Within three months, Perry-Hoyle was operating in the black. Within three years, the agency ranked within Birmingham's top five. Perry's ten-year plan projects that the firm will rank as the number-one ad agency in the state by 1983, and so far, they're right on target.

Southern women bent on successful careers don't waste any time going after them, and they don't bother with modest dreams. At the age of twenty-two, Verda Gibbs is director of public relations for Nashville's Top Billing, Inc., the largest and most aggressive talent/management agency in this capital of country music. She landed the job less than a week after graduating from Middle Tennessee State University.

"Some people say it's a minorities trend. You know: if you're black and female, you've got it made. But this is a competitive business, and I don't think sex and color have much to do with being successful here."

Nor do I: Verda's boss is the powerhouse president of Top Billing, Tandy Rice, who is generally conceded to be the shrewdest talent rep in town. Agent for such media heavyweights as Kitty Wells, Billy Carter, Tom T. Hall, and Jerry Clower, Rice is a man not easily dazzled nor given to tokenism. He is as likely to be featured in the press as any of his superstar clients, and he has got more than a grain of grit of his own. Accepting the management of Cornelia Wallace's show-business career after her divorce from George Wallace, Rice stared down a corps of skeptical reporters who wondered aloud just what it was Cornelia would do to justify the hefty fees to be charged for her personal appearances. Cornelia Wallace doesn't have to do *anything*, said Rice, rightfully; she's a "media event."

She's more than that: she's a Southern woman.

In these days of a revamped nouveau-chic South, that seems to be more than enough to suffice, and for good reason: you can't travel a mile in Dixie without stumbling across at least one native daughter who tears into life with such flair that she is cause for celebration. I traveled some 46,000 miles of Southern backroads, and I met more of them than I could fit into this book.

I haven't told you about Harriett Prevatte, a free-spirited Southern artist who plies her trade on the Square in New Orleans' French Quarter. She's just beginning to realize the advantages of growing up Southern:

"There was a lot of emphasis on manners, on behaving always 'as a lady,' the kind of thing I thought was ridiculous at the time but I appreciate now. I got that from my mother. Dad treated me as if he expected me to do anything a guy would do. So I know how to use a hammer and a saw, and how to change a tire, and that kind of thing. Lately, I've found myself becoming more feminine, and I don't fight it. There are certain things after all that I really *enjoy* about femininity, but I've always determined my own life."

> *I'd be willing to pay the price of a military*
> *draft that includes women if I knew*
> *I'd have absolute sexual equality. I don't*
> *see that femininity should give you protection*
> *against a military draft. For one thing,*
> *we've got too many women around, anyway.*
> —HARRIETT PREVATTE

I haven't told you about seventeen-year-old Teresa Taylor, who lives in Thorsby, Alabama, and works after school in her family's Rebel Café, and thinks softball is every bit as important as boys. She has lived her whole life in the South, she says, and she guesses she'll die here.

> *I might get married when I'm about thirty.*
> *But I want to enjoy life first.*
> —TERESA TAYLOR

And I haven't told you about Rose Thadford of Port Gibson, Mississippi, who knows the grindingly hard work of playing the traditional role as wife and mother of three daughters while working daily alongside her husband, sharing fully in his labor, at their Texaco service station.

Or Susan Todd, who owns and operates the Page One Bookstore in Natchez and likes, better than anything else, to "get into some grungy old clothes and pack up my husband and kids and go fishing all day long."

> *I just ignore the feminist movement.*
> *I think of it as a Yankee thing.*
> —SUSAN TODD

There hasn't been room to tell you about Sandra Bell, a reporter for the *Natchez Democrat,* who shares with her husband, Dick, a partnership marriage and a nine-year-old son. Bell hates housework, smokes little black cigars, and thinks Southern women are capable simply because they've always had to be.

> *They only pretended to be fragile.*
> *But lots of them ran the plantations, you know.*
> *And they're still tough, because they have to be.*
> —SANDRA BELL

I wanted to tell you too about Marie Woodard, a mellow black retired schoolteacher in McComb, Mississippi, active in the Freewill Baptist Church and the civic-minded Elite Club and just about every other group in town that gets things done.

> *I never felt limited, I don't think, as a woman*
> *or because of my race. But I've been more*
> *fortunate than others who had to struggle hard*
> *to work and try to go to school too.*
> *Black and white people are coming back to the*
> *South, and I think most everyone is doing very well.*
> —MARIE WOODARD

You should meet Inez Wooten Henry, assistant to the president of Berry College near Rome, Georgia. Henry arrived at Berry some sixty years ago with forty cents left over form the sale of a calf, eyes that "popped out on stems" at the sight of the campus, and a compulsion to work her way through school. The founder of this unique work-study college took her in, and Henry never left. After graduation, she stayed on to serve as Martha Berry's private secretary, travel companion and "flunkie," and then moved on into administrative work for the college. She is a woman rooted in the past, but her eyes even now are on the future.

> *I hope we continue to enjoy being women and*
> *being feminine. But my thinking is that Southern*
> *women never have minded walking out and wading in*
> *to do what had to be done. So I hope too that*
> *we continue to share in the world's work.*
> —INEZ HENRY

Micki Fuhrman, billed as the brightest young country-music artist to be showcased by Shreveport's "Louisiana Hayride," deserves a chapter of her own. So does Heidi Betterton, the up-tempo sociologist at Southeastern Louisiana University in Hammond. And a dozen others do, too. All are true-grits honky-tonk heroines who manage to play out regional clichés while embodying, simultaneously, all the real-life qualities behind the clichés. All share the down-home values—the old love of courtesy and custom, the regional identity, the traditional respect for place over time, the familial ambience, and the yahoo courage of their own convictions—that distinguish Southern women from women who live elsewhere. All are determined survivors, concerned with the fundamental problems of living, and keenly aware that happiness is to be found in the textures of everyday life. All favor to one extent or another the traditionally Southern velvet-hammer approach, giving the pendulum of power as it is divided between the Southern sexes a crazy rebel tilt.

They know the difference between form and substance. And the difference sets them free to establish their own standards of feminism. They've always enjoyed, by exploiting Dixie's special social loopholes, more freedom than most, and they're not ashamed to admit that they're not anxious to stray too far from this reality: they may do a man's work and lobby for a man's pay, but they want as well to continue to tend the baby, dust the piano, arrange the geraniums on the sill, and see what's for dinner.

The best of both worlds, as Ginnie Raymond says.

The vitality of their grass-roots history, their populist traditions, and their feeling for the land persists, less evident in the ascendency of Southern politicians than in the women themselves—the women who perpetuate such community events as the Pilgrimage in Natchez, who safeguard such traditions as Sacred Harp singing, who contribute such individual talents as that of Ethel Mohamed, whose quicksilver fingers weave past memories with future hopes into tapestries painted with random bits of colored thread.

Reason enough, I think, to celebrate the women of Dixie.

If Redneck Mothers, Good Ol' Girls, and other Southern Belles now reign as trash-with-flash, pop-cult national heroines, it don't make them no never-mind. And it suggests that other regions of the nation might profit just a mite by undergoing a process of selective Southernization. That is what this country craze is all about, don't-you-know: it's not a matter of the Americanization of Dixie, but, instead, the enthusiastic Dixification of America's heroes and heroines.

A matter of true grits.

> *We all stayed right here. None of us ever went*
> *north. Well, I did have a cousin who got married, and*
> *she let that old fool cart her off to California.*
> *But it don't count, 'cause she always was crazy. Not*
> *good-crazy, you know, but crazy like them people outside.*
> —GRETTA TOWNSEND